A WOMAN IN DEFENCE

Karina Molloy grew up in County Donegal and, as a young woman in 1981, fulfilled her dream of entering the Irish Defence Forces.

She retired after a 31-year career, where she claimed many first achievements for a female recruit, including attaining the rank of Senior Non-Commissioned Officer.

She is part of the Women of Honour group that was set up in the wake of the military #metoo movement – detailing allegations of sexual abuse, harassment and discrimination in the Irish military – which advocates for change and accountability.

A Woman in Defence is her first book.

A WOMAN IN DEFENCE

A Soldier's Story of the Enemy Within the Irish Army

Karina Molloy
with Kathryn Rogers

HACHETTE
BOOKS
IRELAND

First published in 2023 by Hachette Books Ireland

A CIP catalogue record for this title is available from the British Library.

ISBN 978 1 39971 230 9

Typeset in Sabon LT Std by Bookends Publishing Services, Dublin
Printed and bound in Great Britain by Clays Ltd, St Ives plc

Hachette Books Ireland policy is to use papers that are natural,
renewable and recyclable products and made from wood grown
in sustainable forests. The logging and manufacturing processes
are expected to conform to the environmental regulations of
the country of origin.

Hachette Books Ireland
8 Castlecourt Centre
Castleknock
Dublin 15, Ireland

A division of Hachette UK Ltd
Carmelite House, 50 Victoria Embankment, EC4Y 0DZ

www.hachettebooksireland.ie

In memory of my beloved parents,
Raymond and Eileen Molloy.

Mum, you always hated me saying, 'I'll do it later.'
But I did it later. Sorry it was too late for you.

Dad, I hope I've finally made you proud.

Also, in memory of Susan, Caroline and Maria.
Remembering you all with pride.

Contents

Glossary

2IC	second-in-command
2LSB	2nd Logistics Support Battalion
AO	area of operations
ARW	Army Ranger Wing
BMR	Battalion Mobile Reserve
BQ	battalion quartermaster
BQMS	battalion quartermaster sergeant
chalk	a group of soldiers rotating to or from a mission
CO	commanding officer
CQ	company quartermaster
CQMS	company quartermaster sergeant
CS	company sergeant
DS	directing staff
EO	executive officer
EOD	explosive ordnance disposal
EUFOR	European Union Force Bosnia and Herzegovina
FCA	An Fórsa Cosanta Áitiúil (former title for local defence force)
FN	Fabrique Nationale (rifle)
GOC	general officer commanding
GPMG	general-purpose machine gun
HMG	heavy machine gun

Inf Bn	infantry battalion
IRG	Independent Review Group
Irishbatt	Irish Battalion HQ, also A, B and C companies in Lebanon
MINURCAT	United Nations Mission in the Central African Republic and Chad
MP	military police
MST	military sexual trauma
MWA	morale, welfare and activities
NATO	North Atlantic Treaty Organisation
NCO	non-commissioned officer
NSE	national support element
PDFORRA	Permanent Defence Forces Representative Association
PTI	physical training instructor
PTSD	post-traumatic stress disorder
PX	post exchange (army retail outlet)
Q	quartermaster
QMG	quartermaster general
ROE	rules of engagement
RTU	return to unit
SAG	Special Assault Group
SAS	Special Air Service (British Army)
SFOR	Stabilisation Force in Bosnia and Herzegovina
SRAAW	short-range anti-armour weapon
UNIFIL	United Nations Interim Force in Lebanon
UNMEE	United Nations Mission in Ethiopia and Eritrea
WSC	Women's Service Corps

Prologue

Urgent whispers outside alert me. They're coming for me. I lie on a thin mattress on the floor, bracing myself for whatever is about to go down. My pulse beats hard as I watch and wait in the pitch darkness. *They can't kill me*, I remind myself.

The door creaks open, more whispers, and I hear a metallic sound roll across the concrete floor of the small room. A moment of stillness and then a heart-stopping BOOM! A thunder flash of blinding light and a massive explosion rents the air. I flinch, shrinking into the mattress as the shockwave, the noise and light engulf the room and overload my senses.

BOOM! A second deafening bomb blast and a dazzling burst of crackling light vibrate the room.

Fuck! My heart hammers hard in my chest. The

self-assurance that *they can't kill me* has crumbled. *Christ, they've lobbed two stun grenades at me in a confined space. Maybe they can kill me.*

A click of a switch and the fluorescent light flickers on in the room. I see the outlines of two directing staff (DS) coming at me. I'm even more panicked now, trying to scramble to my feet, coughing amid the cloud of smoke, but my balance is off.

The stun grenades have done their job: overwhelm the senses; disorient the enemy; keep injuries and death to a minimum. I'm squinting, still blinded by glare from the explosions. My ears are full of high-pitched ringing, and the DSs' roars seem distant. 'You! Fucking up! Get dressed! Now!'

Blinking, wincing, I think I recognise one DS, and I'm nearly sure it's the sergeant major of the Army Ranger Wing. *Oh, Jesus, I'm in trouble now.* Their faces are close to mine, but their voices still sound very far away.

The room is spinning. I'm shaking, stumbling around, still unsteady, grabbing my fatigues. Adrenaline is racing through my system, and my ears feel like they are stuffed full of cotton. The men quit the room as I dress, but they don't go far. They bang, pound and kick the door. One of them is yelling. 'Tell me what you're doing!'

Seriously? I think.

My mouth is dry with shock, but I croak a reply. 'I'm pulling on my fatigues.' My voice sounds strange and distant.

'Tell me what you're doing!'

'Putting on my belt.'

They continue to pound the door, continue to shout. 'Tell me what you're doing!'

My hands are trembling. 'Pulling on my boots.'

My head throbs from the explosions or maybe lack of sleep or the constant hammering on the door. I'm not thinking straight but, as I go outside, the twisting cramps in my lower midriff remind me it could be a long time before I see a toilet again. I squint down the hall and spot my two tormentors. They're temporarily distracted, standing at the exit, looking outside. I pat one of the pockets in my fatigues and, reassured, lurch to the tiny toilet outside my room.

I try to shut the door quietly, but I'm trembling too hard, and they hear the click of the lock. 'You! What the fuck do you think you're doing!' one of them screams. I see them running towards me through the wide gaps in the toilet-door slats. They set upon the wooden door, punching and kicking it, and I can see their black eyes peering in at me.

'Tell me what you're doing!'

I'm sure as hell not going to tell them I'm changing a tampon. Things are bad enough. I'm not about to bring that heat upon myself. 'Urinating!' I reply.

They're banging and kicking the door harder now. Their faces come up close, obstructing the light streaming through the gaps. 'Tell me what you're doing!'

I feel my face burn red with humiliation and my stomach sick with anxiety.

They kick and punch the door again, until I fear it will come off its hinges. 'Tell me what you're doing!'

'Urinating,' I insist, desperately trying to insert the tampon. My heart is hammering. My hands shake and I see their eyes and feel their hot breaths through the gaps in the door.

'TELL ME WHAT THE FUCK YOU'RE DOING!'

It's four o'clock in the morning and I am beginning to wonder the same thing. *What the fuck am I doing?* This is crazy. I'm sick and exhausted, and I'm not even 12 hours in this place. I am the first woman to attempt the Army Ranger Wing selection course, and the rangers furiously kicking the toilet door are determined I will fail.

1

Childhood

My brother's battalion, sandwiched between several warring factions in Lebanon, was under intense fire at times. Three Irish soldiers were killed during that mission, but he managed to return from his first peacekeeping tour without a scratch. It was 1980 and he was young and single, and the lump sum in overseas allowances from the army burnt a hole in his pocket. So he went out and bought a motorbike. That's how, weeks after returning safely from a conflict zone, he badly injured his leg in a horrific road accident near our Donegal home.

Soon after he came home from the hospital, Dad and I happened to be in the hall. We could see my brother sitting in the living room, his badly scarred, stitched and bandaged leg resting on a stool. Then from somewhere in the house came the sudden loud bang of a door slamming. I still don't know how he moved so quickly considering the state of his leg but, in one fluid movement, we saw him dive to the floor and under the protection of the chair opposite. I stood motionless and stunned for an instant, but then, as I rushed to help him, Dad caught me by the arm. 'Leave him,' he said quietly, drawing me back out of my brother's view. He didn't want him to feel embarrassed by what we'd seen. 'Walk away now and just leave him.'

That was the first time I began to suspect that my brother had been through more in Lebanon than he had told us. I now know that I'd witnessed an episode of post-traumatic stress disorder (PTSD), but no one had heard of it then. That frightening glimpse into my brother's invisible wounds still didn't stop me from rushing to apply when the Irish Army opened its doors to its first female recruits the following year. The truth is nothing would have stopped me.

I grew up in Ardara, a small village by the ocean in Donegal. The town is in an isolated area surrounded by wild, rugged scenery but sheltered from the worst of the Atlantic winds by the steep slopes of Slievetooey. Tucked in a valley where the Owentocker river flows into the bay, this was a close-knit and insular community consisting of just a few hundred people in the 1960s. Even though we lived among them, we didn't feel part of that community.

Growing up, I was always aware my family were regarded as outsiders.

Ardara was a very traditional and conservative place back then, full of passion for GAA and, in many quarters, the IRA. My father, Raymond Molloy, was English of the old stiff-upper-lip British variety. It ensured that although he was treated with courtesy and respect, he was always eyed with a certain suspicion. His bloodline was pure Donegal, however. My father was actually born in New Zealand, but his father and generations before him were from the village.

His father, Peter Molloy, emigrated and served as a British Army officer in Burma during the Second World War before he and his British wife, Ethel, moved to New Zealand. However, they moved back to England when my father was only months old and he was raised in Surrey.

When my father was in his late teens, his dad took the family back to Ardara to run a tweed business, established by my great-grandfather, James Molloy. Unfortunately, his Murlinn Hosiery & Tweed Manufacturing Company was already in a decline like most of the textile industry in Ireland during that era. My grandparents quit the business and returned to England, leaving my father to continue.

A type of social apartheid existed between Protestants and Catholics in those days. Yet my father, raised in the Church of Ireland, fell in love with a Catholic. Eileen Phillips was from Kilcar, a Gaeltacht village in Donegal, and faced excommunication if they both didn't vow to raise their children in the one true church. So my father made the decision to convert to Catholicism, and they married in Kilcar in 1956. When my father returned to Ardara with a wife who hailed from a village a whole 17 miles away, it sealed our status as blow-ins.

By the time I came along, my parents were living in a rented house in the village. My eldest brother Garry was born four years ahead of me, and my other brother, Alan, was two. My dad was an avid reader, and Mum always said he chose my name, Karina, because he had just finished the Leo Tolstoy novel *Anna Karenina*.

I'm sure Dad thumbed his nose at good saints' names like Mary, Bridget and Catherine because he enjoyed being a nonconformist. Our family was complete when Geraldine arrived four years after me. Dad, never a devoted mass-goer, stopped attending mass altogether when we had all been confirmed.

Our only playmates belonged to a local Church of Ireland family. So, living isolated from the rest of the village children, I grew up roughhousing with my older brothers, being tied to trees, dangled upside down over heights and getting shoved into rivers. I didn't care. I fought, tumbled and ran wild with them through the countryside. We climbed trees in our orchard garden and spent hours fishing in the river beside us. I couldn't bear cooking, sewing, knitting or crocheting and don't ever remember playing with dolls, even though I had a Crolly doll from the namesake village not far from us.

I was mesmerised by war films and westerns and

groaned when my mother insisted on watching a romantic movie or a musical. I was an unruly tomboy, wearing my brothers' worn trousers and other hand-me-downs. But on Sunday mornings, my mother would drag a comb through my tousled hair, tie it in neat pigtails and make me wear a pretty dress for mass. I hated those mornings.

My father loved adventure, sports and the great outdoors, but his interests were niche for the time. His feats of derring-do were reported in the local newspaper before I was born. In 1955, the *Donegal Democrat* reported that 'a gallery of excited spectators' watched in 'breathless amazement one of the most thrilling performances ever witnessed in the district' when he drove up a bridle mountain path on a motorbike. Dad would have been the first to admit that not a lot went on in Ardara in those days.

In the early 1960s, Dad was also one of the pioneers of surfing and fashioned his own boards and wetsuits. As other kids played GAA, we were thrown into the Atlantic Ocean to become surfers and swimmers. He also drove us on 40-mile round trips to Burtonport every week to learn judo, something of an exotic sport at that time.

Dad treated me the same as my older brothers – everything they did, I did. I loved to go hunting in the local woods with him. With his shotgun slung over his shoulder, we'd head out in the frosty mornings during pheasant season. Our trained gundog, Roy, a beautiful Irish setter, set an enthusiastic pace, eagerly sniffing the way ahead. I can still remember crunching through the dew-wet brown, green and ochre foliage of the forest floor, hoping to flush out our feathered game.

Hours later, we'd bring home a brace of birds that Dad liked to hang in the house for days. We weren't rich, but we were one of the few families in Ardara who ate pheasant for dinner.

My father was the sole provider for the family for many years, making his living in the family tweed and knitwear business. He ran the equivalent of today's online businesses. His customers, mostly American, ordered from brochures or adverts, and their knits were shipped across the Atlantic from our house.

As a child, I remember being in the car as he drove along pot-ridden, winding roads through some of the most isolated parts of Donegal. He'd stop at the end of remote bothareens to collect jumpers from elderly women supplementing the family income with their knitting. My mother was a ferocious knitter too, and I remember her sitting up nights sewing buttons or our personal label 'Molloy's of Donegal' on the cardigans. However, the demand for handmade knitwear was steadily declining in the face of cheaper machine-made alternatives.

My mother, always industrious, managed to buy a plot of land on the Portnoo Road at the other end of the village. Located on a hill studded with granite rocks, the site had a panoramic view of the Atlantic Ocean. My father was tasked with building a massive house, and Greenhaven Bed and Breakfast became their business. Dad continued building until, at full capacity, the place could accommodate

22 guests. I grew up with visitors constantly coming and going, giving us enticing glimpses of the faraway places they came from.

Even though I hated sitting still, I loved school and had a passion for learning. For a long time, I had no idea what I wanted to do when l grew up. I was clearer about what I *didn't* want to do, and that was anything most women did. I didn't want to do secretarial training or business studies. I didn't want to be confined in an office or behind the counter of a shop. All the traditional career options for women, the 'nice' professions, were too sedentary for me. I loved the outdoors and doing anything athletic, relishing the feeling of motion and running, climbing or swimming. I craved the freedom of being out in the fresh air and the rush of adrenaline and endorphins I got from pushing myself faster and harder.

However, I had a eureka moment about my future the first day I attended Glenties Comprehensive School. While running around the basketball court under the instruction of our PE teacher, Mr Barnes, it dawned on me that he was getting paid to teach sports. *Wow, I want to be like Mr Barnes!* I thought. *I would love that job.* I was always single-minded about things and, from that day, Mr Barnes' job was my dream. I put all my Leaving Cert eggs in the PE basket.

No one had been hugely surprised when one of my brothers joined the Irish Army after leaving school, it wasn't hugely surprising as our family had multi-generational ties to the military. As well as Dad's father serving in Burma, my father's only brother was an officer in the Royal Navy. My maternal grandfather had served in the Irish Army during the Emergency and one of my cousins became an explosive ordnance disposal (EOD) officer – a bomb disposal expert – in the British Army. My father also served four years in An Fórsa Cosanta Áitiúil (FCA), now known as the Reserve Defence Forces. He was about to accept his commission to become an officer, but times were hard, and the volunteer position required a major time commitment. With a failing business and five dependents, he had to turn down the commission, something that became his lifelong regret. Both my brothers also served in the FCA.

It wasn't until my brother started coming home at the weekends, telling me they'd been climbing mountains or shooting on the range that I started feeling pangs of envy. He did his recruit training in Athlone, where he showed exceptional promise and won one of the prestigious recruit prizes for Best Shot.

He was then stationed in Finner Camp in Ballyshannon in Donegal, about 30 miles from home, where he was best known in the camp by his nickname, Buddha. My brother was a fan of the martial arts star and actor Bruce Lee. He shaved his head and even fashioned wooden nunchaku with which he would train after his day's work. Through him, I became fascinated by Bruce Lee and his life and philosophy and even joined the Bruce Lee fan club. Robert Redford was my childhood heartthrob, but Bruce Lee became my idol. By extension, I later became interested in all things Eastern, including meditation, Buddhism, alternative medicine and healing.

Alan's job seemed like an adventurous one, but I had my own dreams. And my heart was set on getting into Thomond College in Limerick, the only place in Ireland where they trained PE teachers. I had blinkers on and never considered anything else. Nothing would do me but to study hard and go to Thomond.

Then came the day when I returned to school to collect my Leaving Cert results, trembling as I opened the envelope and scanned the sheet of paper inside. My eye instantly settled on the 'D' in honours biology and my heart sank in bitter disappointment as the honour was essential for admission to Thomond. I tried hard not to cry as I left the school.

However, my father was waiting outside to drive me home, and as soon as I sat in the car and met his questioning gaze, I burst into tears. 'I'm not going to get Thomond with *this*,' I cried, offering him the offending results in my hand.

My starched-collar dad couldn't cope being trapped in a car with his highly emotional daughter. 'We'll talk to your mother,' he said, setting his eyes on the road ahead and putting his foot on the accelerator. 'Your mother will know what to do.'

But I was inconsolable because I knew no one could fix this. I was crushed because I had no plan B.

2

The British Army

As the plane soared from Aldergrove airport in Belfast, I watched the world below dwindle into a patchwork of lush greens before it disappeared behind white cotton clouds. I sat back in my seat, knowing the wheels would touch down in London within the hour, taking me one step closer to fulfilling my new dream of becoming an army nurse. A British Army nurse.

The journey from crying in my father's car to flying for an interview with the British Defence Medical Services was separated by a year during which I sat the Leaving Cert again.

While I was studying, the Irish Defence Forces advertised

that it was going to recruit the first cohort of female officer cadets for the new Women's Service Corps. The advert said the post offered an attractive annual salary of over £5,000 per annum.

My focus was still on the Leaving Cert and becoming a PE teacher, but I couldn't have applied even if I'd wanted to. The first cadetships were only available to university graduates with working experience.

My second attempt at a Leaving Cert was in vain, and I failed to get into Thomond again. I had to accept that the dream I'd held for years was over, and my confidence was severely knocked. Crushed by the disappointment, I was lost for a while.

I knew the Irish Army had its own version of PE teachers called physical-training instructors (PTIs). I asked him if the army might be a backdoor route to a career in physical education.

'The army are only taking female cadets,' he said. However, he planted a seed when he added, 'But you can join the British Army.'

My mother, always concerned about my tomboyish attire, attempted to steer me towards nursing, a far more feminine career direction than that of a PE teacher. She had a photo of me as a child in a nurse's uniform, complete with a stethoscope and medical bag, so her attempts at brainwashing had begun early. I always had a fascination with medicine and agreed to apply to the two training hospitals, the Mater and St Vincent's. However, unemployment levels were sky high at the time and demand for the training positions was huge. I didn't even have an honour in biology, so it was no surprise when I didn't get in.

I researched the British Army but found nothing about female physical training instructors. However, I sat up straighter when I read that they recruited and trained nurses. I realised this could be a way to combine my interest in medicine and my love of physical training, adventure and travel – I knew the British Army was stationed in exotic places worldwide.

Unlike the Irish Army, the British Army trained their own nurses. I could join as a nurse cadet, do basic military training and then train as an army nurse for three years.

'I want to become a nurse in the British Army!' I announced to my parents, and couldn't understand why their faces fell in unison.

I was stubborn. I wouldn't listen to their petrified objections. *It's far too dangerous*, they said. I dismissed all their concerns and applied, and received a letter for an interview in central London.

I was naïve. We were a non-political family, and I hadn't been exposed to republican sentiments about the British Army. The only time I ever remember anything about the Troubles being aired in our house was Bloody Sunday in 1972, when British soldiers shot 26 unarmed civilians during a protest march in the Bogside area of Derry, killing 13 of them.

Events in Northern Ireland meant nothing to me at ten years of age, and I was blind to the news about the massacre on TV. I sat on the big padded arm of my daddy's chair, playing with the dog, singing away to myself. The next thing, I felt a sharp whack across the head, and I recoiled in shock. My mother had come from behind me, her face dark as thunder.

'How dare you sing when all those people have died?' she cried.

I put my hand to my stinging face, and burst into tears at this undeserved 'clip around the ear'. Of course, her anger had nothing to do with me. It was a very dark day in the history of Northern Ireland, and she struck out because she was stressed and fearful. The Troubles had just escalated, and she was married to a British man, so she must have been worried sick about what would happen next. My parents managed to hide their fears from us most of the time because that's the only childhood memory I have of the Troubles.

Being a sheltered teenager, I didn't understand the depths of the sectarian divisions out in the wide world. The British Army held no negative connotations for me. I had been taught to believe there were good and bad people in all walks of life, and armies consisted of highly trained professionals. Like everyone that age, I also thought I was immortal, and the dangers of joining the British Army held no fear for me. My heart was set on a new goal of being an army nurse, and nothing could dissuade me.

I really didn't do my homework. Using all my savings, I bought a return ticket to London and flew out from the former Aldergrove airport in Belfast. Within hours, I sat before the recruitment officer, and everything seemed to be going well. I explained where I was from, adding, 'We're only one hour from the border.' This was the height of the Troubles, with civil unrest, the dirty protest and hunger strikes, and yet I thought this might be helpful to my application.

The officer eyed me carefully. 'You know that if you join the British Armed Forces, you won't be able to return to the Republic of Ireland whenever you like anymore,' he said.

I looked at him in confusion.

'For security reasons, two Special Branch officers will have to be assigned to you anytime you want to go home because you could become a target.'

I listened in growing dismay to the impact my joining the British Army would have on my personal and family life. As a member, even as a trainee nurse, I would have to make an application to return home, and it would only be permitted on limited grounds.

This stark information put a whole different light on becoming a British Army nurse. I would be a permanent exile from my home if I joined. I flew back to Belfast deflated, disheartened and upset. I knew straight away that the cost of joining the British Army was too high. It just seemed everywhere I turned, I faced insurmountable barriers.

3

The Interview

My brother in the army tried to cheer me up. 'We're hearing the army may start bringing in female recruits for the new female officers to train,' he said. With that, my dreams of training as a physical training instructor in the army were resurrected.

However, my parents weren't about to let me hang around at home and twiddle my thumbs on the off-chance that the Irish Army *might* change the rules and accept women. While looking for a job, I got a phone call from my old PE teacher, Kevin Barnes.

Kevin was working on the UCD campus as the assistant director of their vast, new sports complex, and a position had opened for a sports assistant. The interview with the director was a mere formality. I got the job on Kevin's recommendation and started on a six-month probation period straightaway.

The title of sports assistant was a lot grander and more glamorous than the reality. I was one of six sports assistants, and our jobs included scrubbing toilets, showers and changing rooms. When the judo team came in, we had the mats waiting for them. When the athletics team was booked, we took the hurdles out. It was pretty dull, manual work, but it was mostly outdoors, which suited me.

Best of all, the job had prospects. If I passed my six months' probation, I would be a member of UCD staff and could enrol for free on any course the following September. It was a huge perk, and my plan was to study for a science degree.

Months later, however, in March 1981, adverts for the 'enlistment of women in the defence forces' appeared in the national newspapers. I pored over the ad with excitement and the idea of a science degree went out the window. The army was a way I could achieve all my real ambitions. It would involve lots of training and adventure, and I'd become a physical training instructor at the same time.

The advert read:

The enlistment of 40 women recruits in the defence forces will take place in the near future ... Applicants for enlistment, who may be married or single, should be in good health and be between the ages of 17 and 32 years.

I wrote away for the information leaflet and application form. The leaflet mentioned that we would be part of the Women's Service Corps and listed the roles women would undertake in the army:

> *These will include appointments such as drivers, clerks, radio operators, air-traffic controllers, photographers, grooms, printers, librarians, telephonists and military policewomen.*

I didn't think about it properly. 'Clerks, librarians, telephonists' meant filing and answering phones. The inclusion of 'grooms' should have told me we were being hired as hairdressers for horses and 'drivers' meant chauffeuring officers. For me, however, the army had become synonymous with sport, training, shooting, adventure, travel and becoming a physical training instructor – everything I wanted to do with my life. At no stage did I suspect we wouldn't be proper soldiers.

The leaflet stated that the minimum height requirement for women recruits was a tiny 4 feet 10 inches. (Years later, they upped it to the same as cadets, which was 5 feet 2 inches, meaning many of the first recruits would never have got in.) Educational requirements were only Intermediate Certificate level.

My mother was dead set against me joining the Irish Army. She didn't want me entering what she saw as a man's world. I think her greatest worry was that no man would ever marry me if I joined the army. This, in her eyes, would be the end of me.

'Why would you want to do something like that? Go and apply again for nursing.'

My army brother was equally opposed to me following in his footsteps. 'I swear, Karina, you'll be so bored in the army,' he warned. 'They're not even going to let you be a soldier.' He was preparing to leave the Irish Army and was seeking adventure and new experiences in the French Foreign Legion.

Two of the sports assistants I worked with were ex-army. One was a retired sergeant called PJ, a fair-haired, wiry and incredibly fit former member of the army gymnastics team. He took me under his wing and gave me good advice.

'If you have to apply, don't use your Donegal address, or you'll end up in the Western Command,' he said. 'Use your Dublin address, and maybe you'll get into army headquarters. The further away you are from headquarters, the less opportunity you have of making an impression.'

So I used my Stillorgan address when I returned my application to the secretary of the Department of Defence. Even though I was not a prayerful person, I prayed every night. My anxiety rose when I read media reports about the vast numbers of applications for the 40 available posts. If I had known that over 4,000 women had applied, I would have lost all hope. But weeks later, my prayers were answered when I received a letter telling me to go to Collins Barracks for an interview in May.

I was in a whirl of excitement about the possibility of joining the army and becoming a physical training instructor, but I could see my mother was heartbroken.

'Look, Mammy,' I said, 'I can sign up for three or four years and get it out of my system. Then I can leave. Look at your youngest son – he's leaving.'

'Yes, and look where he's going,' she replied.

'Well, there's no way they'll allow a girl to join the French Foreign Legion, so you don't have to worry about that.'

She was understandably anxious. Women had never trodden this path before, and she didn't want her daughter to be among the pioneers.

My father, however, was delighted. He had hoped to follow his dreams vicariously by seeing his sons become army officers. But neither of my brothers shared his ambitions. Garry had no interest in the military at all, he followed in my maternal grandfather's footsteps to become a highly skilled carpenter.

So I was my father's last chance, and I was also a daddy's girl, always eager to please him. I spent my whole life trying to impress my father, to get his approval and praise. I think I was always striving to break through his reserve, to see him express his delight and excitement in my achievements, but of course that was never going to happen. My father was averse to displays of emotion and remained a stiff-upper-lip-style Brit to the end.

I remember entering a race in Ardara as a kid, but Dad shrugged and said he was too busy to go. However, when I returned, he gave me a blow-by-blow account of what I should have done in the race. He had got a ladder and climbed up on the roof with a pair of binoculars to watch me run on the GAA pitch even though it would have been quicker and easier to stand on the sidelines. I'm sure he was proud of me, but it wasn't in his nature to express it. I didn't realise that for a long time, unfortunately, and often felt I failed to meet his expectations.

However, my dad recognised that I had an ambition and drive for military life that wasn't in my brothers. His dreams were within his grasp once again and immediately he began applying pressure on me to become an officer. 'Now listen to me, Karina. There are officers, and there are enlisted ranks, and they are always separate. Their uniforms are different – even the colour of their shoes is different,' he explained. 'Commissioned officers are like higher management in the army, but you'll enter as enlisted ranks.'

He explained the two ways enlisted ranks could become an officer. 'You can go in as a recruit like you and apply later for a cadetship. Or you wait until you become a non-commissioned officer and apply for a Potential Officer course.'

He was determined that I would become an officer.

When I told my boss, Kevin, that I was interviewing for the army, he was bewildered.

'Why would you do that?' he said. He was astounded that I'd consider quitting a good job in UCD for the army. Everyone knew that the pay in the defence forces was appalling back then.

However, retired sergeant PJ supported me and helped prepare me for the interview. We rehearsed potential questions and answers. *If they ask you this question, you say that. If they ask that question, this is the answer.* By the day of the interview, I felt fully prepared with all the buzzwords and army terms.

My hair was styled, and I smoothed down my smart skirt and checked that my shoes were still shiny as I approached Collins Barracks. I prayed that the interview would go well. At the barracks, I was sent to a gymnasium, where I joined hundreds of other applicants sitting in rows. I was shocked to realise the girls were being interviewed in a line of open partitions in full view and hearing of everyone else waiting behind.

This only happened in the Eastern Command. I learnt later that the other commands around the country recognised the historic nature of the new recruitment drive and that female candidates were interviewed in a private room before a panel of officers.

Eventually, I was called for my interview. I sat at a desk in a partition, facing a sergeant, a slight man with dark hair and a moustache. I memorised his name as PJ had asked me.

The sergeant asked my age and checked my educational qualifications. 'I see you have two Leaving Certs – that's good,' he said. When he asked, I rattled off everything I knew about the army, including work from bomb disposal to cash escorts to serving overseas. The sergeant nodded and scribbled frantically. I felt it was a flawless interview.

He shook my hand and said I'd be hearing from them soon. He had a great poker face, but I left the hall beaming.

I have this! I thought. I felt so happy. I got the bus back to the other side of the city and went straight to an evening shift at UCD. PJ was on the same shift.

'So how did it go?' he asked.

I was full of nervous glee. 'Really well, PJ. I got to use all the information you gave me. It couldn't have gone better!'

'Who interviewed you?'

PJ had only retired from the army months earlier, and having served in Collins Barracks, he recognised the sergeant's name.

'Okay, I'm going to make a few phone calls and see what I can find out.'

I was delighted. I hoped PJ could confirm my suspicions that I was a shoo-in.

At the end of the shift, PJ pulled me aside.

'Well?' I said, a smile spreading across my face. I couldn't read his expression, but I was still very confident. 'Am I in? Am I in?'

But PJ couldn't quite meet my eyes. 'No. He said your application has been rejected.'

I'll never forget hearing those words. They were like a punch, and I reeled with a sense of shock, deflation, shame, confusion and bitter disappointment. PJ looked stricken as my face crumpled and I burst into tears in front of him. Even writing about this 40 years later, I get a lump in my throat remembering that night. I was devasted at this news.

'Why?' I eventually managed to sob. 'Why won't they accept me?'

PJ had scribbled down the three reasons given by the sergeant for rejecting my application. I still remember them today: *Too well educated, knows too much and will not take orders.*

I was bewildered. *Will not take orders* was probably true, but *too well educated* and *knows too much*? I thought of my father's advice to always research the job I was going for. 'What the hell?' I sobbed. 'What am I going to do now?'

I didn't expect PJ to have an answer, but he did. 'Well, what I'd do is go upstairs,' he said, indicating the ceiling with a jerk of his head.

My head was swimming. 'Kevin can't help me get into the army.'

'Not Kevin,' he said, using a forefinger to point towards the ceiling again. 'The director!'

He had to tell me that the director was a retired army commandant, which explained why two of his staff were ex-army too.

'Really? Would he help?' I said, hardly daring to hope.

'Go and see him first thing tomorrow and plead your case,' he said. 'I'll have a word with him too. Things might be in your favour tomorrow. Do you know what's happening here?'

Much of the UCD complex was blocked off for the 'Eastern Command'. I hadn't realised this was the Eastern Command of the Irish Army. Their annual athletics championships were taking place in UCD, meaning the general officer commanding and all the high-ranking officers would be in attendance.

'All the director has to do is walk across to the track tomorrow, casually drop your name to the right person, and your name could be taken off the rejection pile,' PJ said with a wink.

I was always a bad sleeper but had even poorer sleep than usual that night, and the following morning I went upstairs to the director's office, trembling with anxiety. 'I really want to join the army,' I said. 'If you could do anything – *anything* – I'd be really grateful.'

PJ had already talked to him, but the director sat me down and spoke to me as if I was his own child. 'You know, I wouldn't want my daughter to join the army.'

I assured him I'd thought about it a long time.

'But you're only five months into your probation period here. You know, if you don't pass the training, your job won't be here for you afterwards?'

'I know, but I still want to join the army.'

'You're walking out on a good job, and if you do one more month, you can go to university here. Do you realise that you're giving up the chance of getting a valuable education?'

I wasn't listening to any of it. I was always resolute and single-minded when I wanted something. Nothing would have changed my mind.

In the end, he sat back in his seat and shrugged in defeat. 'Okay, if that's really what you want, leave it with me and I'll see what I can do.'

I waited on tenterhooks for the next couple of weeks,

praying, and then praying some more, that the director's influence would work.

As soon as I saw the brown envelope bearing the 'harp' postmark of a government department, my stomach lurched. I'd been disappointed too many times. I tore the envelope open and, in my panic, could only see a blur of words at first. It took an interminable time to find the phrase 'successful in your application'. When I managed to calm down, the rest of the letter informed me that they would contact me with the date for my medical.

For 40 years, I never told a single living person about how I failed to get into the army on my own merits and had to use a retired commander's influence. The truth is that I felt dishonourable, and I felt substandard and undeserving of my place. It didn't matter that the sergeant's reasons were foolish. I'm not so hard on myself now because I didn't waste the chance I received, and I did my place justice. I also realise that many of the girls in my platoon had fathers and other relatives in the army and may have used their family connections to get their places too.

But, for a long time, I was deeply ashamed of the real story behind my admission to the defence forces and, for decades, it remained one of my darkest secrets.

4

Curragh Camp

The chattering of a tall blonde woman with a big suitcase breaks the heavy silence in the waiting room of Cathal Brugha Barracks. I sit tense and nervous, hugging my sports bag to my chest. When the woman pauses for breath, I hear the stop and start of motors at the gates and soldiers' boots crunching on the concrete outside.

Mostly, I listen to her speak with the confidence of someone who has been in the army all her life. Her father, uncles and brothers are in the military, so she is the authority on everything 'army' among us.

One of the other girls pipes up, wondering if we'll be leaving for Curragh Camp soon.

'Oh, no, not for a while anyway,' the blonde says. 'We

must be attested first, and then they'll bring us to the dining hall for lunch.'

Her words strike panic in my chest. *Oh, Christ! What does 'attest' mean? Is there another test?*

She is right. A sergeant arrives to lead us into the main building in the barracks. Then, a few at a time, we are sent into a room for our attestation. We are each told to place our left hand on a bible, raise our right hand and swear an oath of allegiance to the country:

I, Karina Molloy, do solemnly swear that I will be faithful to Ireland and loyal to the Constitution and that while I am a soldier in Óglaigh na hÉireann, I will obey all orders issued to me by my superior officers according to law, and I will not join or be a member of or subscribe to any organisation without due permission.

Then I sign on the bottom line, and that's it – I'm no longer a civilian. On the morning of Monday, 15 June 1981, I become number 300043 and the property of the Irish Army. I am one of the 38 women who make history as the first female recruits.

I was in such a whirl of excitement and apprehension that I actually have little memory of that momentous event in my life. Did I read out the oath at my attestation? Was I asked to repeat the words? I don't remember. Our contracts stated that we were non-combatant members of the Women's Service Corps, but it took a long time before I came to understand the implications of that.

The day had started early when my ex-army mentor, PJ, arrived to collect me in Stillorgan. I had already consulted him about what I should pack.

'Well, don't bring your make-up or heels,' he said, which was fine because I didn't own either. 'No girly-girly shit. Bring a good pair of runners, tracksuits, warm jumpers and training gear.'

The army has a saying, *Hurry up and wait*, and like the good soldier he was, PJ collected me far too early, so we sat outside Cathal Brugha Barracks a full hour before I was due that June morning. I remember him plying me with advice.

'Now, Karina, you keep the head down. That's going to be hard for you because you're so tall but, seriously, don't highlight yourself. And don't volunteer for anything because it's bound to be a dirty detail – cleaning toilets or something – and for God's sake, Karina, don't question any orders ...'

I stored all of this information in my head.

As soon as we saw other girls arriving with suitcases, I knew it was time. Most arrived with their parents. Luckily, I didn't need to hold my parents' hands because my mother wouldn't have come anyway. She was still implacably opposed to me joining the army. I said farewell to PJ, grabbed my bag, showed my acceptance letter to the gate policeman and entered the barracks and a whole new way of life.

My attestation didn't leave as deep an impression as my first visit to the army dining hall that day. The sergeant told the ten of us to leave our suitcases by the door and line up with the other male recruits and soldiers for lunch. I watched as the cook shook a steel pan of eggs that spattered in inches of blackened grease. One after another, he scooped two fried eggs with a spatula and let them slop onto a plate.

Bile rose at the back of my throat as he shoved the plate at me. My mother was a domestic goddess before her time, and, for 19 years, I had been spoilt with good food. I sat in the dining hall with the other girls, listlessly stirring grease around the plate. I surreptitiously pushed aside the tea too. The tea had stewed in stainless-steel dispensers for so long that the teaspoon almost stood to attention in the mug. My first visit to the dining hall was not a good introduction to the military. *How am I going to survive this?* I wondered. I had heard my brother moan about the terrible food but had always thought, *How bad could it be?* Now I knew.

Instead of eating, I used the time in the dining hall to assess the strengths of my competition. I never thought for a minute about making friends. Each girl was a potential rival, and I eyed the blonde, in particular, with suspicion. She was tall, athletic and knew far more than I did. I didn't like that.

Some of the girls wondered where the rest of the recruits were. The job adverts told us that the army was recruiting 40 of us, yet only ten sat at the table. It required the blonde to explain that there were four commands in the Irish Army – the Eastern, Southern, Western and the Curragh.

We were the recruits chosen by the Eastern Command and we would meet girls selected by the other three commands when we reached the Curragh Camp.

Later, we learnt that the Western Command girls had been attested on 10 June, five days ahead of the rest of us. It was years before we heard an explanation for that. Apparently, the Western Command press office had heard that the Department of Defence was getting cold feet about women entering the army. Amid a general election, a decision was made to postpone the entry of female recruits indefinitely. However, before an order could be issued to delay the women's arrival, someone in the Western Command pulled a fast one and called in their ten recruits for attestation. When the women signed on the dotted line, they became permanent, salaried members of the army, and the Department of Defence couldn't get rid of them. So the female recruitment proceeded as planned. If this is true, we owe a debt of gratitude to the male officer who brought forward the attestation of the Western girls because God only knows how long they would have delayed the entry of female soldiers.

After lunch, we were shepherded onto a minibus headed for the Curragh Camp. Motorists driving through the vast expanse of the Curragh plain usually see a dark green wall of trees off one side of the motorway, way off in the distance. Above the treeline are the tops of a church bell tower and a chunky red-brick structure that is part of the old British water tower. For most people, these are the only glimpses they'll ever have of the Irish Defence Forces training centre, better known as the Curragh Camp. As our minibus sped through the Curragh, edging ever closer to that camp, I felt both a sense of excitement and trepidation about the life concealed behind those trees.

I'd watched enough American war movies to have absorbed the trope of the psychotic drill sergeant. My brother had also warned me about 'beasting' – the routine abuse and brutal training ordeals endured by 'red arse' recruits. (Anyone less than three years in the army was routinely referred to as a red arse.)

As soon as we alighted from the bus, were we going to have our own psycho sergeant screaming abuse and spittle in our faces? Would we have to drop to the ground and give him 50? Would we spend our first night jogging the plains or scrubbing the toilet floors with toothbrushes? It had already been a long day and I didn't know if I could face relentless hours of torture.

I distinctly remember the bus travelling the curve coming up the hill into the Curragh Camp and looking down to a hollow on my left. There, I spotted the obstacle course. It all started to feel very real. I hoped we wouldn't have to try out on the obstacle course for at least a few days until we broke in our boots.

My first impression of the camp was not good. Everywhere I looked, I saw red-bricked, grimy buildings. The whole camp, our new home for the next 16 weeks, was industrial looking, grim and quite depressing.

I saw the giant water tower and the church to our left, and then the bus made a sharp right turn. We passed signs in gold lettering for the military police HQ and another sign for MacDermott Barracks on the right, and then the bus pulled into a road marked Clarke Barracks. We stopped outside one of the many red-bricked buildings where big letters on the gable read 'C Block'. We'd soon learn that the Curragh had seven barracks, each named after the executed leaders of the 1916 Rising.

We streamed out onto the road, dragging our belongings with us. The bus driver said, 'Good luck, girls,' with an amused chuckle and drove off. Straightaway I saw the sergeant march towards us, a small but stocky man with the ruddy complexion of someone well practised in roaring heated insults at recruits. I eyed him nervously, expecting it all to kick off at any moment, but instead his face broke into a big toothy smile.

'Welcome, ladies, welcome,' he beamed, throwing his arm in the direction of the open door of Block C. 'Make your way inside now, girls, and make sure to mind the step.' We shuffled forward, doing as he directed, and he stood there rocking on his heels, nodding to each of us in turn and rubbing his hands together with jovial pleasure. Sergeant Fintan Morrissey, our platoon sergeant, seemed far more genial uncle than psycho sergeant. This was nothing like the cruel and abusive hazing I had braced myself for, so it was all a bit perplexing.

Entering the block, we got the overpowering smell of fresh paint as the entire two storeys of the block had been overhauled and painted in our honour. The showers and toilets had also been refitted – and the urinals removed.

Shower curtains were hung for the first time and the wooden windowsills gleamed with new gloss paint. Everything was spotless and fresh for us. We soon learnt the other blocks were dilapidated and damp, but standard army accommodations were deemed unsuitable for our more delicate female sensitivities.

The first order of business for the sergeant was to assign our billets or rooms. We lined up as he ran a finger down a ledger and asked for each of our numbers. A few of the girls nervously admitted they had already forgotten their numbers.

Sergeant Morrissey shook his head with a look of sad disappointment. 'Ah, now girls, you may be remembering your numbers. Jesus, don't be trying to make life difficult for yourselves here from the very beginning. Don't forget your numbers, girls.'

Two of us from the Eastern Command were allocated to the same room on the ground floor. Metal-framed beds with sagging springs and thin mattresses were lined up on three walls of the room. At the end of each mattress was a 'bed block', a perfectly square arrangement of elaborately folded sheets and blankets. Our cases were to be placed, handles to the wall, on top of the locker. My sports bag had to be flattened pancake-like so it didn't catch the eye from the door. Not even a dust mote was allowed to rest under our beds. The army had rules for everything.

For the next couple of hours, more girls poured in from the other commands and four billets over two floors filled up. I watched all of them, assessing them, wondering how fit or fast they were. I had no interest in making friends. I was there to become the best soldier. My father's words were ringing in my ears: 'You win best recruit and you become an officer.' I only felt a duty to succeed.

I knew nothing about psychology or parents foisting their failed dreams on their children. My brother had won Best Shot as a recruit, and my father expected no less from me. I had a mantra running through my head: *I must win at least one prize*. Enjoying the experience didn't come into it. My priority was to be the best recruit.

I was anxious, however. Many girls came from boarding schools and were used to sleeping through the attendant noise of echoing halls and dorms. I'd had the privilege of having my own room for 19 years and yet always had problems sleeping and had been an insomniac from an early age. Sharing with eight other recruits was going to be an enormous test of endurance for me. It was my ultimate nightmare. How could I possibly become the best soldier if I was permanently sleep-deprived?

It was lights out at 23.59 and I lay back in bed for my first night in the Curragh Camp. The historic nature of the day and the accomplishment of being one of the first women to make it into the Irish Army never entered my mind. The only thought rolling around my head that first night was, *Please God, let me get a few hours' sleep.*

5

Recruit Training

Shrieks of laughter reverberated through our block, and suddenly one of our fellow recruits burst into our room. She struck a mock-model pose at the door, her lips pouted, a hand on her jutting hip. Her pigtails swung over our new physical-training (PT) uniform – a white V-neck tennis shirt, a tiny white tennis skirt with blue trim and long white socks.

'Well, what do you think, girls?' she said as she sashayed through our room catwalk style. We laughed uproariously.

Then, she swivelled in her socks, flipped up the rear of her little skirt and, in modern parlance, 'twerked', wiggling her army-issue frilly white knickers at us. Her audience whooped and cheered.

'Can you believe it?' she screeched. 'We're supposed to wear this stuff in public?' And with another 'twerk' of her lacy undies in our direction, she was gone, darting off to entertain the next room.

Our PT uniform caused much hilarity but most of us were cringing behind it all. I held up my own pair of frilly white knickers, covered in row after row of ruffled lace. The army was sending us training dressed more like saucy schoolgirls than soldiers.

There wasn't a lot of time to think about it, however. Our early days as recruits were head-spinning as the army threw vast amounts of information at us to absorb and learn. In the movies, the American military rose to the chirpy bugle call of the reveille. We had orderly sergeants pounding heavily on our doors while letting out a few choice roars. However, everyone was up long before the sergeant started yelling at us to get outside. From day one, everyone was expected to be up, dressed and ready to go on parade by 07.00hrs.

The job of transforming us from civilians to soldiers began on our first morning with Sergeant Morrissey teaching us how to fall in as number four platoon. I was anxious to learn and please, but that task was not made easy as all the drill in the army was conducted in Irish.

When the sergeant bellowed, '*Luigh isteach!*', it was double-Dutch to me and, by the confusion around me, it was obviously incomprehensible to everyone else too. Learning to 'fall in' was a rigmarole organised according to height. It made sense when I got my number – I was number three, the third tallest in the platoon.

But then Sergeant Morrissey began the task of teaching us to march, and everything fell apart. '*Buíonn, aire!*' he bellowed. '*Do réir dheis, go mear máirseáil.*' ('Platoon, attention! By the right, quick march.')

Haltingly, we turned in every direction, not knowing what we were meant to do. It could have been a comic scene from that year's hit movie, *Private Benjamin*. Fortunately, Sergeant Morrissey had backup in the form of two section non-commissioned officers (NCOs), and eventually our rag-bag platoon, wearing assorted civvies, marched in three uneven columns to the clothing stores for our first uniform.

No formal (number one) uniforms were issued for a long time. The army wouldn't waste resources on recruits who might yet be discharged during the 16-week course. Instead, we were handed a pile of white PT gear and ordered to get kitted out in the army's workaday fatigues, shirt, tie, beret and boots.

When we questioned the oversized fatigues, we were told they only came in men's sizes. The shirts worn under the fatigues were men's sizes too. Thankfully, everything was held in place by the canvas webbing belts cinching our waists. However, the biggest problem was with the boots, which were also only available in men's sizes.

'Don't worry,' I said with naïve confidence. 'It's probably temporary.'

It took the army another two or three years before they introduced proper women's footwear to the uniform. In the meanwhile, ill-fitting boots caused terrible problems, from blisters to shin splints. But we wore everything and got on with it.

However, mutinous mutterings continued over our PT kit. The guys wore army-issue shorts and vests for physical training, but there was nothing vaguely military about our tennis skirts and frilly knickers. We couldn't run in the flimsy white plimsolls issued with the uniform, so we were ordered to wear our army boots instead. We lined up outside the barracks for our daily runs in minis and boots – years before Madonna made the look a trend.

Lieutenant Maria Flynn, the officer in charge of our physical training, led us on two-mile runs in the mornings. I regarded the lieutenant with a mixture of awe and envy. The daughter of a colonel, she qualified from Thomond before joining the army as a cadet. She occupied the job I planned to get.

When we took off for our runs in our frilly knickers and boots, the entire camp ground to a halt. I know an ex-army member who still fondly remembers looking up and seeing us pass as he dug a ditch 40 years ago. We were so busy concentrating on trying to stay in step that, mercifully, we couldn't see the entire camp laughing.

After our morning runs, the platoon had time for a quick wash before heading to the dining hall yards from our barracks. The dining hall served congealed food amid nicotine-stained, peeling walls, and plastic stacking chairs and rickety old Formica tables. Many of us survived on Weetabix or beans on toast. I struggled with the fare on offer throughout my time in the army.

At 08.15hrs, we lined up on parade in front of our block to be inspected by Sergeant Morrissey and our platoon officer, Lieutenant Maria O'Donoghue. She had been among the first female cadets to be commissioned the year before us and trained by the Women's Royal Army Corps in Camberley in Surrey.

If Sergeant Morrissey was our genial uncle, the lieutenant was like our formidable maiden aunt. She was dark and neat, but her expression was darker, and her demeanour stern and intimidating. Even though she was slight in stature, she was a woman not to be crossed.

Looking back, I can only imagine how much pressure she would have been under. She was in her early or mid-twenties and was given the responsibility for the military education of the first platoon of women to enter the army. That was an enormous undertaking. All eyes were watching her and us, and plenty were willing us to fail, so she had to be rigid and uncompromising.

We were reprimanded if our ties weren't perfectly straight or our boots weren't shining. My short, curly hair grew rapidly, so I got a sharp tap on the shoulder when a curl reached my collar. I had to pin it or snip it off later.

As the sergeant or Lieutenant O'Donoghue inspected us, a corporal followed with a pad and pen, noting who got reprimanded for what.

When there were multiple reprimands, the entire

platoon was punished, and we had a couple of recruits who inadvertently got everyone into trouble. The army refers to them as 'heat seekers' because they are always drawing trouble on themselves and those around them. Fellow recruits would press their uniforms and send them out looking immaculate. But the minute they got on parade, their hair would stick out or their berets would be crooked.

The male instructors lost their heads with us at times. 'Yis shower of feckin' eejits! And yis are supposed to be the best of the women who applied for the army. Well, God feckin' save us from the rejects!'

However, they never were as abusive to us as they were to the male recruits. We often heard the instructors turn the air blue screaming at the male platoons. 'Feckin' eejits' was as bad as it got for us.

The punishments were as inventive as they were varied. One day we were ordered to march *ar sodar máirseáil* (double speed) to MacDonagh Square while clapping our hands in the air. We had a vast audience that day. No one paid a blind bit of notice to the male platoons marching. But all the men liked to stand and watch the female platoon and provide a running commentary on our marching skills, or lack of them.

Marching has been used to move mass numbers of troops effectively and speedily from one place to another since ancient times. For a long time, our marching was neither effective nor speedy as foot drill was not easy to learn. As recruits, we stretched our arms when marching so that our thumb knuckles reached the shoulder of the person in front. We broke into twos and practised our *deas agus clé iompaígí* (right and left turns) for hours. It took a long time for most of us to get it.

The main square for the training of recruits was MacDonagh square. After our inspection outside the barracks, we marched to the square for another inspection at 08.30hrs. The defence forces were churning out recruit platoons in the 1980s, so the square was always busy. We were number four recruit platoon, so there were three male platoons before us and two more behind us, all marching on the square.

Before starting the day's training, we were allowed 15 minutes for a smoke break. Nearly everyone, from officers to recruits, smoked, so these breaks were frequent. In some billets, girls had to put up with chain smokers lighting up in bed. Communal areas like the dining hall, the rec room and training rooms were full of smoke.

Everyone in the platoon was randomly split into sections from our first day – each group containing nine or ten recruits. Dividing us into sections made it easier for us to learn and for instructors to teach. By 09.00hrs, our section NCOs appeared on MacDonagh square to march us into one of the training rooms for weapons, fieldcraft or signals training. Alternatively, the timetable could dictate that we stay on the square for foot or arms drills.

One of the first things we learnt was the unique art of crafting our blankets and sheets into the neat square 'block' demanded by the army. The bed block was about discipline, maintaining high standards and attention to detail. The blue line down the middle of the sheets had to be perfectly straight and tucked into expertly folded blankets. It was said to be 'character building'. However, most girls said it was a pain in the arse and resorted to using sleeping bags, so their bed block remained permanently made.

In signals training, we started by learning the phonetic alphabet: *Alfa, Bravo, Charlie, Delta, Echo, Foxtrot, Golf, Hotel, India, Juliett, Kilo, Lima* … In weapons training, we learnt how to strip the FN (Fabrique Nationale) rifle and the GPMG (general-purpose machine gun). Huge levels of new information came at us fast and hard.

Instruction with our section NCOs finished at 16.30hrs, just as the dining hall started dishing out dinner. However, we still had a lot of homework to do. The corridors of our block were chaotic as we broke up in pairs or small groups and spent hours marching up and down, still figuring out one foot from the other.

'Left, right, left, right … stop! This isn't working. Start again.'

I also had to polish my boots, fight over the ironing board and press my shirt and uniform every night. There was little downtime, apart from Saturdays when we had to be back in barracks by 23.59hrs. The girls who lived near the area returned to their families and the rest of us took the bus to Newbridge for the day.

We had no lie-ins on Sundays. I hadn't seen the inside of a church since I left home two years earlier, but we were paraded to mass whether we liked it or not. The occasional non-Catholic was still forced to go on parade to the church and was left standing outside until mass was over. Compulsory mass in the army continued for years.

We got one weekend off a month, and I often didn't even go home then. I stayed in and trained and got very efficient at making my bed block and reorganising my locker. I'd shake my head when I heard girls talking about their great weekends away.

Jesus, you shouldn't be out drinking or clubbing if you want to make the most of this.

Looking back, I took the whole thing too seriously. At no stage did I think, *Molloy, get over yourself now and try and enjoy this time in your life.* I enjoyed every minute of recruit training because I loved to learn. But I wish I'd allowed myself to have more craic with the other girls and to chill out sometimes. I put so much pressure on myself to do better than everybody else. 'Serious' is the best word to describe me back then. I never relaxed.

Recruits came and went for the first week. A girl in the bed beside me disappeared on our second day at the Curragh, and was replaced by a girl from Dublin the next day. Another recruit was sent home because she had lied about her age. When all the toings and froings ended after about a week, the number four recruit platoon consisted of 38 women.

However, mutinous mutterings continued over the gym kit. We all felt demeaned running around a military camp in tiny skirts and lacy knickers. To this day, I'm not sure who was responsible for the rigout; I imagine the decision came down from the higher echelons of the defence forces. Not knowing what to do with women in the army, they resorted to what they knew best – subjecting us to hoary old gender stereotypes and dressing us like cute schoolgirls.

However, events overtook our plans to make a complaint when we arrived at the gym for a lesson in rope climbing. The commanding officer of the gym looked out his office window and looked from the length of coil hanging from the ceiling to our bare legs and miniskirts and realised the PTI had an upskirt view of frilly knickers.

He had the common sense to spare everyone's blushes. 'Get those women tracksuits!' he barked at our section NCO.

We all bought our own blue tracksuits from Dunnes Stores, and the bizarre scenes of the first and only Irish Army platoon to train in frilly knickers came to an abrupt end.

6

Non-Combatants

Towards the end of July 1981, the sergeant marched us into a lecture hall six weeks into our training, around the third or fourth week of July 1981. Several of the officers and non-commissioned officers (NCOs) were assembled in front of us.

'What's all this about?' we whispered among ourselves. The officers' expressions were solemn.

'This is to inform you, ladies, that the Women's Service Corps [WSC] is to be disbanded,' an officer announced.

We glanced at each other, unsure what this would mean for us. All 38 of us had signed a contract with the WSC rather than the Irish Defence Forces. According to a Department of Defence memo, the WSC was intended 'to release male soldiers from certain duties in order to fill more active military functions'. The army had also discussed plans to pay women less than men and to terminate the service of any woman who became pregnant. Thankfully, equality legislation put the kibosh on those plans. However, the WSC didn't even have time to get off the ground before it was disbanded.

'As you ladies did not sign a contract with the army, you are free to leave if you wish,' the officer said. 'However, if you choose to stay, you are no longer a member of the Women's Service Corps. Your platoon will be fully integrated into the army.'

I remember looking around at the others, wondering what, if anything, this meant for us. I met other confused expressions and shrugs. Training continued as usual, and even though our old contracts were thrown out, we never signed new ones.

We weren't aware of it then but disbanding the WSC was the first real injustice to the female recruits. If the corps had remained, it would have meant rapid promotion through the ranks. But as soon as the defence forces disbanded it, we had to vie for promotional opportunities in an old boys' club that often closed ranks and actively impeded the advancement of women. It also had more unfortunate implications for us in the coming years.

Officially, we had just been absorbed into the main body of the army, but we were only starting to realise that we were still very much restricted in what we were allowed to do.

As non-combatants, we began to see differences between our training and that of the male recruits. Our platoon never went 'on the ground' as the male recruits did, marching across the mountains and over rough terrain on a 24-hour exercise. I wanted the opportunity to do what the male recruits were doing, so I resented these omissions.

My platoon only experienced two route marches during our 16 weeks of training, and the longest we marched was six miles. The only reason the route marches were challenging was because our equipment, boots and uniform were designed for men.

Our backpack was not designed for the female body. The 1958 pattern webbing backpack was made to sit on the small of a man's back, but it was too long for women, and the straps and waist belt didn't fit. It towered over some girls' heads and stretched so low that it hit off their backsides, chafing their hips badly.

No matter how many pairs of socks we wore, the boots never fitted. They slipped up and down, making marching a far more painful experience than it should have been.

The disparity between the treatment of the male and female recruits was never so apparent as the day Sergeant Morrissey announced that number four recruit platoon was to be given the afternoon of 29 July off. 'The officers have kindly decided to give you time off to watch the British royal wedding,' he beamed. 'I'm sure none of you wants to miss Lady Diana Spencer marrying Prince Charles!'

Lots of the girls were delighted, of course, but I could hardly believe my ears. Neither could the male recruit platoons, who were hard at training while we were supposed to 'ooh' and 'aah' over Princess Di's wedding gown.

When we signed up, we were told that recruit training was 16 weeks; if we passed, we would emerge as two-star privates. To become fully qualified soldiers in the defence forces, we would return to the Curragh shortly afterwards and undertake our three-star course.

During the three-star course, privates learnt advanced military skills and tactical training. They marched up mountains, crawled through rivers, dug trenches, learnt map-reading, used weapons in night firing, and had chemical, biological and nuclear training.

The final week involved ground training in the Glen of Imaal and being put through the infamous 'scratch' challenge. Scratch was an extreme obstacle course, a form of beasting that involved lots of mud, water and pain. NCOs screamed abuse in soldiers' ears and took them out of their comfort zones into full combat zones.

It was a week of full-on psychological warfare where the army tried to break its soldiers. The three-star course would provide our first true physical challenge, and I looked forward to it.

Then ten weeks into our training, the army had another announcement for number four recruit platoon.

'I've good and bad news, recruits,' said our platoon officer after telling us to *seas ar ais* or 'stand at ease' outside our barracks. 'The bad news is that recruit training is being extended from 16 weeks to 18 weeks.'

A general groan and a concerned commotion rose from the platoon. 'What's going on?' the girl beside me whispered. 'They can't do that, can they?'

'Ladies, your attention, please,' continued the officer. 'The good news is that you will pass out as three-star privates at the end of the 18 weeks.'

This time there was an excited murmur of approval in the ranks. Everyone was beaming at this news, but my heart sank into my ill-fitting boots. The officer confirmed that instead of the three-star course, we'd spend the two extra weeks learning clerical duties, such as typing, filing and how to run an office. I was gutted. We were not getting full training as soldiers.

That evening, a few of us were queuing for fish and chips outside the Wes Café, where half my wages were spent. We met a few male recruits and told them about our three-star status. I saw the guys' jaws drop in astonishment and outrage. They didn't take the news well either.

'Well, feck that!' one lad said. 'You're passing out with three stars and we have to come back here and kill ourselves to get the same thing?' It was a big bone of contention for the male recruits, spawning a lot of resentment against the women that continued for years.

'Why do you lot get all the special treatment?' they complained, even though we had no say in the matter.

We talked about it in our room that night.

'God, the lads aren't happy about it, are they?'

'I'm not happy about it either,' I said. 'I wanted to do the three-star course. I think we're going to be missing out on so much.'

'Missing out on misery, you mean!' replied one of the girls. 'Are you daft, Karina? Thanks be to God we don't have to come back and spend weeks freezing our arses off in muck and rain.'

The other girls agreed. No one else shared my frustration over the latest changes to our training.

'Get a grip, Karina. Why waste time training us for combat when we're non-combatants? Be grateful that we're getting away with it. We're getting our three stars, and we're out of here.'

No one recognised that the army had just placed a major barricade between us and full gender integration and equality.

I decided to push all thoughts of disappointment aside. *Just focus on getting on a physical training instructor course*, I thought. *That's the ambition and that's what I'm here for.*

I consoled myself thinking that clerical training wasn't as bad as the classes the female cadets endured. They had to train in make-up, grooming and deportment while the male cadets were off doing other things, like heavy-weapons training. It's still hard to believe, but while the men were busy blowing stuff up, the female cadets were left to try on lipsticks and parade up and down the barracks balancing books on their heads.

The truth is, the first female soldiers of the army were like weather vanes, blown around in every direction. Our contracts were torn up and our Women's Service Corps disbanded. Our training and schedules were constantly in flux, constantly changing at the whim of every civil servant or general. We never knew what was going to be happening next.

Looking back now, I realise we were guinea pigs in the hands of an organisation still suffering from culture shock. When the government introduced an act to provide for the enlistment of women in 1979, the army's hand had been forced. The all-male environment was already brushing up against equality legislation and anti-discrimination laws. It was also out of step with the mixed-gender militaries of other Western countries. But the defence forces were dinosaurs, slow to adapt to any modern notions of gender integration. The truth was, when the army took on 38 female recruits, they still hadn't figured out what to do with us.

7

Prize Giving

The instructor handed me the primed grenade. 'Prepare to throw!' he barked. I took my stance, left leg forward. This was the culmination of an enormous number of drills. We had practised within an inch of our lives, flinging dozens of blue-coloured dummy devices, and now I held a green grenade. Finally, I was about to throw the real thing.

I stood, heart thumping, in the throwing area with two instructors. We were in the purpose-built grenade range, a concrete trench in a secure location. All the girls had received a safety briefing designed to scare the shit out of us, warning us of all the things that could go wrong. I had already watched one girl break down in tears on the grenade range.

I kept a tight grip on the grenade, the fly-off or safety lever firmly depressed in my hand. Then, with a deep breath and a violent twist, I pulled the pin. The instructors watched my hand, beady-eyed and alert. We were still safe if I kept the lever depressed. If I accidentally released the lever or dropped the grenade, we had six seconds before it exploded. It was just enough time to be dragged ignominiously around the safety blast wall behind us. The rest of the girls were in the holding bay, another walled area of the trench, watching me through a slatted opening.

Don't fuck this up. Don't fuck this up, I thought.

I spread my arms; my empty left hand aimed towards the target – a wooden box low in the gravelled throw area before us. My right arm was stretched behind me, gripping the live grenade.

'THROW GRENADE!' roared the instructor.

'GRENADE!' I cried as instructed, and flung it over the trench wall, releasing the lever of the device as I did so. We were allowed a second or two to see the device land before ducking below the concrete wall for safety. I stood too long, waiting for the grenade to stop rolling, hoping against hope that it was on target.

'Get fucking down, Molloy!' the instructor bawled in my ear as he wrenched my shoulder and flung me to the ground. I'd never make that mistake again. My ears were ringing and my body was winded even before the grenade exploded, and a cloud of dust and gravel fell on my metal helmet. These days, recruits have ear protectors and body armour, but we had none of that in the early eighties. I got to my feet, dusted myself off, pocketed the pin from my first grenade and was handed my second.

'Prepare to throw!' the instructor barked again, and I took my stance, left foot forward.

I still have that first pin I pulled along with a grenade casing that I picked up that day, even though I've thrown many grenades since.

Near the end of our recruit training, we received big news. The quartermaster general of the Irish Defence Forces, a brigadier general in rank, would carry out the final inspection of our kit. A general – an actual general – was coming to inspect the recruit platoon's kit. It was unheard of. The order could only have come from the chief of staff, and I imagine the general was disgusted that he had to conduct such a lowly deed. All that concerned me was impressing the general to keep up with my brother and bring home one of the top recruit awards.

My hopes of winning the Best Recruit award were high in the early days of recruit training. I distinctly remember the day we met our section non-commissioned officer (NCO) for the first time.

'Right, girls,' he said, clapping his hands. 'I'm sure you know we have the best female recruit in this room, so this must be the best section. Let's get on with this.'

I was delighted and astonished at this announcement. *Wow, how the hell did he know that? This is the first time I've met him! Gosh, these guys are so perceptive to realise that I'm the best soldier.* I looked around at the other eight girls and I had no doubt that I was a far better soldier than any of them. *Winning Best Recruit is going to be easier than I thought.* My father had drilled it into my head that I would get the Best Recruit, and I never doubted it.

Within a few weeks, I realised I had no hope of winning the award. With growing dismay, I watched recruits who were faster, stronger and better than me.

Always practical, I quickly relinquished my dreams of winning Best Recruit and focused my efforts on winning the Best Shot prize. Even though we signed a contract saying we were non-combatants, we still had full weapons training.

We learnt to handle and strip the general-purpose machine gun (GPMG), a hefty machine gun that weighed 31 pounds, including its spare parts and barrel bag. The weapon of choice for the Irish Army then was the Fabrique Nationale (FN) rifle from Belgium. The rifle weighed ten pounds and was 43 inches long – a mere 15 inches shorter than some of our girls.

The rifle also had a considerable kick. Ten at a time, we took turns on the range, and those who didn't get the rifle properly set into the crook of their shoulder ended up black and blue from the recoil. One of the section NCOs taught them to protect themselves by tucking a wad of field dressing behind their bra straps.

At the end of our first rifle session, Sergeant Morrissey appeared flushed with excitement. 'Amazing! We've got two great shooters here, girls!'

I always imagined hitting the targets with rock-like steadiness and eagle-sharp eyesight. I had no fear of using weapons because I'd often fired my father's shotgun when we were hunting. I still remember Sergeant Morrissey, beaming with avuncular pride, his cheeks even redder than usual as he declared, 'Recruits Curran and O'Riordan – well done, ladies – your ability to shoot is outstanding!'

I gazed at the two girls in a mixture of shock and envy. *Holy fuck. Them?* They were the most unlikely sharpshooters. One of them was so quiet, I'd nicknamed her *'The Librarian'*. But as they say, it's always the quiet ones. The two gentlest, most reserved and feminine girls on the platoon turned out to be the most lethal.

It came as a major blow to me to discover I was one of the worst shots in the platoon. I couldn't shoot a target to save my life. I barely scraped by in range practice and, as a result, I also had to relinquish any dream of winning Best Shot.

My shooting capabilities remained poor until years later when I met my partner, an ex-army ranger. He explained where to set the sights via a diagram on the back of a cigarette box and taught me that hitting the target was all about breathing. When I returned to do my annual range practice, everything fell into place, and my shooting improved immensely, but it was 25 years too late to get Best Shot.

Jesus Christ, I better get Best Kit or my father will take me out and shoot me himself, I thought. The Best Kit award involved the perfect presentation of everything the army issued us, including everything stored in our lockers and bed space.

Paula McCosker was the only other recruit from Donegal, and she happened to be in my room and section. She was skilful at folding shirts because she had worked in a shirt factory before joining the army. Everyone knew I was desperate to win Best Kit and saw me eyeing Paula's perfectly folded shirts.

I asked her to share her secret. I still remember her standing in front of me, hands on her hips. 'No way, I'm not telling you!' she said. 'What makes you so sure you'll get Best Kit anyway?'

Paula teased me for ages before she relented, and I learnt the sacred art of shirt folding. After that, I felt sure the Best Kit award would be mine.

In the fortnight before the general arrived, we had surprise inspection after inspection. Towels had to have the perfect fold, and T-shirts and shirts had to be crisply ironed. Everything had a place and had to be placed properly and in the correct direction. Our platoon officer found fault with everything and told us to get our act together. *You girls are not up to scratch!*

Then, finally, it was D-Day, and amid much pomp and ceremony, the general arrived. He and his entourage went upstairs first, where he met the other Recruit Molloy, an All-Ireland camogie player. Ann Molloy got special dispensation to leave barracks to play her county matches and she stored her camogie sticks in her locker.

'So, you're the camogie player,' said the general, standing in the middle of the room. He could see the contents of her locker from there.

'Yes, sir!' she said, standing to attention. Unfortunately, Recruit Molloy's camogie sticks failed to stand to attention in the locker.

'Did you fire those fecking camogies from here?' he roared.

The general arrived downstairs; the expert shirt folder, Paula, had the first bed on the left as he entered our room. As the general inspected her kit, he ordered her to open her poncho. Upon hearing this, my heart hit my boots, and I panicked. *Fuck, fuck, fuck!*

We all carried rolled-up rubber ponchos under our backpacks. They covered us and protected our packs and equipment in a downpour. No one had inspected the ponchos before, so I never thought to clean mine. Beads of sweat broke out on my forehead and more trickled down my back. *Oh God*, I thought. *There's my chance of Best Kit gone.*

Paula unwrapped her poncho and, to everyone's horror, revealed a great lump of dried-in mud on the front of the garment. The general summoned himself to his full height and pointed to the offending stain.

'What is THAT?'

Paula was standing to attention, eyes ahead. 'That would be MUCK, SIR!' she replied in her full Donegal accent.

A cloud of confusion passed over the general's face. The men usually stumbled, lied or prevaricated with excuses, so he wasn't expecting a direct response. He stood stunned for a moment and moved on.

The following inspections passed without incident, until the general reached me. I was sweating profusely at this stage, thinking of my dirty poncho. But the poncho was not my undoing.

Anytime we took out our FN rifles, we had to clean them, which I did share with my fellow section members during the lesson. To clean the gun barrel, we needed a pull-through – a cord with a brass weight to which we attached a 4 x 2-inch flannelette for cleaning. Pull-throughs were always in short demand, and I was often fed up waiting for one. So, to use an army phrase, I decided to 'relocate' a pull-through. I popped it in my pocket so I'd always have one.

This was a massive no-no in the army, and it was a cardinal sin to take anything that wasn't personal ordnance. If it wasn't signed for, it belonged to the stores. Somehow I managed to miss that memo and made the mistake of displaying it as part of my kit. I was clueless, thinking I would look good having a piece of equipment that no one else had. *I'll be the only one. The general will think I'm so resourceful and motivated.*

Of course, the general spotted the pull-through straight away and spun towards Lieutenant O'Donoghue and Sergeant Morrissey. 'Why has this recruit got ordnance in her kit that she wasn't issued?' he demanded.

If looks could kill, Maria O'Donoghue would have murdered me on the spot. She glared at me so long and hard that I thought I could see her teeth grinding. I was devastated. I wanted to crumple into a ball and cry but, minutes later, we were ordered outside, where we had to fall in for the general's departure. Lieutenant O'Donoghue departed with him, leaving us with Sergeant Morrissey.

The sergeant, a master of understatement, waited until they were out of earshot. 'Well,' he said, arms behind his back, rising up and down on the balls of his feet. 'We had a few feckin' surprises in there, ladies.'

As Lieutenant O'Donoghue announced the prizewinners in the lecture hall later, I was despondent. I felt totally gutted and foolish. I'd sabotaged myself and destroyed my last and only chance of a prize. Our section NCO was right – the Best Recruit award went to one of the girls in our section, but it was Maeve Magennis rather than me. Joint winners of the Best Shot award went to our resident snipers, Mary O'Riordan and Bernie Curran.

I mentally listed off the two or three rivals likely to win Best Kit. Then somewhere in my gloom I heard our platoon officer call out the name 'Recruit Molloy, K'. I couldn't believe it – I'd won Best Kit! The lieutenant added some acerbic commentary such as 'by the skin of her teeth' and 'a controversial decision', but I was beyond caring. In my head, I was already dancing. *I won! Jesus Christ, I fecking won!*

We heard that the official prize-giving ceremony would be held at our passing out then we went back to training. My heart was pounding with excitement. I could hardly wait until the evening, when I could walk 15 minutes up to the only public telephone and break the good news to my father.

'I got Best Kit, Daddy!' I said.

He paused on the other end of the phone. 'What happened to Best Recruit?'

'Em …'

'I thought you'd at least get Best Shot.'

'Well …'

I made whatever excuses I could.

'Okay, so you got Best Kit.'

My father was just being his usual dispassionate and reserved self. He couldn't be anything else. When I eventually hung up, I realised that he hadn't said the words 'well done'.

I walked back to the barracks, went straight to my room and burst into tears. I must have cried for an hour that night, thinking of how I must have disappointed my father.

8

Passing Out

The day of our passing out was miserable. Dark clouds sat heavily over the Curragh Camp, and the rain pelted down at times. The grounds were pocked with big black puddles of water. Nevertheless, the platoon was in a flurry of excitement as we fell in outside our block for our last time as recruits. We all stood to attention, looking immaculate in our starched and pressed uniforms and black berets.

Our number one and two uniforms arrived late into training, only a short while before our passing out. The shoes were stodgy-looking brown brogues. Laced and clunky, they bizarrely came with a two-inch chunky heel unsuitable for marching or standing on parade. We called them 'nuns' shoes'.

The significance of being issued with brown shoes didn't dawn on us initially. Only officers wore brown shoes in the army. Yet the female other ranks continued to wear brown shoes for another four or five years until someone finally noticed the mistake.

Dublin-based designer Ib Jorgensen designed all the women's uniforms. He revealed that the army had requested 'glamorous' uniforms like those he'd created for the Aer Lingus air hostesses. This request was probably another indication that female soldiers were regarded as more decorative than useful among the senior army ranks. Whoever sourced our footwear, however, ruined the army's objectives. We couldn't look remotely glamorous when the lumpen brogues were worn below our skirts.

The number one dress uniform for ceremonies and formal occasions consisted of a green fitted and belted jacket over a matching skirt with a front pleat. After months in fatigues and an all-male environment, the uniform was popular with our platoon. We liked the skirts and enjoyed standing out from the rest of the army.

Our new hats, a green pillbox style with a scoop, failed to arrive in time for our passing out, so we had to wear our plain berets instead. We loved our hats, but later female recruits ridiculed them as 'ashtrays' and 'bedpans'.

The army also issued us with six pairs of tights in the shade *Tivoli* every six months. This allocation was clearly decided by someone who never wore tights because I often laddered two pairs a day when I started working. We received handbags too as part of our uniform. The female officers got the same bag, but theirs was made from leather, and ours was PVC – a subtle reminder if ever we needed one of the differences between officers and 'other ranks'.

The final weeks of recruit training flew past, even though the admin course was even more boring than I'd feared. I learnt that everything about the army is different from civilian life. The last sentence of every military letter is 'For your information and action'. Signing off, we would use the rank and surname of the officer for whom we were typing the letter. (Officers never typed their own letters.) My eyelids drooped and my head bobbed during interminable lessons on how to answer the phone and complete the in-out log book. By the end of the course, I was more determined than ever to get on the physical-training instructor course as fast as possible.

The different treatment meted out to the male and female recruits became evident again we got closer to passing out. Traditionally, all recruits performed an arms drill at the passing-out ceremony. However, Sergeant Morrissey broke the news that we would only be doing foot drills.

'There are concerns over your skirts,' he said. 'They might be caught by the cocking handles when you have to lift them.' He was referring to the part of the drill where we had to *tóg airm* or pick up arms from the ground.

'Sure, that's just daft,' I said. 'We could move the rifles out so they won't catch our skirts.'

I'm certain the explanation was just an excuse. Even

with the introduction of new equality legislation, equal rights were still a pipe dream. Patronising attitudes were prevalent across society, and women were controlled and 'protected' rather than empowered. That's why women were non-combatants in the army, and why those who strayed from society's strict moral expectations were still being incarcerated in Magdalene laundries. The men in army headquarters or the Department of Defence decided that the public wasn't ready to see young Irish women marching with rifles. It was far too dangerous and unladylike.

The platoon was bitterly disappointed to lose our arms drill. Our families were attending the passing-out parade, and we knew a display of marching skills would not be a particularly riveting performance – the Irish Army is not known for fancy foot drills like other militaries. Fortunately, two of our platoon, former girl guides or scouts, choreographed a foot-drill display we could be proud of. We rehearsed for hours at a time on MacDonagh square and, nearer the date, the Curragh army band started rehearsing with us.

Only days before the parade, we discovered we'd be marching to the cringeworthy tune of 'Thank Heaven for Little Girls'. Ironically, we would conclude our drill with a track from the musical *Annie Get Your Gun*, a show that was based on an actual female sharpshooter.

'They're fine with Annie getting her gun,' I said, 'but they won't let us be seen with rifles.'

The ground was saturated as we set off in formation

to MacDonagh square on the morning of the parade. The sergeant and platoon officer led the way, with two non-commissioned officers (NCOs) alongside. We had only marched a few yards when I felt my legs getting wet. Mud was spattering on my tights as we marched.

Within seconds, we realised as a collective what was happening and began spreading out and slowing down. The row in front of me was no longer within touching distance of my thumb knuckle, and the row behind dropped back too. We kept two arms' lengths between us and marched more slowly, to reduce the impact of our shoes in the wet.

The two male NCOs had heart attacks as they saw our formation spread out and slow down. One of them ran at us, roaring, 'What the feck is going on? Touch up! Touch up!' No doubt he was thinking, *Jesus, these women are passing out and they still can't bloody march*. 'Touch up!' he screamed again.

'We can't. We're minding our tights,' came the reply.

The guy's face turned from outrage to confusion and, after glancing down, to comprehension. He'd only ever dealt with trousers in the rain before. 'Oh, shit. Right so,' he said, before passing the information up the ranks.

On the square, Sergeant Morrissey kicked off our foot-drill display with a single command: '*Buíonn aire. Do réir dheis, go mear máirseáil!*'

Then it was just us 38 women. We performed the rest of the display without further commands. We managed to pull it all off, including the deceptively complex figure of eight routine.

As a prizewinner, I also practised leaving formation, marching to the commanding officer, taking one step forward and saluting. Then there was another palaver about accepting the award in the right hand and bringing it smartly down to my side, taking one step back, saluting again, turning and marching back. Finally, I had to put my hands behind my back, where an NCO relieved me of the prize, so my two hands were free to march on. Everything is choreographed in the army, even accepting a small wooden plaque.

My parents sat in the viewing stand erected for all the families, with my brother who was soon to depart for the French Foreign Legion. He wore his uniform under duress from my father, and I'm glad he did because a local newspaper took photos of us, sibling soldiers, in Irish Army uniform together. They're the only ones I have. My parents were not the type to display emotion, but I still have all the photographs and their broad smiles betray their pride. Even my mother had reconciled herself to my career path by then.

I looked around, feeling proud and happy that night at our celebration party in the Keadeen Hotel near the Curragh Camp. We wore the matching platoon rings we had designed to mark the occasion. Each signet ring bore the female biological symbol and the letters 'FF', standing for *fianna fáil* or 'soldiers of destiny'. Thirty-eight rings were made in gold or silver by a Newbridge jeweller, and they remain the only ones of their kind in the world. (The silver was offered as a more affordable alternative because recruits earned very little money.)

I felt honoured to be part of that historic group and that night's celebrations. I also felt grateful that I got the opportunity to join the army and relieved that I didn't waste the space that should have gone to another girl.

It was only after we left the Curragh that we realised we were handled very cautiously in recruit training. Sergeant Morrissey, a real gentleman, treated us as if we were his own daughters. All who had taught us were gentlemen. They trained us very well, but they coddled us. We didn't face the same rigours as the men and, in that sense, the army didn't do us any favours. It meant we weren't prepared when we went for promotion and went into competition with the men on NCO courses.

Real army life came as a terrible shock to me anyway. Compared to my NCO course three years later, I would look back fondly on my 18 weeks in recruit training and liken it to a Butlin's holiday camp.

9

Army Headquarters

I carried a tea tray to the general's office and rapped on the door. I was new in army headquarters and among a skeleton staff who worked on Saturday mornings.

'Who is it?' the general demanded.

'Private Molloy, with your tea, sir!'

'Bring it in!'

I opened the door, balancing the tea tray, and hesitated for half a second at the sight that greeted me. The general was standing in his office, wearing nothing but his underpants.

The officers often changed into their uniforms in the

office as they had no changing rooms. But the general did not ask me to wait outside or even reach for his trousers. He just stood there in his white Y-fronts.

If he wasn't going to be embarrassed, I decided I wouldn't be either. Instead, I affected a nonchalant attitude. 'Good morning, sir,' I said, placing the tea tray on his desk, and I turned around and walked out.

When I returned to my office, I told a colleague, a young captain.

'Maybe he didn't hear you when you knocked,' he laughed, 'or didn't realise you were a girl.'

But the general had heard me and had replied to me. I'm still unsure what he intended to achieve with his Y-fronts display. Maybe he was making a point, *Don't think you're going to get special treatment around here.*

I made sure he didn't get to make that point again. I left his tea so late that he was in his full uniform by the time I arrived. Often, he had to call the captain demanding his cup of tea before being served.

My first posting was decided weeks before passing out. I was called to a 'final approval' interview in the Curragh. I sat across the desk from our platoon officer and sergeant and listened to a review of my recruit performance.

'Now that you're approved, where ideally do you want to go in the Eastern Command?' Lieutenant O'Donoghue asked.

Three Eastern Command girls volunteered to join a drivers' course. One girl went for the Signals Corps, responsible for the defence forces' communications and information systems. Another became one of the first women in the military police.

I knew exactly where I wanted to go. 'I want to be a physical-training instructor,' I said.

The lieutenant rolled her eyes in irritation. 'There may be a course next year but, in the meantime, you must work,' she snapped. 'The Eastern Command is looking for a female to volunteer for army headquarters. How about that?'

Army headquarters in Parkgate Street was a short walk from Collins Barracks, where all nine Eastern Command girls were to be billeted after we left the Curragh.

The lieutenant saw my hesitancy. 'You don't have to answer that now,' she sighed.

For hours afterwards, I thought about the job. I remembered PJ saying the closer you are to army headquarters, the better your opportunities are. However, I also thought of him warning me never to volunteer for anything.

The Eastern Command girls were brought together that afternoon, and again the lieutenant mentioned she was looking for someone to volunteer for a job in army headquarters. The response was silence, until I decided to take a risk and raised my hand.

'Okay, Recruit Molloy, you're off to army HQ,' she said.

The sergeant noted it in his book, and it was done. I was posted to the quartermaster general's (QMG's) branch as the first and only female soldier working at army headquarters. 'Q' appointments, as they are known, are about logistics, administering barracks and looking after supplies.

I soon realised I should have listened to PJ's advice about never volunteering for anything. First, army headquarters was open on Saturday mornings and, being the lowest in the pecking order, I had to be there most weekends. Second, there was nothing casual about Parkgate Street, so I had to wear my number-one uniform – skirt, jacket and nylons. I spent a small fortune on the tights, which were only available in Arnotts or Clerys department stores. Also, as the only private in the quartermaster general's branch, I was appointed the unofficial tea lady of army headquarters, and my first job every morning was to serve tea to all the officers in the branch.

On my first day, a young captain was tasked with orientating me. He stopped as we approached the first of numerous double doors along the corridors of army HQ. 'We have a dilemma here,' he said.

'A dilemma, sir?'

'As officers and gentlemen, we always open doors for women, but other ranks like you are expected to hold doors open for officers.'

'I don't see the problem, sir.'

'Well, I don't know how officers will feel about a woman opening the door for them.'

'But you'd expect a male private to open the door for you, right, sir?'

'Well, yes.'

'Well, there you are, sir. I'm a private, regardless of gender, so I open doors for officers.'

He didn't look convinced, but I opened the door for him and we continued.

'The older guys will have a hard time coming to terms with that.'

Having already been exposed to the general's Y-fronts, I wondered if the captain was overestimating the officers' chivalry.

Army headquarters was full of officers, but I wasn't expected to salute all of them. Members of the army only salute when wearing their headdress, so saluting is chiefly conducted outdoors.

All the Eastern Command girls moved into our billets in Collins Barracks a week after our passing-out parade. We had a whole, newly painted block to ourselves and a huge rec room with a tiny TV, but we all had to share one room for sleeping.

I had to walk to army headquarters in full uniform as I'd no place to change out of civilian clothes. Cars slowed, heads swivelled and people pointed. My appearance on the street nearly caused car crashes. I found the ten-minute walk a mortifying ordeal. Finally, I copped on and requested my own locker in Parkgate Street. To the disgust of the civilian female typists, I got a locker wedged into our small toilets. It was a relief to walk to Parkgate Street in anonymous civvies.

As nine women living among 500 men, we were also

considered strange curiosities in the barracks. Everyone gawped as if we had two heads when we walked around in uniform. Even entering the dining hall, the place fell into a hush as the men turned to stare. It was so intimidating that we always tried to go in pairs whenever we wanted to eat.

'We're like fecking unicorns in this place,' I said.

It wasn't just the men who regarded us as oddities. The cleaners were as bewildered as any in Collins Barracks. I remember one of them planting her mop in astonishment, looking us up and down and laughing aloud. 'Youse are not real soldiers, are youse?'

Meanwhile, I desperately watched for the next physical-training instructor (PTI) course. Every week, a newsletter, *Routine Orders*, was pinned on the notice board in Collins Barracks. Every week, I combed through its listings of all the upcoming courses. Finally, in the second week of January, a new PTI course was advertised. The army demands everything in writing, so I wrote a letter of application for the course and sent it up the chain of command.

The colonel in army HQ called me in upon receiving my application. 'You know, we want someone who will stay in the office,' he said, 'and you've only been here a couple of months.'

I never realised my boss could refuse to recommend me. However, he must have read the expression on my face. 'Of course, I know this is really important to you,' he said hurriedly. 'So reluctantly, I'm going to recommend you for this course.'

I still had to wait to see if I was accepted. One girl from each of the four commands was guaranteed a place.

Meanwhile, Geraldine Acheson joined the Eastern Command, exchanging her place in the Curragh Command with another girl. She was an athlete who competed for Ireland as a middle-distance runner.

Shortly after, I got a message to report to a female officer, whom I'll call Officer Williams. I'd had no dealings with her and wondered why she wanted to see me in her office. There was no preamble. 'Do you think it's fair that you should go on the PTI course instead of Private Acheson?' she said.

I was friendly with Geraldine as we ran together, but she never said she was interested in doing the PTI course. 'Has Private Acheson even applied for the course, ma'am?' I asked.

Officer Williams glared at me for questioning her. 'She would be a more appropriate candidate for the Eastern Command girls as she's an international athlete, so I think you should rethink your application, private.'

I had no intention of rethinking my application. 'I think it's up to Private Acheson to apply, ma'am and, if she does, we can compete for the place,' I said.

She glowered as she dismissed me. I left bewildered about why she was trying to meddle with the applications for the PTI course. It was none of her business. Geraldine never had any intention of applying for the course because it would have interfered with her competitions and training.

I soon forgot about Officer Williams, but she didn't

forget about me. She popped up several times as an obstructive presence in my career.

Being busy in our roles, the Eastern Command girls failed to notice that no other female recruits passed out from the Curragh. But, as time slipped by, it gradually dawned on us that no new female faces were arriving.

Slowly, the original 38 women began dwindling in number too. By 1987, 20 of the platoon were married, 17 to fellow soldiers. Some left to have families and the rest of us carried on as increasingly rare unicorns. It would take nearly a decade after we passed out before the next female recruits entered the army.

10

The PTI Course

My application for a place on the PTI course was successful, and I was happy to return to the Curragh for six months. However, on the third morning the company sergeant (CS) stuck his head out his office window overlooking the gym and let out an almighty roar. 'Corporal Molloy, get in here!'

Overnight, I'd been promoted to acting corporal – privates weren't allowed to apply for the physical-training instructer (PTI) course. However, army headquarters wanted to train four women as instructors, so they tweaked the rules, and the three other women and I were given acting ranks as corporals. The men were not happy.

I dashed to the CS's office, wondering if our tracksuits were the issue. Everyone was given two tracksuits, one black and one blue, and the class was ordered to wear the black tracksuits on arrival.

However, that morning, one of the girls sniffed her tracksuit and wrinkled her nose. 'Girls, we can't wear these for the third time. Let's all change into the blue tracksuits.'

So we went on parade at the gym with 13 guys still in their black tracksuits and all four girls in their nice, clean blue ones. It didn't dawn on me that there might be a problem, until the CS roared for me.

He was almost simmering behind his desk as I hurried in. 'What the hell are you lot doing in different tracksuits to everyone else?'

Why did he pick on me? I wondered. 'The black ones were dirty, CS, so we decided to change to our blue ones.'

His eyes popped out on stalks at this. 'This is the army! You don't get to decide what you wear! You don't break rank. You all wear the same colour. Do you understand, corporal?'

'Yes, CS!'

I was feeling a bit hard done by as I wasn't the one who had decided to change our tracksuits.

'Why did you ask me rather than the other girls to come in here, CS?'

The CS couldn't believe anyone would question him. 'You're here the longest, Molloy, so you're the most senior!' he bawled.

I was the longest there by a week. A basketball referee course had started in the Curragh the week before the PTI course began, and I had managed to get on that as well.

The CS was beside himself at this stage. 'Anything else that goes wrong with the females from here on, it's your problem. Do you understand, corporal?'

'Yes, CS!' I replied.

However, as I went to leave, the CS added, 'By the way, congratulations, you passed the referee course.'

I left the office grinning, despite getting bawled out. I was among the eight of 20 students who had passed the basketball course, so it felt like a considerable achievement.

All four women were billeted to accommodation in Clarke Barracks, close to the gym. Initially, it was a pleasant stroll from the accommodation to the gym but, as the course progressed, every muscle began to ache, and that 'stroll' became a herculean effort.

The classes were more like physical torture than training. The instructors taught us to control a PT class, for example, by ordering us to run laps or do shuttle runs in the gym, frequently interspersed with squats, lunges and press-ups. Then, they called upon us, one at a time, to take the class and continue. We ran around that gym for hours as each of the 17 students had to take a turn to teach. It was little surprise that we couldn't walk by the end of the first week.

Whenever we did something wrong, we heard, 'Give me 20, now!' or 'Get up the rope!' When Patricia O'Shaughnessy was sent up the ropes for a misdemeanour,

Ann Molloy called up, 'What's the weather like up there, O'Shaughnessy?' Unfortunately, the CS overheard her.

'Why don't you go up there and find out for yourself, Molloy?' he said, and we all watched as the two women kept each other company up the ropes.

By week three, we had to physically lift our legs to get out of bed and needed help getting up from a seat. 'Oh dear God, would someone please scratch my head for me?' I remember wailing. 'I can't lift my arm anymore.'

We couldn't even bear to walk to the dining hall in the evenings and might have starved only Ann Molloy had a car. She drove us 500 metres to the Wes Café, where we refuelled with chips.

We were taught the three Fs of being a PTI – to be *fair, firm and friendly* with our students. Modules included training recruits, battle PT (training soldiers to make them fit for battle), training with Olympic apparatus and unarmed combat training.

One day, press photographers arrived to get shots of the first females on the PTI course. As we practised a blend of martial arts and modern combat techniques, one of the photographers joked, 'Girls, draw blood! It'll be great for the pictures!'

I was paired in combat with Stevie, a gymnast who had a stocky, muscular build. We were always trained to stop short of striking a fellow student in the face. Maybe the baying snappers made me overenthusiastic, but I went in for a blow and didn't pull back in time, so I punched him right on the nose. My unarmed combat partner started spurting blood. The instructor wasn't happy that I had injured a student, and I was mortified as Stevie mopped his face and pinched the bridge of his nose to stem the bleeding. To be fair, though, the photographers were happy.

I aced the academic side of the course but was a dismal failure at gymnastics. Ann Molloy and I were the worst gymnasts by far of 17 students. I was 5 foot 9 inches, and Ann was an inch shorter – it's no accident that the best female gymnasts are also the shortest. Our instructors were dedicated, however, and had the patience of saints, trying to teach us. During that course, I learnt that the army was excellent at training and instruction. Everything was drilled into us by constant repetition. Subjects were rotated and timetabled to the millisecond, and, when the soldiers were flagging, the instructors redoubled their efforts. There's no training like army training.

The biggest problem for Ann and me was our lack of upper-body strength. No one knew then that weightlifting was how women could achieve this. A few years later, all the physical-training schools started weight training but, back then, the penny hadn't yet dropped.

We spent six months trying to do a backflip before accepting that we wouldn't get there. The instructors lowered their ambitions and helped us to perform a simple cartwheel. At the end of six months, I still barely held a handstand for five seconds.

Even worse, however, I also found that I wasn't a good instructor. I had the knowledge but lacked the confidence to deliver it, finding it nerve-wracking to stand up in front of a class. We were often called upon to instruct the class, and, as soon as it was my turn, the shaking, sweating, butterflies in my stomach, dry mouth and rapid heartbeat started. I stumbled over my words and got tongue-tied while trying to shout out orders.

I suffered in comparison with the others too. The men on the course were corporals who had gone through their non-commissioned officer (NCO) course. They had been taught to stand in front of a platoon and give orders and instruction, so they all exuded confidence. And while none of the girls had completed a Potential NCO course, they had experience in coaching or singing. Patricia, who was a few years older than the rest of us, was mature enough not to give a shit. She delivered everything with confidence. But public speaking remained a nightmare for me.

I don't know where I found the energy to have a romance during the course, but I did. One night at the Wes Café, I spotted a guy with the distinct '*Fianóglach ARW*' shoulder flash of the Army Ranger Wing. Being fascinated with the rangers, I was more interested in the unit than the man, but I agreed to have a coffee with him. He was a quiet and serious man and nothing like the typical macho rangers we'd meet around the Curragh Camp. We only went out together for a few weeks until we realised we weren't compatible, but we remained friends. The brief romance is only worth mentioning because it backfired on me later.

The PTI course was long and arduous, taking students

away from their families for six months. Yet, every year, the successful men got a handshake, boarded their transport and returned to their units.

About a month before we finished, Thomond-trained Lieutenant Flynn, who was in charge of the course, announced we'd have a proper graduation ceremony. 'The highlight will be a display of gymnastics for your families to watch,' she said, delighted at her idea.

Ann and I exchanged a horrified glance. *Oh, dear God, no!* The instructors tried to choreograph a routine that brought out the best in each individual. Stevie was a whirlwind on the floor and the high bar. Sharon was a dazzling gymnast, and, even though the gym was equipped for men only, she displayed strength and agility on the men's high bar rather than the asymmetric bars.

Everyone on the team did their best to conceal my inadequacies, but my contribution was what you'd expect at a kindergarten performance. I managed a couple of cartwheels but couldn't even get into the splits with the rest of the team. So, while everyone else was red-faced with handsprings, somersaults, split leaps and general exertion, my face was red with embarrassment.

Ultimately, I qualified as a PTI, with additional qualifications as a basketball referee and a senior lifesaver award. However, I failed to distinguish myself in those six months due to my less-than-stellar instruction abilities, and came tenth out of 17 on the course.

My certificate is printed with the words, 'This is to certify that *he* has qualified' and '*he* has special qualifications'.

The instructors doctored the girls' certs by scribbling an 's' in front of the masculine pronoun.

My report card reads: 'Private Molloy was a dedicated and capable student. She excelled academically but would appear to have limited experience in the practical aspects. A quiet personality and rather withdrawn in the group.'

Being quiet and withdrawn was never considered an asset in the army, but I was still determined to advance. I just had to find a route up the ranks that didn't involve a lot of standing in front of people and barking orders.

11

The MPs

'Private Molloy, outside now!' Two military police roared this from the door of the gym at Cathal Brugha Barracks.

The entire gymnastics display team was there, and as everyone turned to stare, my cheeks burnt as bright as the MPs' red berets. It was never good news when the military police arrived for a soldier. The MPs were responsible for the prevention and investigation of offences and took their policing of the defence forces seriously. They never called to bring you out for a chat. Still, what came afterwards left me reeling. The ensuing investigation gave me the dubious distinction of being the first woman to be charged with an offence in the army. I still can hardly believe how it happened.

After leaving the physical-training instructer (PTI) course, I was naive and assumed I'd be moved to the Curragh to train new female recruits. However, the army didn't recruit any more females. I thought I might be sent to the large gym in the training depot in Cathal Brugha Barracks, but I wasn't eligible for any PTI vacancy because I hadn't passed an non-commissioned officer (NCO) course.

Instead, I was sent straight back to the office in army headquarters and soon realised that I wasn't going to get anywhere near a gym.

I had no chance of advancement, and thus leaving clerical work, until I passed the NCO course. The course was the starting point for anyone with leadership ambitions and the only chance to move up from private to corporal. I applied every year but I knew I hadn't a chance of getting on the Potential NCO course for at least two years.

I felt increasingly disheartened and demoralised by the job, realising I was nothing more than a glorified typist and tea maker in army headquarters.

Then, one day, a middle-aged couple checked into my mother's guesthouse in Donegal and everything changed.

The husband glanced at a photograph of my brother and me in uniform on the piano. It was the one taken by the local newspaper on the day of my passing out. He asked how we were getting on in the army, and my mother explained that my brother had left for the French Foreign Legion and that I was unhappy in my job.

'All she ever wanted to do was become a physical-training instructor and, even though she passed the course last year, she's still stuck behind a desk,' she explained.

The man's wife nudged him and said, 'You can handle that, darling, can't you?'

Only then did my mother realise that her guest was a senior officer in the army. Within weeks, I was rescued from my dull office job and posted to the Eastern Command gymnastics display team in Cathal Brugha Barracks. The team performed at fairs and festivals as part of a public-relations exercise every summer. I was thrilled to get out of the office, even if it was only for two months. However, being a brutal gymnast, I ended up co-compering the show with a male soldier.

That summer, I also met my first serious boyfriend. It was a slow burner rather than a lightning-bolt moment between us; my attraction to him was a gradual process. As the only woman on the display team, many of the guys just ignored me. Some of them feared the others would rib them if they talked to me, while others were just plain hostile to the idea of women in the army. It was something the other girls and I first encountered on our PTI course and when we moved into Collins and later McKee Barracks.

But GI was an accomplished gymnast and a more confident young man than most. He didn't have any of that callow self-consciousness or toxic masculinity about him. For weeks, we exchanged lots of banter and laughter. He was a couple of inches shorter than me, which wasn't ideal in my mind. However, he also had blond hair and blue eyes similar to the idol of my teenage years, Robert Redford.

And the more I learnt about GI, the more I admired him. He was an excellent athlete and a remarkable soldier who had completed a Special Assault Group course, a version of the rangers course. Increasingly drawn to each other, we became a couple.

That summer, I also organised training for the women who had volunteered to compete at the All-Army Athletics Championships. Anyone representing the Eastern Command had to wear their official red tracksuit at the event, so I was ordered to go to the clothing stores, where I signed for and collected six tracksuits for the women's team.

When the event ended a few days later, I collected the tracksuits, but one of the girls refused to return hers. I asked her repeatedly to produce the tracksuit but she wouldn't do it.

'Jesus, will you just give me back the tracksuit, please? All the other girls have returned theirs. It's not yours. It belongs to the army.'

'Well, it's mine now,' she said.

I returned to the clothing store, handed back five red tracksuits, and explained to the company quartermaster (CQ) that the sixth girl refused to hand back the sportswear.

He glared at me in response. 'You owe me a tracksuit, Molloy,' he said. 'Give me back the other tracksuit!'

'I've told you, CQ, Private X won't give it back. There's nothing I can do about it.'

That's where I learnt the power of the signature in the army.

'Molloy,' he said, 'you signed for the tracksuit, and it is your responsibility to get it back to me. Get the bloody tracksuit back to me or I'll charge you its price.'

It was a branded Adidas tracksuit with the Eastern Command insignia, so it was costly. The tracksuit was an expense I couldn't afford. If the girl wouldn't give it back, I decided I'd take it back.

The corners of our aluminium locker doors were slightly flexible, so I prised the girl's door back, peered in and tugged the tracksuit out through the gap. I stole it out of her locker and returned it to the CQ. *Feck her. It's not hers to keep.* I didn't give it another thought in the days following.

When the military police arrived at Cathal Brugha gym and called me outside in front of everyone, I still had no idea what was happening. I knew it wasn't a good thing to be called out by the MPs, but I was confident that it must be a case of mistaken identity. Then one of them addressed me: 'Private Molloy, there's a charge against you. Private X has charged you with theft of a tracksuit.'

My jaw dropped in shock. I was horrified and told them everything. I said Private X was holding on to property owned by the army and explained how the clothing store's CQ hassled me to return the tracksuit. 'I didn't steal it!' I argued. 'She did, and I was only returning it to the stores.' I looked from one to the other of the men waiting for them to say, *Okay, we understand now so this will be dropped.*

But they didn't, and that's not how things work in the

army. The army only sees things in black and white: I stole. Ergo, I must be punished.

On 27 July 1983, I was charged with the offence of 'conduct to the prejudice of good order and discipline' and became the first woman to be charged with an offence in the army. The section of the offence was 168: 'improper possession of property or cash'. The punishment was one pound in old Irish currency, which was far less than I'd have paid for the tracksuit. It was only a token fine, but it was a blot on my army record.

I was long enough in the army to know that if a soldier gets charged with anything, their career can mysteriously stall for several years. Thankfully, the ranks above me must have recognised shades of grey because my career continued to progress. Nevertheless, it was an important learning experience on the power and responsibility of the signature in the army.

12

The Preliminary Course

Remove the magazine and carry out safety precautions. Okay, done. I start stripping the Fabrique Nationale (FN) rifle, working fast, noting all the parts and springs and laying them out in the order they are removed. The students all around me are on their hands and knees too, frantically working on their rifles, each trying to outpace the other under the watchful eyes of the non-commissioned officer (NCO).

Okay, rifle disassembled. Now, get it back together. I start to reassemble the receiver by putting the bolt into the recess. But one guy is already getting to his feet, his rifle fully assembled. *Come on, Karina, come on.* I can feel my heart beating faster.

Place the rest of the bolt into the rear of the carrier at a 45-degree angle. Holding the receiver by the rod or what we call the rat's tail, I try to place the receiver back into the weapon using the guide rails. In my peripheral vision, I see more guys standing up. *Oh God, is that one of the girls finishing too?*

Christ, what am I doing wrong? It's not aligning properly! It should slide into place along the rails, but it doesn't. I pull it back and try to realign everything again. The bolt carrier won't go into the recess. More guys are jumping to their feet, rifle assembly completed. I'm so absorbed in my struggle that it's almost by osmosis I realise everyone else is up and ready with their FNs.

I'm still on the floor, head down, scrambling, stuck. I'm furiously disassembling the bolt again to see if I did something wrong there. I can almost feel the NCO's eyes boring into me as the guys smirk among themselves. *One less to compete with.*

It's never a good idea to be first at anything in the army – it draws too much scrutiny on yourself – but it's even worse to be last. My hands are trembling, and my heart is beating so loud, it feels as if the entire barracks must be able to hear it. *Jesus Christ. Think! Think! Check again. Yes, the bloody hammer is in the cocked position. So what the fuck am I doing wrong?*

'Everyone who has completed the task, fall in!' the section NCO orders. Then, he roars at them to get downstairs, and I listen to their boots on the steps and the NCO's boots following them. And then there's silence. *He's gone! They're all bloody gone!* It feels nearly worse than when they were all watching me. I'm on my own, on the floor, wrestling with my damned rifle.

It feels like forever but, finally, miraculously, the bolt carrier suddenly slides into place. There are no more hitches and I finish the rest of the rifle assembly in record time. I test the action by pulling the trigger several times. Finally, I get my gear back on, slap my beret on my head and dash down the stairs. I run outside, my heart pounding and discover ... no one. *Fuck, the section is gone!*

I glance around me wide-eyed. The barracks is a massive place, and my panic levels have soared to Defcon 1. I've had a long and frustrating wait to get on a Potential NCO course, so I cannot fail on the final day of this preliminary course. I must get a place on the 22nd Potential NCO course or be forced to wait another year for the next one. *Where the hell is my platoon?*

I knew I had to be patient and serve my time before I got the chance of a place on the annual NCO course. But it was a frustrating time. After two glorious months with the gymnastics display team, I was sent back to the office. GI and I were still together, but I was back typing, making tea and feeling thoroughly depressed about my job. I'd applied for the NCO course in 1983 but wasn't selected. Meanwhile, I watched as the Southern Command selected three women for their Potential NCO course. Those three women became the first females in the defence forces to complete the course and reach the rank of corporals. Hearing that the other girls were progressing while I was stuck in an office made me even more discouraged.

Finally, the *Routine Orders* newsletter listed the next NCO course and three women in the Eastern Command were selected to try for it starting in January 1984. Another girl from the Western Command was allowed to try for it too.

First, however, we all had to attend and pass a two-week preparatory course. Seventy or eighty soldiers went on the preliminary course. Not everyone could get a place on the Potential NCO course, so it was a competitive two weeks.

Most of the guys were in the infantry and were used to doing 24-hour duties where they were always armed. Their units still gave them a full preparatory course before the official preliminary course.

Women only handled rifles on our annual range practice. The three of us from the Eastern Command got a single day's training, so we knew we were at a severe disadvantage when we started.

This might help explain why I was last to assemble my rifle and ended up standing panicked, head swivelling in every direction of Cathal Brugha Barracks. The barracks was vast, so I didn't know whether to run right or left. A passing NCO must have seen the terror in my expression.

'They've gone that way, love,' he said, pointing towards C Block.

Sweat was pouring off me as I ran around the barracks

to C Block. Officer Williams was the course commander for the preliminary NCO course. She had tried to deter me from applying for the PTI course, but we'd had no contact since, so her position as head of this course didn't bother me.

She was addressing the soldiers as I caught up with the platoon. Of course, army regulations didn't allow me to simply scoot in at the back and line up with the rest of them. I was late, so I had to approach the officer, salute and ask permission to fall in. As I approached to salute, Officer Williams gave me a dismissive flick of her hand, waving me away in an expression of pure disgust. Burning with humiliation, I put my head down and joined the last rank. My pulse rate still hadn't returned to normal when we were ordered to '*lig amach*' or 'fall out'. The course was over, so everyone scattered in all directions to catch transport back to their units. I fretted. I was last to reassemble the rifle and now the course commander had flicked me away as if I was a piece of dirt. *Oh, Christ, I've blown my chance at getting on the Potential NCO course.*

At that moment, I heard my name being called. Corporal Carrick, one of the course instructors I knew from recruit training, approached me. One glance at his grim face confirmed this was not good news. *Oh, Jesus*, I thought, my pulse already racing.

'Karina, she put you on the rejection pile,' he said. 'She says you're not NCO material.'

He didn't even have to say who 'she' was. My eyes glanced towards Officer Williams as she walked away from

C Block. I felt the world swim around me. The corporal said the list of those granted a place on the Potential NCO course had already been decided.

'You should know I fought for you and your section commander stood up and fought for you.'

He continued talking about their meeting when all I wanted to do was scream, *Say it! For fuck's sake, say it!* But I couldn't even speak. I gazed at him, naked terror in my eyes, unable to exhale. My future hung in the balance.

Then he said it. 'Keep it to yourself, Karina, but she had to give in to us. You've been selected.'

I could finally exhale after two weeks of stress and dread. A united front from two NCOs had saved me. As I desperately struggled to contain tears of relief, the corporal added, 'Don't make us regret this, Private Molloy. Don't let us down.'

13

1 x Female

'Please don't leave,' I pleaded. 'Please don't leave me on my own.'

My head was in my hands and I could hardly talk for the sobbing that racked my body and, still, I begged her. 'Please, please don't leave.'

It was early Friday morning in Cathal Brugha Barracks, barely a week after we'd started what was to be a four-month non-commissioned officer (NCO) course, and Margaret, a fellow platoon member, couldn't muster the will to face another day. She was trembling, broken and her face pale. My stomach churned with anxiety.

I had to make her change her mind, but I couldn't even get her to meet my eyes. 'I'm sorry, Karina, I can't take this any more,' she said. 'I just can't do it. I have to get out of this place. I can't hack this anymore.'

My mind raced. *Jesus, how am I going to survive this on my own?*

All four women had made it through the preliminary course to the Potential NCO course. However, only Margaret and I had turned up the following Monday morning, a miserable grey day in January 1984. The NCO courses are always held in the coldest and wettest conditions.

Geraldine Acheson didn't turn up because she got a better offer – an athletics scholarship to America. Geraldine made a quick exit from the army and never looked back.

However, the girl from the Western Command couldn't face the abuse from the NCOs of the Eastern Command training depot for four more months and refused to return. Her decision was not a surprise after our experience of preliminary training. It was like Dorothy says in *The Wizard of Oz*: 'Toto, I've a feeling we're not in Kansas any more.' Reality hit, and we entered an unfamiliar place where NCOs screamed in our ears, swore at us and, generally abused privates until they cracked, all for their own amusement.

As we were the only women among 60 or so men, anyone might naturally assume that the army would put us in the same section. At least then we might have the same sense of companionship and support that the guys shared. But, no, the Eastern Command didn't put us in the same section. They didn't even put us in the same platoon. The course was split into two platoons and the timetable meant we never saw each other during the day.

It had been a long and lonely first week for both of us. As the only women, we experienced little of the camaraderie the guys enjoyed. Many on the course resented our presence entirely and objected because they felt they couldn't talk trash around us. Others feared being derided by the other guys, so they ignored us. It was more juvenile than the schoolyard at times. Exclusion was very much part of my experience for many years in the army. We were marginalised and isolated at every turn.

As women, we heard all the mutterings as we moved between barracks and offices. The guys objected to orders to remove pornography and posters of page-three girls from the walls of locker rooms, tea rooms and anywhere the female soldiers would share. I lost count of comments like, *You know, we had to clean up this fucking place just because you bloody shower were coming in.* Many men relished this macho, misogynistic and exclusively male atmosphere, and seemed completely threatened by the arrival of women.

Margaret's mind could not be changed. After a week, she had taken as much abuse as she could handle. So that first Friday of the Potential NCO course, she was gone from the barracks by noon, and I was left as the only woman for the next three months and three weeks. I felt a knot in my stomach all that morning. I never felt so isolated and vulnerable.

Around noon that day, the lecture hall door burst open, and our platoon sergeant roared, 'Private Molloy, get out here!' I was startled. Everyone's head turned, no doubt thinking the same as me and wondering what I'd done. The sergeant marched me off across the square.

'The course commander wants to see you now.'

'Why, sergeant?'

My mind was racing, trying to figure out why I was in trouble.

'You bloody wait until he decides to tell you!'

He led me across the square and up a flight of stairs to the course commander's office. I marched in, turned right, saluted the course commander sitting behind his desk and stood to attention. I was surprised to see my section NCO and platoon officer standing on either side of the commander. Behind me, breathing down my neck, was the platoon sergeant. I felt even more anxious now. What had I done to merit the attention of this military line-up?

'Private Molloy, your female colleague has left,' the course commander announced.

I was confused. *Is that all?* I looked from one to another of the men staring at me. 'Thank you, sir. I'm aware.'

He glowered and turned to my section NCO, demanding his training diary. I saw him flicking through the book containing progress notes on his students. I don't imagine there was much in there as we'd only been on the course for four and a half days. He looked at my section NCO and then fixed narrow eyes on me.

'You have done nothing wrong so far. So, stick around, and see how long you last,' he said. 'Now get out.'

I was stunned. They dragged me out of a lecture and marched me in front of the course commander to tell me Margaret was gone. I felt I was being told I'd soon follow. As far as I was concerned, his tone made the message clear – my days were numbered. They were going to sit on me, as the army expression goes, until I quit too.

Being the only female on the course would be a logistical headache for the unit. Margaret and I lived in McKee Barracks but also had an entire billet to use as a changing room at Cathal Brugha Barracks. During on-the-ground training, they would have to set up separate accommodations for us. The army never liked making exceptions, and now they would have to do this for one person. I was 1 x Female on their interminable lists. However, that was their problem, not mine.

My initial sense of bewilderment was replaced by rising anger as I left the course commander's office. I recalled what he said and the tone he said it in. His words were like a red rag to a bull. *You bastard*, I thought as the sergeant marched me back down the stairs. *You fucking bastard*. I was in a hot fury by the time I reached the bottom. *We'll see how long you last*. I formed a mental image of myself on the square at the end of my course.

My entire career in the army was as good as over if I didn't pass the Potential NCO course. I would stay a private and could never get promotion if I didn't complete it. I fumed, thinking about what he'd said and his barely veiled threat that they would get rid of me.

To the day I die, I'll never forget leaving that office and walking down those stairs. If I ever needed motivation, I had it then. He wanted me off that course, but it just backfired on him. *You think my days are numbered? Just watch. Come hell or hight water, I'll be on that square on 11 May.*

14

Swimming with Sharks

I glided through the pool, enjoying the freedom of moving through the shimmering blue warmth. It was soothing to be lost in my own watery bubble. Even the pungent smell of chlorine and the roars of men echoing around the tiled walls faded into the distance, and I felt relaxed as I pulled my way rhythmically through the water.

Our platoon was in the public swimming pool in Rathmines, booked for our exclusive use early that morning. Anyone who could swim got into the lanes and powered through lengths of the pool. The soldiers who couldn't swim were at the other end, learning to tread water and float.

I nonchalantly noticed one of the instructors diving into my lane. During my six weeks on the Potential non-commissioned officer (NCO) course, I had few dealings with this person. I got the usual reprimands from him like every other NCO, but he was just another instructor, one of many, and he had his own section to take care of. We swam in opposite directions and had no need for any interaction.

The first time we passed each other in the pool lane, I passed it off as an accidental collision. He was doing the front crawl, ploughing through the lane with strength, and his arm may have brushed between my legs.

However, the second time we passed each other, there was no mistaking it. I distinctly felt his fingers grab my crotch, clawing at the most intimate part of my body. I recoiled to the wall in shock, trying to catch my breath. As soon as I was sure he had swum away from me, I scrambled out of the pool.

At first, my eyes darted in panic, but everyone else was swimming or splashing about, and no one saw what had happened. 'Molloy!' one of the other instructors yelled. 'Class isn't over. Get back in the pool!'

It must be a defence mechanism, a survival tactic, but in the immediate aftermath, I shut down. What happened seemed unreal, like an out-of-body experience. *Did that really happen at all?* I got back into the pool with the guys who couldn't swim, far from my assailant who was still swimming as if nothing had happened. My heart was pounding, but I was in such disbelief that I wondered if I had imagined it. I said nothing, told no one and bided my time until I could get out of the pool.

In the changing room afterwards, I couldn't get washed and dressed quick enough. I was shaken. I'd always felt fortunate to have a lithe and streamlined body, able to do what I demanded of it. I felt strong, athletic and powerful even in a swimsuit. Yet, I felt as exposed and defenceless, at that moment, as a little girl. It highlighted for the first time concerns around trust, safety and security in the army. I was surrounded by men all the time, and this incident shook me to the core because it showed how vulnerable I was.

Even though what happened was none of my doing, I also felt a sense of deep shame. The only one who should feel ashamed was the instructor, but the feeling persisted. I felt sick to the pit of my stomach. It was unspeakable what he did, so unspeakable I couldn't talk about it.

From early in the Potential NCO course – probably due to the course commander's encouragement – I was made a 'heat seeker'. The 'three Fs' that I'd learnt in the PTI course – fairness, firmness and friendliness – went out the window. Instead, I was victimised, targeted and abused at every turn.

Unfortunately, everyone else in number-one section also got to share the limelight. Whenever there were dirty details, my section got them. If stairs had to be polished or toilets cleaned, my section was always called upon to do it. Because I was in number-one section, the others got landed with all the shittiest jobs too.

When it became known that I was a heat seeker, the platoon was even more determined to give me a wide berth. My section couldn't distance themselves enough from me. They resented having the only woman foisted upon them and being crucified for it.

Two men, however, didn't follow the herd. Both were married and more emotionally mature than the others. One of them, nicknamed Cosi, was a slight but fit man with a shock of raven hair and a moustache. He had a good heart, saw that I was alone and scared and took me under his wing. The other man, Jock, was a kindred soul mostly because he was another heat seeker. He was a tall, heavy-built man from Scotland who had a different accent and a different religion. He also wore glasses, was well-read and academically minded without an athletic bone in his body. For any or all of those reasons, he attracted unwanted attention from the NCOs too.

'We're watching you, you Scottish bastard. You're this close to being fucked off this course ...'

The NCOs sat on both of us, day and night.

Jock and I were sitting on the pavement outside the men's changing rooms one afternoon. It had been a tough day, and we were worn out. We'd been screamed at, abused and run ragged, and I knew he felt as dispirited and wretched as me. I was still startled, however, when he lowered his head to his knees and started sobbing.

'I'm just so tired of this badgering,' he said, wiping his eyes with the palms of his hands. 'How the hell are you doing it, Karina? Why the hell are you still here?'

'They want me to quit, so I won't,' I said. 'I'm just a stubborn bitch, Jock.'

He laughed at that.

But there were many times I felt so disillusioned that I could have quit. Reprimands were countless. 'Drop and give me twenty,' was my middle name. The NCOs looked for any excuse, a hair out of place, a beret at the wrong angle. I was constantly second-guessing myself and anxious. Most days after training, I had to report to the orderly sergeant for 'sixteen-thirty details', as they were known, because our training finished at 16.30hrs. I scrubbed entire flights of stairs or toilet blocks and completed mind-numbing chores for hours, only for them to return, pick faults and hurl more abuse.

I made a disastrous mistake the first week. We memorised the serial number for our own rifles and signed for them each time we collected them from the stores. In my anxiety to avoid being last, I never checked the number before I signed for a rifle one day.

To assume anything on an NCO course is to make an ass of yourself. I fell in outside the stores. However, the guy who did what he was supposed to do and checked the serial number realised his Fabrique Nationale (FN) rifle was gone. The NCO in charge stormed out and ordered everyone to check their weapons. My heart sank and my face burnt with shame, as I returned to the stores with the wrong rifle.

It was a stupid mistake. I didn't have it ingrained in me to check the serial number like infantry, who were used to handling arms most days. I was also flustered and in haste, constantly waiting to be tripped up and ended up tripping myself up. They destroyed me for that mistake, humiliating and abusing me all day.

The NCO course was a steep learning curve, and I struggled to find my groove in the early weeks. Bullied by the instructors and rejected by many of my peers, my self-esteem was sometimes on the floor. I cried a lot in the privacy of my billet, but I still refused to quit. I really was a stubborn bitch.

Cosi and Jock were my saving graces. Cosi was the opposite of me. While I was constantly alert and taking the course very seriously, determined to do nothing wrong, he was laid-back and cool.

'It's a long four months, Molloy,' he'd say. 'Take it easy or you'll give yourself a heart attack.'

I was also lucky that our section NCO, a reserved and intelligent man from Dundalk, wasn't the typical chest-beating goon who thrived in the Eastern Command training depot. He didn't appreciate the abuse his section was receiving. I wish he had been strong enough to stand up to the commander and other NCOs, but I understand that he was badly outnumbered.

The course emphasised leadership. It aimed to turn us into military instructors capable of effectively training others in combat techniques and motivating soldiers under our command. I quickly had to overcome fears of standing in front of a class or bellowing orders in the middle of the square.

We all had to take turns being the platoon's orderly sergeant. On the first day, we were told it would be done in alphabetical order. I heaved a sigh of relief that my surname was halfway through the alphabet, meaning I could watch and learn for a couple of weeks. On the third morning, however, the NCO called, 'Private Molloy, front and centre!'

What the fuck? I thought. *Why's he calling me?*

'I know it's out of turn,' he said, 'but I'm curious to see what a female voice sounds like on the square. Take over.'

I turned bright red. He made it sound as if I was an alien. *Curious to see what a female voice sounds like?*

I learnt to be hypervigilant on that course because the moment I let my guard down, they pounced on me. The minute I relaxed in the pool, I was sexually assaulted by an NCO.

In the hours after the pool incident, I had remained in a daze, not knowing what to think or how to deal with it.

My boyfriend, GI, and I had arranged to meet for lunch that day in the barracks. I wondered if I should tell him what had happened. I didn't know if I could even say the words, but GI came rushing towards me, wide-eyed and frantic.

'What happened at the pool today?' he said.

I was stunned. I had told no one. 'How did you hear about that?'

A sergeant friend had witnessed this NCO loudly

bragging in the mess about what he'd done to me. 'Did you see the fucken ass on Molloy?' he'd brayed to everyone. 'I gave her a good groping in the pool this morning.'

My assailant had gone on in that vein in front of maybe 50 men from every unit in the barracks. They'd all had a good laugh over their morning coffee.

GI always said he disliked the mess society in the place, and now I knew why. I was shocked, angry and humiliated all at once. It was even worse that everyone knew and that no other NCO condemned him for his vile behaviour. I couldn't bear the thoughts of facing this man again. I was sickened and tears brimmed over.

But GI shook me out of it. 'No crying. You can't go there. You have to stay angry and you have to deal with this. You're not even a third of the way into this course. If you don't put a stop to this now, they're going to destroy you.'

My first instinct was to bury this and try to forget it, but I knew in my heart GI was right. That NCO was emboldened by the laughter of his peers. He, or maybe more of them, could come after me again.

'He can't get away with this,' said GI. 'Report the incident and make a stand. Go straight to the top – the course commander.'

The course commander couldn't ignore an official complaint even if he wanted to. So I dashed off a hand-written note requesting a private interview at his 'earliest convenience' and handed it to my platoon sergeant.

'What's this all about, Molloy?' he said.

'I'd rather discuss it with the course commander, sergeant.'

I didn't have to wait long. I was in the lecture hall that afternoon, and the platoon sergeant called me out and marched me across the square.

'Are you going to tell me what this all about, Molloy?' he asked again. 'Are you finally going to leave us?'

You wish, I thought.

'I'll speak to the course commander first, if that's okay, sergeant.'

I climbed the same stairs I'd been on six weeks earlier, feeling even angrier, if that was possible.

In my innocence, I thought the course commander and me would meet in his office as I'd requested a private interview. Instead, I marched in to see my platoon officer, my section NCO and the company sergeant (CS) of the Training Depot standing behind him. My platoon sergeant joined them. The course commander was surrounded by all his henchmen.

'What's your problem, Private Molloy?' he said.

My heart sank at the prospect of relating the details of the pool assault in front of five men.

'Well, it's about what happened ...' I began, but I was cut short mid-sentence.

'If it's what happened in the pool, I'll stop you there,' he said. 'I must inform you that your boyfriend has assaulted [my assailant].'

I was stunned as this could have only happened in the few hours since lunchtime.

'And if you decide to take this further, your boyfriend will be charged with assault.'

I looked at the other men, but none would make eye contact. I continued to stand to attention in silence, my mind racing.

'We want a decision now, Private Molloy!' he said. He didn't give me an opportunity either to think about it or discuss it with GI. I didn't want GI to be charged with an assault that might derail his career for years.

'Okay, I won't take this any further,' I said. 'But I'm not swimming again.'

I went back to the lecture hall in a daze, and it wasn't until the day's training was over that I talked with GI again and learnt that he hadn't laid a finger on my assailant.

'I cornered the bastard,' he said. 'But I never touched him, although I wanted to.'

I had to steel myself to face that NCO every day for the next few months. When he inspected the platoon, he often stood within six inches of my breasts or behind. It was deliberate intimidation. I never flinched even though my skin crawled every time.

I was determined not to leave because of him and the other thugs in the place. I dug my heels in. Guys were walking out and being fired off the course in those first six weeks, but I hung in there, despite their best efforts.

No one ever tried to deny what happened in the pool. The course commander acknowledged it happened during that meeting with me. The whole army knew what had happened because army men are worse than women when it comes to gossiping. My friend Caroline worked in the Eastern Command military intelligence branch and overheard a general officer commanding discussing it. However, it was clear that the perpetrator was allowed to act with impunity. There was never any suggestion that he would be punished or charged.

The army is a small place and I saw that NCO again. Thankfully, by then, I outranked him and handled him with the disdain and loathing he deserved. His career continued, but the army learnt no lessons. Years later he was sent to a training establishment where, once again, he had contact with young women entering the army.

15

Scratch

I sat in the back of an open truck as it rattled its way along the hour-long journey to the Glen of Imaal in Wicklow. More than 50 of us were transported in convoy on a gloomy grey morning in early March. After two months of class work and training at the barracks, we were finally facing two weeks of on-the-ground exercises.

For weeks, I'd been listening to the lads talk among themselves about 'scratch'. All they could talk about was this battlefield circuit and how it would be hell. They'd all experienced a version of this nightmare circuit during their three-star course, and they knew my three-star training was typing and admin. 'You won't know what fucking hit you, Molloy,' they sniggered. The guys were trying to psyche me out, but I could tell they were dreading it too.

I wore my newly issued combat uniform: dark green double-layered trousers with multiple pockets and a jacket with a detachable hood. Even though I was tall, I had a slight build with a neat 24-inch waist. The jacket in army size 'small' fitted, but the trousers, designed for men, were too straight for female hips. However, obtaining the crown jewels would have been easier than requesting a jacket and trousers in my size. Combats in size 'medium' were slapped in front of me. 'You'll grow into them,' I was told.

Sitting on the truck, my heart pounded harder than on my first day as a recruit. I tried to convince myself that it couldn't be that bad. I glanced around me. I was 23 years old and as fit as most of the men, but I didn't have the experience of those in the infantry. *It's going to be tough*, I thought, *but this is what you signed up for.*

I straightened up when we passed through Coolmoney Camp's perimeter fence, mentally bracing myself for what was to come. As the truck lurched to a stop, the non-commissioned officers (NCOs) were already yelling at us to get off. I expected nothing less. *Three minutes to get to your billets, drop your excess gear and fall back in on parade. THREE MINUTES! MOVE YOUR FUCKING ARSES!* We got three minutes to do everything on the Potential NCO course.

All the lads turned right, but I was ordered left. The guys' billets were on a different side of camp than my hut. Never the twain shall meet when the army accommodated men and women. They were worse than the nuns. I ran to the billet – the usual spartan hut with about 20 beds lined against the walls and a few potbelly stoves. I dumped anything out of my rucksack that I didn't have to carry and started running again, my pack bouncing on my back, helmet slapped to my head.

We'd barely fallen in when we were ordered to start running. We set out with rifles raised over our heads. A lot of what happened in the hours afterwards is a blur.

Avoiding injury was at the forefront of my mind. If anyone was taken away hurt, that was the end of the course. *Take it easy. Take it steady*, was my mantra as we ploughed through wooded undergrowth. The last thing I wanted was a broken ankle. *There's no way I'm coming back to start this course again.* I put in 80 per cent effort on the circuit and ratcheted it up to 85 per cent when an NCO bawled in my ear. But I never gave it my all. I was determined I wasn't going to injure myself.

We kept running until we reached a wooded area, and then the orders were to get down and belly-crawl through the mud, icy puddles and over knotted tree roots, cradling our weapons in our arms. The earthy smell of rotting leaves filled my nostrils, but if there was any birdsong, it was drowned out by NCOs howling that we were bags of shite.

'You're not in the fucking girl guides now, Molloy!' bawled one. 'Move your fucking arse!'

We progressed into the leopard-crawl course, moving at

speed on elbows and knees with full 1958 webbing pattern gear on our backs, rifles held in the crooks of our elbows. Then, it was back to another brutal mud run through woods of rowan, holly and birch for a few kilometres until we reached a river. We slid down the bank, and the still morning air was rent with shrieks and hollers as we were immersed in the freezing brown water.

We were directed to a concrete bridge that spanned the river. Freeing our hands by slinging our rifles behind us, we had to reach for the underside of the bridge. Then the idea was to swing along, hand over hand, to the other side. The NCOs were on the bridge, watching our every move on this monkey bar obstacle and an exercise that required all the upper-body strength I didn't have.

I carried 20lbs of weight in my backpack, and everything, including my outsized combats, was heavier because they were wet. But I hung on and moved steadily across the bridge. I almost made it. I had two more grasps of the bridge to go, but the burning muscles in my arms gave in, and I dropped into the river below. I could hardly breathe from the exertion. 'Get fucking back and start again, Molloy,' came the roar from the bridge. So I waded, panting, back to the bank again, avoiding other soldiers dropping like stones from the bridge.

I tried to catch my breath on the other side, envying some of the lads from infantry, swinging across with the agility of primates. The NCOs were screaming at me again. My hands were numb with cold, my arms ached, and my rucksack and combats were saturated and heavy. I didn't make it as far as the last time before splashing into the freezing water. 'Get back and start again!' I heard.

After a third failed attempt, I heard the roar, 'YOU FUCKING USELESS PIECE OF SHITE, MOLLOY. GET FUCKING OUT AND CARRY ON!' So I gratefully clambered up the other bank and carried on. Other 'pieces of shite' were also doing the wade of shame across the river before and after me. And then we ran again at a pace through the undergrowth with NCOs screaming in our ears.

Scratch was (and remains) one of those rites of passage in the army. It was more about the NCOs waging psychological warfare on us rather than teaching us about enemy combat. It came from the army mentality that they had to 'break us to make us'. They tried to push us to the limits, toughen us up, and test our resolve and determination. It was a huge physical challenge but a bigger mental one. It was about developing an unyielding attitude and proving that when we thought we couldn't go on, we could, and we did.

The same circuit started again eventually, and we went through the whole thing once more on our bellies, leopard crawling, bridge spanning, running. I had three attempts each time I got to the bridge, but I never made it as far as I did on my first go. By pacing myself, I began passing guys who had pulled ahead earlier. I knew the route and where to jump and where to land. I still had energy in reserve, but some of the guys were spent.

As I passed two lads doing the leopard crawl, the NCO, viewing us from a height, started screaming down at us. Needless to say, it wasn't, 'Well done, Molloy. You're passing the men. Keep going!' Instead, I heard: 'YOU FUCKING USELESS PAIR OF BASTARDS! WHAT ARE YOU DOING ALLOWING THAT BITCH TO PASS YOU!' He didn't intend to motivate me, but he did. I forged ahead.

By the time we were on the circuit the third time, however, I remember thinking, *I hope to God this is ending soon.* I had to push through cold, fatigue and the agony of blistered feet. It seemed to go on for ten hours, but late afternoon, as the light was fading, we finished.

We marched back to our billets, looking like dog-tired, footsore, shivering pandas. Our eye sockets were the only parts of us not covered in muck. I fell in the door of my hut, wondering if I had the energy to peel off my sodden clothes and boots.

Immediately inside each cabin door was a small room with a single potbelly stove intended for the NCO in charge of a platoon. To save on fuel, the staff at the Glen of Imaal ordered me to use that room.

I made my way in the twilight to the toilets and shower block behind my billet. A flick of the light switch told me they hadn't been used in a very long time. All three shower trays were full of broken beer bottles and human excrement. The toilets were equally repellent, smeared with human filth. I cleaned out one of the trays to have a shower but there were no shower curtains and the door to the unit didn't close. I returned to my billet, dragged a chair to the showers and wedged it against the door.

As the steam rose and the water poured over my aching muscles, I concentrated on staying upright and awake. It had been one of the longest days of my life, but I'd survived my introduction to being a real infantry soldier. I was relieved the day was over, and I'd finally passed the infamous scratch. And I was even more determined to continue.

16

On the Ground

'Okay, Molloy, get up here. You're leading the platoon,' said the non-commissioned officer (NCO). 'Get your compass and map and show me your co-ordinates to get there.'

We were heading out on a section in attack, a simulated assault on enemy positions in the Lugnaquilla mountain area. Our mission was to enter the insurgent-held location via a route march to the mountain's summit, an ascent of three or four miles.

The morning after scratch, the real purpose of our two weeks on the ground began. In the barracks, we studied modules including administration and military law, map-reading, and sections in attack and defence.

When we got to the Glen of Imaal, it was time to put all our blackboard lessons into practice. So, for two long weeks, we trudged about the mountains practising combat scenarios.

After being given the job of leading the platoon, I set off through the morning's drizzling rain and low-hanging cloud. I'd completed a mountaineering course, so I could map-read blindfolded even before I joined the army. It was a challenging ascent as the terrain was uneven and rocky in most parts, with jagged stones dotting the landscape.

We squelched through soggy marsh at times, sliding on mossy rocks, and crossing streams and rivulets. I followed the trail guided by my map, trotting along in my own world and at my own pace.

Halfway up the mountain, a runner caught up with me. 'The platoon sergeant says to slow down and wait for the platoon.' When I looked back, I realised the platoon was strung along the mountain. I'd made a mistake. A leader is never supposed to lose sight of their troops.

To climb a mountain requires a different fitness than running around the barracks. Some of the guys were winded, and arrived red-faced and sweating despite the bitterly cold conditions.

The NCOs arrived and said to prepare to move on up the mountain. 'Continue leading the troops, Molloy,' said one of the instructors, which surprised me. I'd led the platoon for some time and presumed that one of the other guys would take over.

However, as I went to leave, the same instructor heaved

the general-purpose machine gun (GPMG) into my arms, an extra 24 pounds of weight. 'That will help slow you down,' he said with a smirk.

I didn't bat an eyelid because I wasn't going to give the NCOs the satisfaction of a reaction. But it was like carrying a reclining toddler up a mountain while also lugging a backpack and a 10lb rifle.

As I set off, it was one of the many times I felt tears stinging my eyes. But no one ever saw them. In all my time in the army, I never cried in front of a higher rank. I may have cried a lot on that course, but it was always behind closed doors.

I struggled up that mountain, my lungs fit to burst with the laboured effort. But I managed to stay ahead, lead the platoon and get us to the correct location on the other side of the summit, carrying the GPMG. I thought back pain would cripple me at times, but I wouldn't let the NCOs win by giving up.

Later, during a section in defence exercise, we used our entrenching tools to dig a two-man trench as our home for the night. After getting into our mucky trenches, we prepared to defend our position, when an NCO appeared. 'Molloy, get up here for a night patrol.' Several of us were dispatched on a reconnaissance patrol into enemy territory. The key to such patrols was silence. The section was trained to walk in single file, weapons already cocked.

The thick cloud cover meant no starlight to illuminate the way. So we moved blind, in black velvet surroundings. When the lead person came upon an obstacle, he turned to the soldier behind him and whispered, 'Fence' or 'Fallen tree' or whatever we should be alerted to. The message was passed down the line.

It was my first time on night patrol, so I was wound up like a coil. I didn't want to be the one to let the section down by stumbling and alerting the enemy to our positions. Cosi happened to be in front of me. 'Fallen tree,' he'd whisper, and I'd pass it behind me.

We moved like ghosts, but the pressure was mounting the further we went. We didn't know if we were walking into an instructors' ambush, so my heart was beating in my throat. I was nearly afraid to breathe for fear I'd be heard.

Cosi's silhouette turned to pass another message. He whispered in my ear, and I'd already half-turned to the soldier behind before I realised he'd said, 'Gis a kiss!' Jesus, I was so nervous I almost let out a snort of laughter. I felt like shoving him in the back, but we couldn't be caught acting the maggot in the middle of a night patrol. There was always an NCO watching and assessing.

But Cosi's silliness was just what I needed to exhale, and we needn't have worried as no one ambushed us that night. The NCOs were probably miles away, tucked up in a warm bed.

I never regretted trying to file a complaint over the pool assault because the NCOs were careful around me after that. As soon as I stood up to them, they knew they couldn't walk over me. A message went out, and they backed off.

That doesn't mean they didn't continue to make it as hard as possible for me. I could never relax. But the NCOs only gave me one more scare on that course.

We returned to the camp after being out on exercises for two nights. 'Get a shower, a change of clothes and rest,' the platoon sergeant said. The usual routine was to brush the muck off our combats and get our clothes as dry as possible. The staff at Coolmoney Camp always had the potbelly stoves lit when we returned to our billets. They left a basket of peat to keep the fire going and a clothes horse for drying our combats. Nothing was to be placed within four feet of the stoves for fire safety reasons.

I stripped down to a T-shirt and went to bed. I was so exhausted, I fell into a deep sleep. I never heard a thing until I opened my eyes to see two men staring down at me. I scrambled back, startled, my heart beating fast.

'Molloy, don't be getting excited,' one of the NCOs drawled. 'We're here for a safety check.' I didn't know what to think because it wasn't the job of the NCOs to check the stoves. I'm not sure what they were at, but after I woke, they left.

The lads confirmed Coolmoney Camp staff had looked in to check their stoves. They ultimately were responsible for everyone in the camp, students and NCOs.

'None of the NCOs came in?'

'Christ, no. NCOs don't do that. Aren't they supposed to be resting too?'

Yet I had the privilege of two coming into my room.

Incidents like that unnerved me. I felt vulnerable and isolated, especially at night when I'd be instantly alert and rigid if I heard noises outside.

With a heightened awareness of safety, I started to question procedures in the army. I was shocked to read that rapists in the US Armed Forces could only be charged with assault according to their military law.

'Is it the same in the Irish Defence Forces?' I asked the lecturer during military law class.

You could have heard the proverbial pin drop. The entire room froze and the lecturer turned a shade of crimson. 'Erm,' he said, finally, 'I don't know the answer to that question, but I will get back to you.'

I'm still waiting for that answer.

As NCOs, we carried the Carl Gustaf submachine gun, a lighter, smaller weapon than the Fabrique Nationale. We learnt to strip and assemble the semi-automatic then, finally, the day came for us to go to the range and fire it. Unfortunately, my poor sharpshooting skills were evident when the NCO examined the target. His sarcastic assessment still makes me laugh.

'Molloy,' he said, shaking his head. 'You should try hitting the enemy with your fucking handbag because you won't hit him with that gun.'

Despite the training depot's best efforts and my failings on the range, I was on that square on 11 May, spruced out in my number-one uniform.

My father came to Cathal Brugha Barracks for the passing out. Months earlier, I'd told him what had happened in the pool during the NCO course. It was a bad idea because as soon as he arrived, he wanted to be introduced to my pool assailant. My father always had a cool head, but he was determined to do his duty and defend his daughter's honour. I feared he'd punch the guy and be arrested for assault, and I didn't want a scene.

'No, Daddy. No way. I'm not pointing him out for you. So just forget about it,' I said.

He was frustrated and annoyed that day because he knew he was standing in the room with a man who had sexually assaulted his daughter. In hindsight, I should have let him. I would have enjoyed seeing him punch the thug, and the army would probably have turned a blind eye.

I remember on the long drive home, he asked if I'd told my mother about the assault. When I told him I hadn't, he nodded with approval. 'Okay, let's leave it like that. She has enough on her plate,' he said.

Mostly that day, however, I felt relieved and gratified to make it to the end despite the course commander and his cronies' efforts. I was also deeply proud that I'd beaten most of the men, coming fifth out of 55 on the 22nd twenty-second Potential NCO course. My father took some gloss off that achievement, however. 'Oh, so you didn't even make the top three?' he said when I told him.

Even if I'd come first, I knew it would never have been acknowledged. A woman in the Southern Command was delighted to top her NCO course the year before me. However, she was brought before her commanding officer, who told her that the optics weren't good, so he couldn't give her the top prize. It couldn't be seen that an NCO course was so soft that *even a girl* could pass it or, worse, beat every man on the course.

The general officer commanding of the Eastern Command gave a brief address at our passing out. He welcomed the proud wives, parents and 'one very special boyfriend' of all the new NCOs in attendance. He saw the historical significance of having the first female NCO in the Eastern Command because he insisted on getting a photo of us together. Unfortunately, I remained the only female NCO there for over a decade as none of the other women who joined the Eastern Command with me attempted the course.

It was a brutal three months, made unnecessarily harsher by the unremitting bullying and harassment from the Eastern Command training-depot staff.

It required inner strength and resilience to make it through those months, but physically I also paid a heavy price. I joined the Potential NCO course weighing a healthy ten and a half stone, but the stress and physicality of those months meant I was a skeletal seven stone, two pounds when I marched on the square that day.

17

The Right to Fail

I was a bag of nerves as the bus pulled out of Cathal Brugha Barracks late on a Sunday afternoon. The men chatted among themselves, ignoring me. *Well, nothing new there, anyway.* I had a sick feeling in the pit of my stomach, but I kept reminding myself: *They can't kill you. They can't kill you.* It had taken 18 months and three applications to get on this bus. And now I was about to try out for the Army Ranger Wing (ARW), Ireland's equivalent to the SAS.

My father drilled it into me that, if I took on a job, I had to strive to be the best at it. So, in the first year of my army career, I looked around and wondered, *Well, what's the best there is in the army?* To my father, it was becoming an officer. To me, the Army Ranger Wing (ARW) and serving in one of the world's most elite forces exemplified excellence in the army.

From my early days as a recruit at the Curragh Camp, my head was turned by any glimpse of the Fianóglach ARW shoulder tab or badge. The unit's flash fascinated me. The blood sword in the centre of the emblem came from old Irish mythology where warriors sacrificed prisoners or animals before battle. The golden olive leaf crown surrounding the sword was presented to great athletes in ancient Greece and represented elite special forces. The black background on the flash referred to the secrecy of special ops.

Anyone who completed the selection course wore the tab for their army career, but not everyone who passed was chosen to serve in the ARW. A red border around the shoulder tab distinguished serving ARW operatives. From the late 1980s, serving rangers also got to wear the coveted green beret, meaning they stood out from everyone else in the army in black ones.

The ARW selection course was traditionally run twice a year. I applied both times in 1983 and trained in earnest, hoping to make it on the course. I did full press-ups and pull-ups and went running every day. As my father always said, 'Fail to prepare, then prepare to fail.'

The first time I applied in January 1983, my application went straight to 'File 13', army-speak for the bin. My submission wasn't even entertained.

My friend Caroline worked in Eastern Command

intelligence next to operations, where they sifted through the applications. I applied again in October that year, and she overheard a conversation which went something like, 'For fuck sake, Molloy's applied again. Is she mad?' This application went as far as the director of training in army HQ before it was dismissed.

I was furious that I wasn't being taken seriously. 'What are they afraid of?' I complained. 'Why won't they let me on the course? Even if they think I can't pass it, I demand the right to fail.'

I was on the non-commissioned officer (NCO) course from January to May 1984, so I applied again for 'the Wing' in October of that year. By then, I realised as a non-combatant, they would probably never let me try out for the ARW. Still, I threw in my application again just to annoy them.

I met Caroline for lunch soon after and asked whether she had heard anything.

'You'll never believe it,' she beamed, 'but you got it this time – you're on the selection course!'

My face fell. 'Shit!' I hadn't trained, convinced it would never happen. It was now three weeks before the course was due to start.

GI had already completed a Special Assault Group course, the precursor to the ARW selection course. He urged me to postpone it. 'It's madness to attempt this if you're not at the peak of fitness,' he said.

But I thought otherwise. I decided to treat it as reconnaissance for a more serious attempt the following year. To gather intelligence, I sought out guys who had previously taken the course. Those who'd tried and failed told me what they'd experienced in the first few days. The men who wore the Fianóglach ARW tab told me nothing.

On the grapevine, I heard that the ranger I'd dated briefly was one of the instructors. I knew that was bad news. My ex-boyfriend was likely to want to prove there was no conflict of interest by treating me worse than any of the other candidates.

In another blow to my chances, the night before the course I felt the familiar twisting cramps in my midriff that told me my period was starting. The timing was appalling because I always suffered badly during my period.

However, period pain was not going to deter me. I wanted to show that women were capable of being part of an elite army unit. I had lofty notions that I represented all the women in the army. *I'm not going to let down the rest of the girls*, I thought. In reality, the rest of the girls either didn't give a damn or thought I was a lunatic for signing myself up in the first place.

The initial selection course for the ARW lasted four weeks and started at 18:00hrs on a Sunday, the first of many ploys designed to disorientate the candidates. Everyone is psyched to start something new on a Monday morning, and Sunday evenings are a time for an early night.

On the one-hour journey to the Curragh, I began to rethink my decision. Why couldn't I be happy where I was? Was it so bad working in an office? I was in full combats and boots, ready for action, but my heart pounded and my stomach churned. 'They can't kill you,' I kept reminding myself. It was the only consolation I could think of. I looked around the bus to see if I could exchange a few words with some of the men and pass the time. Nope. They talked among themselves and studiously avoided making eye contact with me. The entire journey, no one spoke a word to me.

When the bus entered the Curragh and turned the corner onto Plunkett Square, I felt a rising dread.

There was a sudden flurry of activity, and as I gathered my kit, the men filled the aisle, blocking my exit from the seat. It meant I was the last off the bus, and you never want to be first or last at anything in the army.

As my right boot hit the ground, I heard a familiar voice roar, 'Ranger Molloy, as you're last off the bus, give me twenty!' I looked over to see the stony expression of my ex-boyfriend.

Shit, I thought as I dropped to face the tarmac. *This is going to be a long fecking night.*

I hadn't caught my breath before they ran us straight through the gates into the ARW compound, the only enclosed compound in the Curragh Camp. The gates clanged shut behind us, and all previous ranks were suspended. The 65 candidates, who included members of the air corps, navy and army, were referred to as 'rangers', and the instructors were 'DS' (directing staff).

The guys were led off upstairs to a billet that accommodated them all. I was brought to the ARW gymnasium, a converted stable room on the ground floor.

It was a compact space, so they shoved the equipment aside and lay a mattress on the floor. The toilet was outside in the hall. It looked ancient with a tiny sink, a high cistern with a long chain handle and a door of planks with wide gaps. To have a shower required a long trip through the compound. I opted for a 'ranger's bath', as they called it, using the sink for the duration of my stay.

All hell descended upon us when we were run to the compound's obstacle course. Push-ups, star jumps, sit-ups, pull-ups, climbing, leaping, leopard crawling, log lifting – there was no rest. For the next several hours, we were corralled into a cramped area for a frantic mixture of battle PT and circuit training with beasting and unremitting screaming. *BASTARDS! … USELESS SHITE! … FUCKING MOVE IT!* They bawled at us with ear-splitting volume. It was utter mayhem.

The area was so confined, there was no place to hide. I saw the clenched jaws of men rapt with concentration as they tapped into zones way beyond exhaustion. All the while, other disjointed faces, mouths and eyes zoomed into my peripheral vision, shouting, screaming, howling. It was a vision of hell.

It was long after dark when the 'sickeners', as they called them, finally ended. We were told to fall in for a kit inspection in the hall. The DS turned out the contents on the floor and tossed everything around. I'd heard about this. I was not about to allow them to kick my knickers and bras about the hall, so I had my underwear in freezer bags tucked into my combat pockets and tampons in my inner chest pocket. They booted the guys' underpants around the hall, but if the DS wondered where my underwear was, he never let on.

We were ordered to fall back on parade with our full kit on our backs and told to buddy up. I got two buddies instead of one, and their faces fell when they were matched with me. They knew I was a heat seeker and would bring that heat on them.

'I'm sorry, lads,' I said under my breath.

'Yeah, we're sorry too,' muttered one in reply.

We were ordered to wear our balaclavas backwards and then to run in single file. 'Never let go of the man in front!' One minute we were running blind across tarmac; the next, there were roars and cries as the ground fell away, and I, along with everyone else, stumbled into a ditch. We were a tangle of limbs and backpacks lying in muck and water.

'CRAWL, YOU STUPID BASTARDS! CRAWL!' So then began an endless blind crawl in ice-cold mud. 'IF YOU CAN'T KEEP UP, RANGER MOLLOY, WE'LL DROP YOU TO THE FUCKING BUS STOP!' I sometimes felt the hard blows of elbows or knuckles in my face. I wasn't entirely convinced they were accidental or came from the other candidates around me. At one stage, I got stuck on a steep incline. Forty or so of the guys had gone before me, and it was a muddy morass. Every time I tried to crawl up, I slid down again. I couldn't pull myself out. Suddenly, someone grabbed me by the scruff of my collar, pulled me up the hill and kicked me in the arse. Dignified, it wasn't.

Intermittently, a DS demanded that we stand on a left leg, take a left middle finger, put it into our right ear, put our right middle fingers in our left nostrils, keep our eyes closed and recite a nursery rhyme backwards. I chose 'Baa Baa Black Sheep', and I smiled behind my balaclava. *Bring it on,* I thought. Standing on one leg with my fingers in my ear and nose seemed like a relaxing break compared to press-ups. But I heard men around me cracking in frustration and telling the DS to go fuck themselves! They were off the course. It was one of the many times I realised that women have more mental stamina than men.

Finally, the DS ran us back to the compound, where we stood shivering, cold, wet and blind. It was at about 02:00hrs. 'On our command, take off your balaclavas,' we heard.

We did that just as two DS wrestled a man in combats to the ground. He started screaming, but they punched and kicked him and dragged him out of sight through a ground-floor door. It was unnerving, but we didn't have time to think about it as we were ordered to our billets. My billet was straight through the door where the two DS had dragged the screaming man, but I followed orders and walked in to find all three men having a good laugh. They had either forgotten or didn't know I was living in the building.

'YOU. SAW. FUCKING. NOTHING!' one of them yelled, his finger jabbing in my face.

They were messing with our heads, wanting everybody

on the course to believe that it was one of the candidates who was being beaten.

I didn't care at that stage. *Just leave me alone and let me bed down*, I thought. I knew it wouldn't be for long. I lay down on the mattress in the small dark room. I thought of the guys upstairs, talking, processing things, having some craic, wondering about the man they'd seen being dragged off. There was too much going on in my head to sleep. I might have nodded off for a few minutes, but I heard them coming for me around an hour and a half later.

Shortly after, they threw two stun grenades into the room. Stun grenades cause temporary blindness, loss of hearing and balance and a sense of panic. I knew the potential for injuries from the pressure of the blast or shrapnel or fragmentation from the grenade was high. So throwing two grenades into a small room seemed an act of idiocy.

More concerning for me, however, was the appearance of the sergeant major of the ARW in my room. Why was the sergeant major of Ireland's answer to the SAS lowering himself to beast a student on a selection course? But he and a squat, burly ranger, nicknamed the Tasmanian Devil or 'the Taz' by his unit, rarely left my side from that first night. The latter had jet-black hair, a matching moustache and a snarling demeanour. He was called after the Looney Tunes cartoon character who spun in furious circles in pursuit of Bugs Bunny. Neither were official instructors on the course, so I received five-star treatment.

I slipped into the toilet, but the pair almost kicked in the door, roaring at me to get out. It was intrusive and degrading, but I steeled myself to continue. I suspected there was worse ahead.

We were marched to the ordnance stores where they handed me a weapon and a magazine of live ammunition. Candidates used FNs even though the rangers didn't. I don't know where my head was, but I immediately inserted the magazine. I heard a sharp intake of breath around me and saw the guys shrink from me in dismay. It was a colossal mistake. As I left the stores, I sneaked the magazine off and slipped it into my pocket. Do you think I got away with it? Did I hell. The DS leapt on me outside and destroyed me. I ran circles around the platoon with the rifle over my head, giving the guys a rest.

When they were done with me, they told us to check our weapons for faults. I discovered that a clip that enabled me to attach a sling – a sling swivel – was missing. I raised my hand to let them know.

'You can change that in your own time, Ranger Molloy,' the DS replied. *In my own time?* The only time we had to ourselves was an hour and a half in the middle of the night when the stores were long locked up.

The sling bore the rifle's weight, which would give my arms a rest. So I did what every soldier is taught – improvise, adapt and overcome. I attached the sling over the butt of the rifle. But they weren't having that.

'No, you'll use the rifle without a sling until you get your weapon changed.'

That's when I knew the missing rear sling swivel was intentional.

Every time we ran, I had to bear the weight of the Fabrique Nationale rifle in my arms. Whenever we faced the obstacle course, I had to lie the weapon down to complete most stations. As soon as I did, the Taz ran in and snatched it and threw it up on the barbed wire fence surrounding the compound. I'd had to climb the fence to retrieve it every time. Luckily the Taz was short, so he couldn't fire it too high. On reflection, like all good soldiers, the Taz was just following orders, but it felt personal at the time.

Everywhere I turned, the Taz and the sergeant major were at my ears, screaming. I was their pet project. It was like having my own personal cheerleaders, except they chanted constant abuse and discouragement. *You're fucking useless, Ranger Molloy. You know you're going home, Ranger Molloy. Will we drop you to the bus now?*

We ran to breakfast in Clarke Barracks in the main Curragh Camp at around 06:00hrs. Still there was no rest.

'Ten minutes at your billets and then fall in!' they bellowed.

I ran into the toilet and promptly threw up everything I'd eaten. It was a combination of nerves and period pain. Not for the first time, I asked myself, *What the fuck am I doing in this place?*

18

The 96-Hour Woman

I continued to live on water and nerves for the next 48 hours, unable to hold anything down. The 24-hour clock no longer mattered. Day or night, we did physical training, ran the obstacle course or sat in lectures. Punishments were constant and designed to push candidates to breaking point both physically and mentally. If we got to bed at 03:00hrs, we only had an average of two hours of sleep before it started again.

In the middle of the night, I sat through a lecture on folding a map. *Folding a bloody map? I can do that with my eyes closed*, I thought. So I did. I closed my eyes.

I was jolted awake by a roar. 'Ranger Molloy, stand up

and fold your map.' So I started folding it but, of course, didn't do it the Army Ranger Wing (ARW) way.

'Wrong! Wrong! Wrong! Everyone downstairs!' the instructor bellowed. We had to do a full lap of the obstacle course in darkness before heading back up the stairs to more lectures about building base camps and 'bugging out'.

I lay in my concrete room downstairs that night, wondering what was going on upstairs in the men's billet. The gymnasium was a lonely place. I comforted myself thinking of the amount of snoring that must be going on upstairs. When we fell in on Tuesday morning, I realised our numbers were thinner. Several faces were missing from the line-up.

A pair of Irish Naval Service men approached me before they quit that day and shook my hand.

'Well done and keep going,' one said. 'I don't know how you're still here, but we can't take this shit any more.'

The sergeant major and the Taz were on top of me even more now, following me everywhere. To be fair, they never called me a bitch or referred to my gender at all and never appeared in my room before I was dressed. However, their demeanour was vicious and their abuse was more aggressive, so I knew my presence was driving them crazy. I imagined them saying to each other, *Oh my God, she's still fucking here. What do we have to do to make this one quit?* Those thoughts cheered me and, mentally, I felt strong. If anything, their antics made me more determined to continue, and I was able to zone them out.

Psychologically, they couldn't make a dent in me. But physically, I was hanging on by a fingernail. I was broken. I felt sick, dizzy and weak, and the muscles in my upper body and arms were screaming with pain. I kept going hour after hour, but it took all my reserves.

On Wednesday morning, I threw up my breakfast, emerged from the toilet and had to rest my head against the door. My skin felt clammy, my stomach nauseous and my legs felt like jelly. I couldn't even sleep for the few hours we were allowed and was on the verge of passing out. I had enough. What was the point of going on when I knew I wouldn't make it to the end? I had prepared to fail. Before leaving my home unit, I'd asked a civilian typist to type out my return to unit (RTU) request.

'Are you sure you want me to do this?' she asked. 'Aren't you admitting defeat before you've even started?'

She was probably right, but I was glad I had the letter ready. It was tucked away in my combats, folded neatly and protected by a small freezer bag. The numbers on the selection course had thinned dramatically by then, as 22 of the men had already left. *At least I beat 22 men*, I thought. It made me feel less of a failure. I handed my RTU request to the directing staff (DS), relieved by my decision and expecting to be told to gather my kit and get out.

Instead, the DS read my note and hesitated. 'Carry on, and I'll get back to you,' he said.

I was stunned as he walked away. *Fuck!* I thought. I still wasn't free of the place. Shortly afterwards, I was ordered to go to an office in the compound. I had no idea what was going on.

The admin officer of the unit, a young lieutenant, sat behind the desk. 'Have a seat,' he said.

I was astounded. *Have a seat?*

'I've been in touch with the CO [commanding officer]. He's at a conference today and asked if you will stay on the course until he returns tomorrow?'

The CO, known to the ARW as 'the boss', frequently attended meetings at army headquarters. I'd had a few conversations with him, usually joking about when he was going to let women join. But I had no idea why he wanted to see me. I slumped in the chair with exhaustion and bewilderment. 'Really? He wants to see *me*?'

I was smart enough to keep the lieutenant talking for as long as possible. It seemed like a lifetime since I'd done anything civilised like sit in a nice comfortable chair.

Where is the CO? How long will he be? What time? Why does he want to talk to me?

Reluctantly, I agreed to stay another day. I went outside expecting a DS to be waiting for me, but no one was there. So I lingered in the hall, determined to extend this unexpected breather for as long as possible. Unfortunately, the sergeant major's office was nearby, and he spotted me through the open door.

'Ranger Molloy! Get the fuck down those stairs on the double and get back to class!'

Wednesday continued with more hazing, more runs through the obstacle course, more lectures, no sleep and no food. It was Groundhog Day. First thing on Thursday morning, I was called to the CO's office.

'Well done getting so far, Ranger Molloy, and I would like you to continue. So tell me, what's your biggest obstacle to continuing this course?'

'I didn't train enough,' I said. 'Also, the weapon's weight is a problem. I don't have the upper body strength to keep carrying it.'

'We can sort out the rifle,' he said. 'What if I offer to swap out the FN [Fabrique Nationale rifle] for the ARW's weapon – the HK 33?'

The Heckler and Koch was lighter and more compact than the FN, but he could see I was still hesitant.

'I want a female in the unit,' he explained. 'Someone I can call on for operations, so I won't need to call on bangardaí [female guards] again.'

I thought about it for half a minute, and then I had another spasm of period pain. I thought about three more weeks of this and felt overwhelmed with exhaustion.

I also knew that even though the CO was the commanding officer of the ARW, the sergeant major ruled the unit. Nothing happened in the ARW if it didn't suit the sergeant major, and if he did not want women in his unit, then I would not pass the selection course. I thanked the CO very much for the offer of swapping out my FN but admitted I was too sick and exhausted to continue.

'I'll try again when I'm fitter,' I assured him.

I got my gear and headed for the compound gate. The guard opened it and never said a word as he watched this empty shell of a person stagger out. I planned to hitch a lift to Dublin with the Eastern Command who were participating in swimming championships in the Curragh Camp that week. However, I was so sleep-deprived that I hadn't considered the distance between the ARW compound and the pool complex. Luckily, a vehicle stopped and the driver asked if I wanted a lift. There was a moment's silence in the truck before he added, 'Are you the girl attempting the selection course?'

'Yeah.'

'Fair play to you,' he said. 'Where do you want to be dropped?'

Peaky, one of the girls on the swim team, came running when she saw me.

'Oh my God, Karina. What happened? Have you looked in a mirror recently?'

How does she expect me to look after coming off a selection course?

Peaky shoved me in front of a mirror in the dressing room, and I was startled to see myself peering back out of two black and swollen eyes. I'd probably acquired them the first night when I received several thumps while wearing my balaclava backwards. I still don't believe they were accidental.

I remember calling my father afterwards.

'Oh, so we're finished already, are we?' he said when he heard me on the other end of the phone.

I explained that it was bad timing because I had my period.

'See there now, that's why a woman will never get into a special-forces unit. There's a weakness there and you've just proven it – using your period as an excuse.'

I felt like such a disappointment; that I'd really let him down.

Years later, I was reliably told that some people were outraged when it was heard I was admitted to the course. 'There's no fucking way any woman's passing this course,' was one view expressed. The ARW admin officer came into my office 20 years later and apologised for the 'special' attention I'd received during the course.

I fully intended to return, but it never happened. I would have done, had I known that another female was attempting the course a few years later. But I would have ended up on my own again as she was injured on her second day and was forced to quit. It took a further 20 years before another woman tried for the ARW.

While researching this chapter, I talked to the sergeant in charge of my selection course. Now retired, he became the sergeant major of the ARW and is happy to be referred to as DH.

Each ARW selection course was called after a code word in the phonetic alphabet. DH said I was on the selection course called Mike. He admitted that there was discussion in the unit before my arrival, but he only remembered the comment, 'If she turns up, she has some fucking balls.' They didn't expect me to show up at all.

The ARW used Schermuly stun grenades at the time, but these were tactical grenades only used in live situations.

Instead, he said they used Thunderflashes on the candidates, which were military-grade pyrotechnics. I'm not sure this was much of a mitigating factor. Even Thunderflashes are intended for outdoor use only in order to simulate battlefield conditions – not for use in the confines of a room.

He confirmed that I received 'special treatment' from the sergeant major and the Taz. However, what he told me next took me by surprise. They expected me to be gone within hours of arrival, but after 48 hours I was still there and in the elite echelon of the class. He said the two men stopped trailing me after that. His claims about the men are at odds with my memories because I don't remember them ever leaving me alone.

I never realised that I'd performed so well on the course, but DH insisted that I had exceeded all expectations.

'You were doing really well,' he said. 'You were on your way to making history.'

It was a little heartbreaking hearing that. If I'd had any idea that I was doing so well, I might have stayed.

He confirmed that 22 men left before I did. He also said a further nine applied for their RTUs within hours of my departure. It amused me to think that their egos wouldn't allow them to leave before the only woman on the course.

I was buoyed by the meeting in one way and had regrets in another. But it was positive to learn that I was regarded as a serious candidate by the time I left. I was the 96-hour woman because they ranked the candidates by the hours they lasted.

Women have had some success in elite forces in America. More than 50 have now earned their US Army Ranger tabs. The SAS recently opened to female applicants and, to date, two women have passed the pre-selection course. I hope someday soon we follow suit because the ARW remains the last male-only bastion in the Irish Defence Forces and the only unit where women still do not serve.

19

Overseas

The wave of hot air felt like a hairdryer blowing in my face as I stepped out of the plane. Hoisting the backpack over my shoulder, I blinked against the glare of the bright Mediterranean sun. I turned to Jock, disembarking behind me at Ben Gurion airport in Tel Aviv.

'Feck,' I said. 'It's not going to be fun working in this heat.'

We'd been like a pair of overexcited children sitting together on the chartered Aer Lingus flight from Dublin. It was our first overseas mission, part of the 57th Infantry Battalion serving with the United Nations Interim Force in Lebanon (UNIFIL) in 1985. GI was on the same trip, but our relationship was over by then, and we were just friends. We were ecstatic about leaving our usual routines for a bit of foreign adventure.

I never wanted to go overseas as a private because, as a non-combatant, my posting was likely to be 'mess orderly', which meant waiting on officers in the mess for six months.

Instead, I watched my friends Caroline Hayes and Mary O'Riordan become the first women to go overseas with the army when they went to Lebanon in October 1982. Caroline and her brother Joe were also the first sister and brother in the army to serve overseas together.

So I was a non-commissioned officer (NCO) when I had the eye-opening experience of tackling all the requirements to complete the overseas form, AF673, for the first time. I had to gather certs for my annual range practice, fitness test, doctor's medical, dental check, and a battery of vaccinations and boosters.

At the army's insistence, I had to write my will. Getting my ID tags or 'dog tags' was another reminder of the perils we faced. These had to be engraved with my number, religion and blood type. If I died abroad, the army would remove one tag for administration purposes and pop the second between the teeth of my corpse to ensure no confusion during the repatriation of the body.

Before being deployed to Lebanon, we were also sent to the Glen of Imaal for 'battle inoculation'. The army trained us for combat, but nothing except exposure prepared soldiers for real battlefield conditions. So we were sent into a battle simulation exercise with live-fire training to prepare us for the shock and terror of actual combat.

Crouched low in massive trenches in full combats and helmets, we were handed a wad of cotton wool to protect our ears. The exercise began with an enormous explosion. Then, the army engineers and ordnance let loose, and we experienced enemy shock and awe for the first time. Machine-gun crews fired several thousand rounds per minute on us with general-purpose machine guns and .5 heavy machine guns. Next, engineers released explosive charges laid close to our trenches.

The ground shook, and a resounding roar of heavy artillery filled my ears as devices of death exploded everywhere. I felt the bone-shaking vibrations of shell bursts, the unrelenting rattle and rush of machine-gun fire around me. Each vast explosion seemed to suck the air from around us, leaving only the acrid odour of black smoke and cordite. Vast showers of rubble and soil constantly rained down.

I can't say I was afraid. Army safety protocols are among the best in the world. But the experience resonated with me as a glimpse, albeit a sanitised one, of what many men experienced as they fought in the wars. I remember talking to my father about it. The bombardment lasted only 15 or 20 minutes, but I began to appreciate how days, weeks and months under these conditions shattered the men's nerves and brought on shellshock and post-traumatic stress disorder (PTSD). It was an immersive and intense experience and all part of the preparations for landing in Lebanon.

We were given no time to look around the airport on arrival in Tel Aviv. Instead, we were herded into a vast hangar where rows of white UN trucks were waiting to load us up. We waved at the guys from the last tour of duty who were boarding our plane back to Dublin, and compared their dark bronzed complexions with our white pasty ones. The outgoing peacekeepers cheered, clapped and jeered us. 'Only six more months to go!' they yelled. 'I'll raise a pint for youse tonight, youse poor bastards!'

GI and Jock were loaded onto trucks leaving for different outposts – I hardly saw them again for the next six months. For the next several hours, I sweltered under the truck canvas with dozens of others as we drove mile after mile, looking out on the shimmering haze of heat rising around us.

Some trucks turned off for UNIFIL headquarters in the coastal town of Naqoura. 'Bastards,' muttered some of the veterans. Everyone knew Naqoura was the 'cushy' posting.

Our truck turned inland towards the hills of Bint Jbeil, always referred to as 'the Hills'. We bumped along potholed roads and weaved through checkpoints for another 40 minutes. It was well after dark when we arrived at Camp Shamrock at Irish Battalion (Irishbatt) headquarters near the village of Tibnin.

Camp Shamrock was Headquarters Company, the admin and logistics centre of Irishbatt, an area of around 100 square kilometres. Three other smaller camps manned by A, B and C companies were all contained within this area. In addition, each of the three companies had many other smaller outposts.

Anne O'Sullivan, known as Sully, from the Curragh Command, ran out to welcome me. She had travelled out on the first rotation or 'chalk' two weeks earlier. She was one of the military police (MPs) at home, and that might have deterred a friendship as MPs and soldiers rarely become companions. However, there were no obstacles to our friendship overseas as women weren't allowed fill MP posts in Lebanon, and she had to work as a clerk. The only other woman among the 700 men was Officer Williams.

I was pleased to discover I had my own small room in a block building – a rare privilege in Camp Shamrock, where most guys had to share billets for four or more in a sweaty prefab.

I emerged from under my mosquito net the following day to begin work in the logistics office. However, I was told to go to the battalion HQ at Tibnin House in the village to hand in my personnel documents.

Not familiar with the area, I was nervous about setting off on foot. We were in operational theatre in Lebanon, so I left the camp armed with my Fabrique Nationale (FN) rifle and wearing my bush green fatigues and blue beret.

With its rocky terrain and stone-built walls, Southern Lebanon was supposed to resemble the west of Ireland in the winter. But in summer, the vegetation was bleached yellow. The terrain was dry, dusty and scorched, and the narrow winding road was lined with faded posters in memory of the area's war victims, the 'martyrs', and yellow Hezbollah flags. Females in uniform were a novelty and, even though I walked at speed, the locals' heads turned to stare.

Tibnin House was easy to spot with the big blue UN flag fluttering on the roof. As I ascended the metal steps outside, the front door swung open and Officer Williams appeared with my company sergeant (CS) following. It was a relief to see people I recognised.

'Hi!' I said cheerily.

That afternoon, however, the CS intercepted me. 'You're going to be up on orders for failing to salute an officer.'

My face fell and my mind raced. 'What? When ...?'

'Officer Williams is charging you.'

Oh, Christ, I thought, as I remembered meeting her that morning. My first day overseas, and I was already up on orders. It had to be a new record. 'I forgot, CS. My head was all over the place this morning.'

He could see my shock. 'Look, leave it with me,' he sighed. 'I'll have a word with her and see if I can talk her out of going ahead with the charge.'

My CS sorted it out, and nothing further was said. After that, I made sure to give Officer Williams a full regulation salute: extending my arm fully, then bringing my hand below the beret badge, palm facing downwards, pausing, then cutting away smartly to the side. 'Longest way up, shortest way down,' as we were always taught. After that day, a general would have been proud of the ferocity of my salutes.

Looking back now, I realise the army imposed a lot of extra responsibility on female officers overseas. Female officers were held responsible for their own staff and everyone under their command, but they were also supposed to oversee every woman in the camp. If I stepped out of line, my male company quartermaster or battallion quartermaster should have dealt with discipline. However, because of Officer Williams' gender, the responsibility for all subordinate females in the camp was heaped upon her. 'Get your women under control!' was the standard refrain, so the female officers were often harder on us as a result.

The army likes to keep soldiers occupied, so the daily routine of Irishbatt was busy. There wasn't a lot of downtime except at weekends. Four soldiers were constantly on 24-hour duties at the front gate. Meanwhile, drivers manned the white UN jeeps inside the gate, transporting officers to briefings at UNIFIL HQ in Naqoura or elsewhere.

Soldiers were deployed to checkpoints on the roads, stopping the locals' battered old Mercedes to check their boots. Mechanics worked in 'the pits' maintaining the UN vehicles damaged on the potholed roads. Those on the water truck travelled all day getting water to service the main camp and the smaller outposts. For good community relations, the medical orderlies and the dentist cared for an endless queue of sick and injured locals.

My job in Lebanon was as repetitive and dull as in Dublin. I spent my days filling in Q1 forms to itemise and replenish stocks. I recall almost nodding off as I typed endless lists of stocktake until the words 'body bags' jerked me awake. It was sobering to think that these bags sometimes had to be used.

Sully and I went running most afternoons or evenings, usually staying in visual sight of male soldiers for security. We bonded through a mutual love of running and physical exercise. Then, more times than not, I returned to work in the office in the evening just to pass the time.

There wasn't a lot to do aside from work. The canteen 'bar' opened for a couple of hours every night before the officer cleared everyone out at 22.00hrs. Soldiers drank cans of local Almaza beer while taking part in quizzes or listening to tinny pop music from the tape recorder in the corner. A vodka and tonic was my preferred drink, but spirits were the sole preserve of the officer class. I rarely went to the bar.

The occasional soccer game against the other UN contingents – especially the football-mad Ghanaians – helped pass the time for some soldiers. During unofficial siesta times in the middle of the day, soldiers 'swanned' – as they called it – on a rooftop or some other quiet spot as they topped up their suntans and complained about the heat and the mosquitoes.

Sully and I built our own little suntrap with corrugated iron. As it was away from the prying eyes of the guys, we decided it was safe enough to sunbathe topless. However, word soon leaked out about our 'indecent' exposure. The commanding officer (CO) charged at Officer Williams like a bull. Being the only female officer, she got the flack if we did anything wrong. 'Get your fucking women in check!' he roared.

Of course, we should have had more cop on than to sunbathe topless in one of the most conservative parts of Lebanon. It was hard to forget we were in a Muslim country when we heard the cry *Allahu Akbar!* several times a day from the nearby mosque.

Sometimes, Sully and I wandered into the village for supplies from one of the 'mingi men' in 'mingi' shops. The term 'mingi' had been part of Irish Army jargon since peacekeepers first went to the Congo in the 1960s. Traders there sold their wares shouting *'mingi, mingi'*, the Swahili word for plenty, and the phrase was still used decades later by the army on overseas trips.

Mingi shops in Lebanon were ramshackle places which sold everything from rip-off Gucci handbags to toothpaste. The mingi video store stocked porn films for soldiers concealed behind a curtain at the back of the shop. Tibnin also had two gold shops where the soldiers shopped for jewellery for the women in their lives.

Sully and I often ate in a backstreet mingi restaurant called Chicken George – though 'restaurant' was too strong a word for a streetside shack with a corrugated-tin roof selling deep-fried chicken and soft drinks. We sat at makeshift tables and seats in uniform, still carrying our FNs. It was somewhere to go outside the camp during the day. No one was allowed leave camp at night.

The situation in Lebanon was always volatile as we operated beside one of the most fractious borders in the world. If we ever needed reminders, we only had to pass the stone memorial at Tibnin that commemorated the 18 Irish peacekeepers who had lost their lives. (The number of Irish soldiers lost in Lebanon is as of today 48.)

Sporadic mortar shelling, gunfire or artillery attacks sometimes occurred near the camp. As soon as we heard the order, 'Groundhog! Groundhog! Groundhog!' over the tannoy, we slapped on helmets and flak jackets, and ran for the secure underground bunker. I always had a 'bunker bag' at my billet door, with a few comforts and a pen and paper. Groundhog was always the ideal time to catch up on writing letters home.

During the tour, I was sent for observation to the Swedish Medical Company in Naqoura with suspected appendicitis. My parents received the standard telegram informing them, 'Your son has been admitted to hospital.'

Gender confusion was also an issue for me on the hospital ward. The Swedish had mixed-sex wards, so I shared with two male Fijian soldiers, two Ghanaian and one Nepalese. I overheard an Irishman talking to a Swedish nurse in the corridor one day.

'I'm looking for Corporal Molloy.'

Whenever an Irish soldier was in hospital, the Irish Army in UNIFIL HQ dispatched someone to visit in case they needed anything.

'Corporal Molloy is in there to the left,' the nurse said.

A captain marched in, and I could see by his pinched expression that he considered himself too important for this menial errand. He glanced around the room and only saw the Nepalese, Ghanaian and Fijian faces and, exasperated, he turned to me. 'I'm looking for Corporal Molloy. Do you know where he is?'

I hadn't slept for several nights from the snoring on the ward. I was also fed up with the notion that everyone in the Irish Defence Forces was male. 'No, I don't know where he is,' I replied.

He marched out again. I could hear him attack the Swedish nurse. 'Corporal Molloy is not in there! Can you please tell me where he is?'

The Swedish nurse marched in with him. 'This is Corporal Molloy!' she said, her outstretched hand indicating me.

He went bright red. 'Do you need anything, corporal?' he asked.

'No, sir. I don't need anything.'

He spun on his heel and marched out, and I smiled, instantly perking up.

Our only way of contacting home from the camp was via high frequency radio. The army's equivalent to a switchboard operator connected me via radio to my parents' telephone in Donegal. When either party finished speaking, we had to say 'over', and the signals guy listening would flick a switch to allow the other party to speak.

'Hi, Mammy,' I'd say. 'It's Karina. Can you hear me? OVER.'

I'd usually hear something like: 'Oh, hi Karina! How are you? Is everything okay?'

But I couldn't reply because she forgot to say 'over', so she would sit in Donegal listening to static, and I'd sigh to myself. *Oh, for God's sake, Mammy.* My father loved anything military, so he was the only one who loved using the radio system.

I returned from leave in Cyprus and went straight back to work. I was the only woman working in an office with nine men. Most, if not all of them, were married and years older than me.

One of the officers said he'd noticed I'd been away for my 24th birthday. 'Come up to our billet after dinner because we have a few presents for you,' he said.

Naturally, I was chuffed that they wanted to mark my birthday. I innocently thought they must have bought me a trinket in one of the gold shops in Tibnin.

They were drinking when I arrived at their billet that evening. I was presented with a gift, all prettily wrapped with a bow.

The men sniggered. 'Open it! Go on, open it!' they insisted, so I peeled off the wrapping to reveal something red and flimsy. A pair of red lacy knickers dangled between my fingers – the 'sexy' nylon sort. The men howled with laughter, and I tried to smile gamefully.

'There's a message. Read the message!' the officer said.

I turned the knickers, but there was no tag. And then I spotted the officer's birthday message written in black marker on the gusset. It read: 'I wish I was here.'

They cracked up and laughed even louder as my cheeks reddened like tomatoes. I edged closer to the door, but just as I went to leave, one of the men insisted that I come to his room. 'I have another present for you there,' he said. 'A real one this time.'

'Come in, come in,' he said. Like an idiot, I did. As soon as I stepped into the room, he shoved me down on his bed and began mauling me, demanding a 'birthday kiss'.

'Get off me!' I yelled, trying to fight him off.

All I heard was laughter in the other room. Somehow, I wrestled out of his grip and fled through an exit door at the back of the prefab. Flushed and shocked, I ran straight back to my billet. Sully wasn't there, unfortunately. I was sick to my stomach, wondering how I could ever face them in the morning. I hardly slept a wink that night.

It helped that the person who attacked me apologised profusely the morning after. 'I was really drunk and completely out of order,' he said. He seemed genuinely mortified. The rest of the office went on as if nothing had happened. But the 'birthday' incident shook me. I felt uneasy in the office afterwards, trying to work but maintaining a distance from all of them.

About six weeks from the end of our overseas mission, we had the Medal Day Parade, a big spectacle where the force commander presented a Tour of Duty medal to those on their first posting overseas. I felt an immense surge of pride as I accepted my award for the honour of representing and serving my country overseas.

It was a feel-good day, but the celebratory mood suddenly ended when my CO stopped me on the square.

'Enjoy yourself, Corporal Molloy,' he said. 'Because you won't be getting another trip. You're not suitable for overseas missions. You're unable to mix properly.'

His words came like a punch in the stomach. One or

more men in the office had clearly complained that I wasn't 'having the banter'.

I always envied Sully and the way she was able to play the game. She drank in the canteen as 'one of the lads', but I wasn't comfortable doing that. Keeping my distance felt safer.

I was glad to put the trip behind me after the CO's remarks. The next time I went overseas, I vowed it would be an international camp.

We had no access to our personal data in the 1980s, but, years later, I discovered that the CO gave me the worst overseas report of my entire career. 'Corporal Molloy is a very withdrawn type of individual who does not mix very well with others,' he wrote. 'Her performance left a lot to be desired. She displayed no initiative and did the minimum.'

He conveniently overlooked the fact that I was in the office most nights working while the men spent their evenings drinking. He could have ticked one of three boxes: 'suitable', 'suitable with reservations' or 'unsuitable'. He ticked 'unsuitable', then scribbled it out and ticked, 'suitable with reservations.'

His evaluation could have stalled my entire career. I'm still not sure why it didn't. However, his critical review was crushed under the weight of glowing reports I would go on to receive. By the time I left the army, I had completed the most overseas missions of any woman in the Irish Defence Forces.

20

A Bit of Banter

Hoisting my heavy rucksack into the back of the truck was not a problem. But then I glanced up from my skirt and heels to the truck bed, five feet off the ground. *Fuck*, I thought. *The army doesn't make this easy.*

We had to report in our number-one uniforms for the first day of our Standard non-commissioned officer (NCO) course. First, however, I had to find a way of clambering into the truck delivering us to the training depot in Cathal Brugha Barracks.

A soldier already sitting inside the truck finally acknowledged my existence. 'Do you want a hand?' he said.

Oh, wow, I'm not being ignored for once. This is a good start.

'Thanks. I appreciate it,' I said, holding on to the side of the truck and extending my other hand to him. 'This bloody skirt is such a nuisance.'

He pulled me towards him but only to the point where I was teetering between the truck and the ground. Holding me at that point, he whispered in my ear, 'This is the first and last time anyone's going to fucking help you on this course.' He glared at me for emphasis before yanking me the rest of the way into the truck.

I sighed. *Oh, here we go again – another eight weeks of macho shitheads.* The 'helpful' soldier was my introduction to the Standard NCO course.

As soon as I'd finished the Potential NCO course, I'd applied for a living-out pass, allowing me to live outside the barracks like a normal person. I was relieved to get out of McKee Barracks. I hated how everyone knew my business and how the guys at the gate reported on all my movements. 'So, I hear you were hoorin' and tourin' last night, Molloy. What were you getting up to until two in the morning?'

I'd return to the barracks after a nice night out, and I'd be the talk of the place the next day. The workings of my fellow soldiers' filthy little minds were always far more interesting than the reality.

It was a relief to start living like everyone else. I moved into a house share in Inchicore with Aishling, who remains my best friend today.

I applied for several sergeants' vacancies, but budgetary restrictions in the 1980s meant an effective embargo on public-sector promotion. I was confidentially told I did well in the interviews but as a non-combatant, my lack of infantry experience hindered my promotion prospects as much as the tightened budgets. The only way for me to get more infantry training was to apply for another course.

Meanwhile, I worked as a personal assistant to a colonel in the executive officer's (EO's) office in Collins Barracks. As much as I enjoyed working with him, I found the job tedious. One day, it was so quiet, I put my head down on my desk for a little rest. At that moment, my EO walked in. My head shot up, but not before he and three colonels following him saw me having a nap on my desk.

Needing a challenge, I applied for the Standard NCO course. It was still voluntary when I applied, but it became compulsory for anyone seeking promotion to sergeant a year later. The course objective was to teach us to become platoon sergeants, and it would help me gain more infantry experience in a bid for promotion.

Forty-three men and I began the course in September 1986. Boarding the truck, I wasn't surprised by the soldier's remarks. By then, I was used to the gung-ho, macho attitude that thrived in most of the Eastern Command battalions. 'We don't want any fucking woman on the course,' they muttered, when the truth was that they didn't want any women in the army at all.

Three men on the course worked with me in admin in

Collins Barracks, so at least I had someone to chat with and join in the dining hall.

Then, one or two days into the course, I spotted a vaguely familiar face among us. *Fuck, it can't be.* But it was. The Taz from the ranger course was one of the students on the course. He saw me watching him and we exchanged nods of acknowledgement.

I smiled to myself, knowing he would get a taste of his own medicine on the course. As a ranger, he would be an even bigger heat seeker than me. All the goons in the Eastern Command Training Depot saw someone from 'the Wing' as a challenge. *Let's see if he's as tough as he thinks he is.* They tried to outdo each other to make him suffer.

Thankfully, the seven-week-long course was more academic than the Potential NCO training. We only had two weeks on the ground in the Glen of Imaal. I couldn't believe it when I had to buddy up with the Taz on an overnight exercise. 'Forty-three men on this course and I have to be paired off with him,' I grumbled. While I was sent off on a night patrol, he was tasked with setting up our bivouac, a makeshift poncho-like shelter. When I returned around midnight, he was already under the bivvy, bedded down in his sleeping bag.

'So how did patrol go, Karina?' he asked.

Wow, is the Taz being pleasant?

'Oh, fine. All I want to do is get a few hours' sleep before they come for us in the morning.'

Everyone was bracing themselves for the usual 'surprise' attack at 04:00hrs.

The Taz started to get up. 'I'll go for a walk and let you get changed into your nightie so.'

I was stunned into silence for a few seconds. 'Are you for real, Tony?' I asked. 'A nightie? The only thing I'm taking off is my fucking boots.'

Christ almighty, I thought. *Who are you and what have you done with the real Taz?* I decided to take advantage of his newly acquired chivalrous ways. 'I'll tell you what you *can* do for me, Tony. You could try not snoring.'

And, of course, he turned over and snored for the next four hours.

One of the NCOs gave a platoon-in-defence lecture to the men on the course, discussing the enemy breaking our defences. I was in hospital that day.

'Of course, only one person on this course would know all about penetration,' he quipped, to a chorus of appreciative sniggers.

The snarling soldier who 'helped' me onto the truck told me about the sergeant's comment. Against the odds, we became friends while on exercises together, and he admitted he had negative preconceptions of me before even meeting me.

He wasn't alone. Many men bristled when my name was mentioned because everyone in the army thought they knew me. I had dared to complain about being sexually assaulted, broke their twisted code of omertà, so was deemed a 'troublemaker'. Also, I was a snob and 'uppity' because I didn't use the canteen or NCOs' mess. 'She thinks she's a cut above the rest of us,' they said.

However, I wasn't the only woman who struggled with exclusion and discrimination. Many of us were affected by the toxic masculinity that was rife in the infantry. These men didn't want women, full stop, so sexism and misogyny were endemic across the defence forces.

Living up to my reputation as a 'troublemaker', I reported the NCO's remark to the platoon officer, demanding an apology. Instead, I was told to get a thicker skin. So I confronted the NCO about his vulgar comment. 'I thought you'd have more cop on by now,' I said.

'Cool down, Molloy,' he snorted. 'It was only a bit of fucking banter.'

I heard those words in the army so many times. It was the standard deflection, a convenient phrase to cover up bullying and harassment and make the victim feel like a prude or killjoy. No matter what insults, abuse or inappropriate sexualised comments were hurled at me, I was supposed to accept it because it was 'just a bit of banter'.

21

Fraternising

We were always careful where we went together. We picked quiet, out-of-the-way places where we were unlikely to meet anyone we knew, especially from the army. As an officer, it was frowned upon for him to fraternise with me, a member of the other ranks. Our relationship had to be primarily conducted in secrecy.

The game was up, however, when we were spotted by two female officers at an anonymous hotel bar one lunchtime. My heart sank as their eyes immediately swivelled in our direction, and one of them beckoned to us. My partner, I'll call him Ian, knew one of the officers and I recognised the other.

'Let's say hello, and make our excuses,' I muttered. With forced smiles, we approached the two women.

'Well, what a surprise to see you both here,' said one officer, patting the seat beside her. 'Join us – we're just ordering.'

I sighed inwardly. There was nothing we could do without being rude. So we sat down, politely conversing, until Ian had to leave to order drinks or pay the bill, I can't remember exactly. As soon as he was out of earshot, the two officers turned on me like wolves on prey.

'Karina, I hear you're considering leaving the army,' one of the officers said.

I had only started to look at other options at that stage. I didn't think it was widely known, and I wasn't expecting her to be interested in my career plans. 'Yes, I've been thinking about it.'

'Well, you need to make up your mind,' she said. 'You'll have to leave the army if you want to continue this relationship.'

I felt my cheeks burn, but I concentrated on moving food around my plate. Our relationship was none of her business, but she was as targeted as an Exocet missile. She kept coming for me.

'It can't work otherwise, you know,' she continued. 'You can never socialise with Ian in the officers' mess. He won't be able to bring you to any of the dinners and balls he has to attend. Do you know how awkward it is for him to not have a partner for officers' functions?'

'Well, don't worry,' I said breezily, glancing over my

shoulder, hoping that Ian was on his way back. 'Things haven't got that far yet.'

But the officers were only getting into their stride.

'You really should consider Ian's future,' said one. 'Do you know how damaging being with you could be for his career?'

Their meaning was clear: I was acting above my station, and I would never be admitted to their clubby upper echelons. I was being told I should stick to my own kind.

I refused to engage so, lips pursed, they bristled with disapproval until Ian returned to the table, when they became all smiles and bonhomie again. My leave-taking from the ladies was polar cold. Of course, I told Ian what they'd said as soon as they left.

'The bloody nerve of them,' he said hotly. 'I never asked for their opinion, and neither did you. Ignore them.' But I could tell by his irritation that their comments had hit a nerve.

Relationships between army colleagues only became an issue when women entered the defence forces in 1980. (Same-sex relationships weren't a consideration because they remained a criminal offence until 1993.)

During recruit training, the non-commissioned officers told us that the unofficial rule was that we couldn't date anyone more than two ranks higher in the chain of command. However, it was also an unwritten rule that officers should never date other ranks. Such relationships were deemed to compromise the chain of command, resulting in accusations of favouritism. But, of course, it was more to do with snobbery. The caste system was alive and well in the army, and officers objected to anyone who threatened their rarefied atmosphere. Admitting members of the lower orders into their fold couldn't be countenanced.

I was first introduced to Ian in a Dublin bar by friends. They said a colleague of theirs was tagging along. He was in Dublin for his 'forming up' – meeting with the rest of his battalion before he left for overseas. When I heard he was a captain, I groaned. Many officers treated other ranks like they'd treat something nasty stuck to the sole of their shoe. It was beneath them to make a cup of tea or open their own doors. However, Ian proved relaxed and entertaining that night. He was also heading overseas in three weeks, so I was relaxed around him.

We all returned to an apartment, and Ian and I sat chatting after the others had gone to bed. We arranged to meet for lunch the next day, and that was it. Ian wasn't conventionally handsome, yet there was something so attractive about him. He had the kindest eyes and a warm and gentle manner. Unfortunately, he was probably too easy-going. He opted to go straight to his unit instead of university. It was the only issue we argued about. I thought he was foolish to opt out of college and lose the opportunity to be paid a salary while studying. And without a degree or any qualifications, he had nothing to fall back on. He effectively committed his life and career to the army.

We had so little time before he went away, so we spent

what we had together. We saw each other the night before he left for Lebanon, and he complained that our meeting was lousy timing.

'Do you mind if I write to you?' he asked. 'It will make the trip go much faster for me if we stay in touch.' So we ended up corresponding while he was away. In the days before emails, Skype or WhatsApp, we communicated via the military's overseas post system. We could pick up single sheets of paper in any post office, fold them into an envelope and post them overseas for a penny.

I was suffering from a bad case of itchy feet. I kept applying for overseas duty, hoping one of the other girls would drop out, or the army might increase the quota for females overseas. But nothing came up, and I was increasingly bored and disillusioned. The prospects for promotion were dim because I was a non-combatant. Work in the Q-Planning section, a logistics planning office, was mundane. I was jaded. I didn't want to work as a secretary in uniform for the rest of my life, so I started seeking new challenges.

I sent my CV for new jobs, including trainee nursing positions in England and physical-training positions in girls' schools in Dubai. My colonel called me into his office after I applied for an army discharge in the middle of 1987.

'Karina, withdraw your application for discharge,' he urged. 'Stick it out. I know you find it tedious, but there are big changes ahead with new information technology and computerisation.'

He was like my father, advising me to have patience. He reminded me to appreciate a good pensionable job during those turbulent and recessionary times. 'The army is like normal life with its ups and downs, but there are exciting times ahead. We'll be sending you on courses so that you'll be at the cutting edge of all this new technology.'

The colonel said the magic word: courses. Courses meant I would be learning new and exciting things. It made sense to stay put and see where this new-fangled information technology brought me.

Ian then surprised me by asking if I'd join him in Cyprus on his leave. I didn't need to think twice and said I'd see him in Nicosia. I was scrambling to get the money together when another letter arrived containing a blank signed cheque to book my flight. Overseas personnel received their regular army salary along with the UN overseas allowance. With a double officer's salary, he was better able to afford the fare than I was, so I accepted his kind offer.

When Ian's overseas mission ended, we were still a serious item. He brought me to meet his parents, and I brought him to meet mine.

My father always advised that if I was marrying a man, make sure he was either rich or handy. 'If he's not wealthy, make sure he can do all the jobs you won't have the money to pay for,' he said.

As a test, my father always roped my new boyfriends into some job or other, and he quickly discovered that Ian didn't know his way around a toolbox. My boyfriends always disappointed my father. But Ian and I were happy, even if we had to keep our relationship quiet at work.

However, after we had been together a year, Ian's commanding officer (CO) called him to his office. He came straight out with it. 'I hear you've been in a relationship for a while now,' he said. 'Take this as friendly advice: drop her, or your career is going nowhere.'

I felt hurt when he followed his officer's advice but I shrugged and wished him all the best. I understood his career ambitions. He would need the right woman by his side to demonstrate maturity and steadfastness to his superiors.

I had no desire to become an officer's wife. I had no desire to marry at all and had already refused a proposal from another army man. I had my own career ambitions. So we exchanged a big hug and broke up on the best of terms.

Two weeks later, he phoned me and suggested we start over. I think he was genuinely heartbroken and regretful, but pride wouldn't let me take him back. I also knew it was inevitable that he would dump me again.

He said the same years later when I accidentally bumped into him in Dublin. Whenever we met, he asked, 'Can we try again?' But I didn't believe in second chances. I wondered, if it came to another promotion opportunity, would he choose me or his job? We all have choices – he chose his career as an officer, and I chose to let him live with that decision.

22

Tormented

'Wow, the body on you, Molloy!' Officer X said, circling me while grinning with approval.

'This is fantastic! You know, you remind me of my mistress.'

This was how the officer I would come to think of as my tormentor – a man in his forties or fifties (ancient as far as I was concerned) – introduced himself. I was stunned.

I remind him of his 'mistress'? Is this guy for real?

He swivelled his forefinger at me. 'Why don't you turn around for me now, and let me get a good look at the view I'll have in the office every day.'

Why don't you fuck off?

It was the forming-up period in the Curragh Camp as everyone got to know each other before we travelled to on our mission overseas. The first chalk was only days away, and suddenly I felt anxious. Any time I tried to move away from the officer, he followed. The office felt far too cramped now that he had arrived.

He didn't stop. He came up behind me again. 'I'm going to have great fun with you,' he said, trailing a finger down the shoulder of my uniform. 'We're going to have fun, aren't we, Molloy?'

I glanced at him nervously, wondering if any man could really be this smarmy. I looked for some backup from my sergeant and the private sitting in the office, but they both appeared remarkably engrossed in the paperwork on their desks.

Before he left the office that day, he approached me again. He flashed what he must have thought was his best lady-killer smile and bent to whisper in my ear. 'I'm going to have you, Molloy!' he hissed, and then he sauntered out.

My jaw dropped in shock and I turned to the sergeant. 'Did you hear that? I can't deal with shit like that for the next six months!'

'Ignore him,' the sergeant said. 'It's only a bit of banter. He'll settle down when he has work to do.'

I hoped he was right. He was leaving his wife and mistress behind, and I hoped he wasn't expecting me to fill either vacancy while on our mission. I had an uneasy feeling about the trip before we even left Dublin.

I'd been looking forward to this trip more than my previous one as it was an international camp, with contingents from all over the world and a huge mix of people. I was a corporal clerk in the logistics office. Female numbers rose on this trip for the first time. Two of my platoon, Sully and her colleague Muirann, were also on this mission. Both worked as military police in Ireland but, once again, they could only serve as clerks here.

Whether it was to protect us from the Irish men or the Irish men from us, our billets were in the Swedish camp due to the larger number of women there, separated from our own camp by a wire fence. Sully and I arrived on the first chalk and shared a room during the handover.

On our second or third night, we were woken by someone rattling our door handle.

'Who the fuck is that?' I said, lifting my head from the pillow. I saw Sully raise herself on her elbow in her bed.

Discovering the door was locked, the night caller started pounding on it.

'Who is it?' I yelled.

'Open the fuckin' door, Molloy; we're having a party,' a male voice replied. Another hollered, 'Yeah, come on, Sully, open the fuckin' door!'

We hadn't a clue who they were and we certainly didn't want 'a party'. We had to be up early the following day for work.

'Ignore them,' I said to Sully.

But our unwanted night visitors replaced their fists with boots and suddenly kicked our door in. My heart pounded

My mother tried to brainwash me early to become a nurse, but I set my sights on a uniform of a different kind. Christmas 1966, with my two big brothers.

In 1981, my army dream came true.
With Mum and Dad at my passing out parade, Curragh Camp.

Passing out parade of the first female recruit platoon,
McDonagh Square, Curragh Camp, 29 October 1981.

Proud prize-winners from the first platoon. I had my eye on best soldier
prize but had to settle for best kit! Left to right: Bernadette Curran (joint
best shot), myself, Sharon McNamara (joint best sportsperson), Maeve
Magennis (best soldier), Mary O'Riordan (joint best shot), Enid Delaney
(joint best sportsperson).

Myself and my fellow colleagues were the first four women ever to complete the physical training instructor course. Pictured here on the last day at Curragh Camp gymnasium, July 1982. Left to right: Corporal Anne Molloy, Corporal Patricia O'Shaughnessy, Lieutenant Marie Flynn, Corporal Sharon McNamara and myself.

During the ground phase of the Non-Commissioned Officer (NCO) course at the Glen of Imaal, Wicklow, 1984.

With my section buddies at the NCO course in the Glen, smiling because the end is in sight. My good pals 'Cossie' (above me) and 'Jock' (door frame, top) kept me going during those tough days.

My first trip to Lebanon was summer 1985, with Irish Battalion 57.

I was the first woman to complete the NCO course for the Eastern Command. At the course passing out parade, Cathal Brugha Barracks, May 1984.

Brigadier General Savino (RIP) inspecting the troops.

On my first mission to Lebanon in 1985, we had to run with bodyguards, as it was not deemed safe for women to run in shorts and vests in a Muslim country.

Lebanon, 2000. Corporal Eoin Ward enjoying a rare break with his bottle of Almaza beer. He was my right-hand man on the mission.

The Lebanon trip in 2000 was my sixth and last tour with UNIFIL. As the company quartermaster sergeant of A Company, I was involved in setting up the new post at 'Blue Line', the territorial boundary between Lebanon and Israel.

Receiving my first overseas medal with the 57th Battalion, given to me by the 'Bull Callaghan', General Brid Callaghan, September 1985. My steadfast friend Corporal Anne 'Sully' O'Sullivan is to the right.

At Camp Tara, the Irish camp in Naqoura, with my French boyfriend at the time, Muinir, in 1997.

On one particularly difficult mission abroad, my sanity was regularly saved by Sunday evening soirées at the French camp. Unlike the Irish army men, the French loved to dance and taught me to rock and roll.

Bosnia, 2002, on a Stabilisation Force mission (SFOR).

Through highs and lows, myself and my women friends in the military supported each other. Left: myself and Corporal Rachel Snee are homeward bound from Eritrea, 2003.

All smiles with Sully after competing in UNIFIL swimming championships, Lebanon, 1985.

At the medal day parade of my friend Gunner Aideen Mulhall, Camp Shamrock, Lebanon, St Patrick's Day, 1997.

I've been lucky enough to have Mark as my life partner for fifteen years, but we were army colleagues for many years before that. This is a rare photograph of us together at the Blue Beret Club, Camp Tara, 1997.

Wearing my medals with pride at the Veteran's Ball, 2016.

Never one to shy away from physical challenges, these days a winter swim does the trick. Mountcharles Pier, Donegal, 2020.

as two men stumbled into our room. They bore cans of Heineken like they were the holy grail.

'Get fucking out!' I shouted, but they strutted through our room and plonked themselves on our beds.

'It's party time, girls!'

In the chaos, we discovered they were two officers staying the night at the camp from their own mission area before flying back to Dublin. They had heard that three girls had just arrived and they'd identified our billet because our names were posted outside.

Sully and I were not in any humour for their antics, and we thumped and shoved the two men out the door. The drunken pair stumbled out, vastly offended. They clearly weren't expecting the hostile reception they received.

The bloody cheek of them, treating us like we were two hookers, here for their entertainment. I was so angry I couldn't sleep.

The following morning, I was still mad. 'I'm going to complain about those thugs. They're not getting away with this.'

But Sully shook her head wearily. 'Oh, please don't, Karina,' she pleaded. 'We have a whole trip ahead of us. You'll only draw trouble on us if you report two officers.'

Sully was so adamant that she didn't want to make a complaint that I reluctantly agreed to drop the idea. I wasn't happy about it, though. *This is ridiculous*, I thought. *Do we have to be nervous about this happening every time we go to bed?*

I set out for work and saluted a senior officer along the road. We fell into step, and he chatted amiably. I mentioned about the incident from last night, when the two Irish officers had burst into our room.

'Oh, really?' he said.

'Yes, they kicked in our door in the middle of the night.'

The senior officer stopped dead in his tracks and turned to me. The warm, collegial atmosphere had evaporated, and he fixed me with steely eyes. 'Molloy,' he said, 'we won't be hearing any more about that. You'll keep that quiet. Is that clear? Those men have had an exemplary overseas trip and are on their way home today.' He added one final warning: 'Remember, you have a long six months ahead.'

In other words, I'd shut my mouth if I knew what was good for me. It was clear that nothing had changed in the ten years we'd been in the army.

Meanwhile, Officer X was a constant thorn in my side, and his behaviour worsened by the day. He looked for any opportunity to brush against me, grab me by the hips or come up behind me and graze his fingers across the nape of my neck. The harassment never stopped.

'Molloy, you're doing terrible things to me, you know. You looked outstanding in that bikini yesterday. Did you wear that for me?'

I didn't care if he saw me rolling my eyes. 'No, sir, I was wearing that bikini for me. I was sunbathing.'

'I think you're just teasing me, Molloy ...'

He loved to whisper obscene comments in my ear when

he could corner me. 'I'm going to do things to that ass of yours, Molloy.'

I'd fiercely elbow him out of my way, but he'd just laugh. He didn't care what he said to me or who was there to witness it. As far as he was concerned, I was his staff, property and plaything. We worked in a vast warehouse, a relocatable tent-like structure called a Rubb Hall, but he'd still manage to impose his lewd presence on my working day. It went well beyond a joke. I shuddered at the mere sight or sound of him.

My sergeant was no help. Instead, he urged me to treat the officer's behaviour with a pinch of salt. 'Think of him as a peacock revealing his plumage – he's only looking for attention.'

It was easy for him to say, when this peacock wasn't constantly chasing him around the warehouse.

Sully, Muirann and I moved into a new prefab with three billets in the Swedish camp. I could hear Muirann breathe in the middle room next door, but at least we had our own spaces and our own front doors. I often opened the window, hoping to find some breeze to break the heat, but all that entered my room were mosquitoes and more hot air.

Despite the oppressive heat and constant harassment, I grew to love being based there. We also had none of the restrictions at night that we had on my previous mission. The town was a metropolis compared to there and we could cross the border to a city which offered an array of bars and restaurants.

I was also dazzled by all the international contingents – including Norwegians, Ghanaians, Fijians, Nepalese and a handful of Finnish officers. The Italian camp, directly across from the Irish one, had quality coffee and espresso machines long before anyone else. Most Irish Army men didn't mix with the other nationalities. They sneered at them because they didn't share the same desire for slugging back copious amounts of alcohol every night.

Meanwhile, everything Gallic, especially the men, enthralled me. Sunday evenings was dance night in the French camp. The French had no female soldiers serving overseas. So, 80-plus men waited their turn to spin, swing and sweat with a handful of Swedish nurses and me at the small parade ground.

Their dance soirées were frantic and fun, all jive and vintage rock 'n' roll. We danced to Elvis' 'Jailhouse Rock' and The Andrews Sisters' 'Boogie Woogie Bugle Boy'. When a set ended, a scrum of non-commissioned officers and officers elbowed their way onto the dance floor to claim one of a limited number of female partners. None of the women could take a break, so the dance soirée was like a marathon four-hour workout.

I loved that weekly dance. It was my refuge, hideaway and safe place, somewhere I was guaranteed not to see Officer X nor a single man from the Irish camp. I'm sure the French were no less sexist than the Irish men, but I didn't have to work with them. All I did was dance and walk away. I cherished those Sunday evenings.

Mental health is a household phrase now, but no one

talked about depression and workplace stress then. All I knew was that I felt unbearable anxiety about going to work, wondering what excuses I could make to get out of the office. Every Sunday night, I danced and forgot my troubles, but every Monday morning, my stomach churned as I went to work. I wasn't in a good place.

23

Tragedy in Camp

The camp seemed notably quieter one morning. I heard none of the usual shrieks of laughter from the nurses' billets, and the normal buzz of activity around the camp was missing. As soon as I entered our shared showers, I knew something was wrong. The girls, usually so outgoing and cheery, were sombre and talking in hushed tones. I wondered if something had happened in the hospital.

What's going on?' I asked one of the women.

She told me a tragic love story. A nurse in the prefab beside us had been dating a fellow Swedish soldier from an ordinary working-class family in the camp. Their overseas tour was ending and her wealthy family put pressure on her to end the relationship before returning home. Apparently, he couldn't handle the rejection. The male billets were in a different part of the Swedish camp, so we didn't hear the fatal shot ring out during the night.

I knew the nurse she talked about. When the nurses weren't on duty, they often dragged chairs into the balmy evening air and sat drinking coffee and eating cake. When they heard that I had a brother living in Sweden, I became part of the family. I still remember a smiling girl with tawny, wavy hair among the blonde bombshells who surrounded her.

Like her colleagues, she was a fully trained soldier, with her semi-automatic weapon in a locker in her billet.

'She is devastated,' the girl's friend confided. 'The commander put her on a suicide watch this morning and removed the magazine from her weapon. We're taking turns to stay with her and watch her until we get her home.'

That night, I was about to get into bed when I remembered that I'd left one of my bikinis drying outside. My mother had sent me two expensive bikinis, and one bra had already been stolen from the washing line. Men liked to sneak into our camp area in the night and steal them as trophies. They also had some weird idea that it might encourage the women to sunbathe topless.

I went out to get my things from the small washing line sandwiched between our prefab and the nurses' one next door. It was dark outside, but I heard the quiet conversation of a few nurses sitting at their front doorstep on their suicide watch. As I started taking my things off the line, the window of the neighbouring prefab opened a few feet away from me. I spotted the pale face of the grieving girl at the same time as she saw me. 'Oh, hi!' I said, but she shut the window again before I could ask how she was.

Poor girl, I thought. I gathered my things, returned to my billet and got straight into bed. It was two or three minutes later that I heard 'tap-tap-tap' at my door. Three taps, muffled yet distinct. I thought it must be one of the nurses from next door. I got up to answer, but even as I was pulling on my dressing gown, I heard cries and an anguished wail.

I opened the door to see a frantic huddle of people on their knees below me. The security light outside illuminated the pale legs of a girl stretched out beyond them, her feet twitching in the dark. I didn't understand for an instant. Then my eyes were drawn to shimmering rivulets of a dark viscous liquid trickling down my front door.

The nurses were already working on her. So too was a male doctor who appeared out of nowhere. I stood in confused horror at the door, staring at the tragedy unfolding before me.

The doctor scrambled to his feet when he saw me. 'Please, it's best if you go back inside,' he said, gently guiding me back into my billet. One of the nurses from next door followed me. Her face looked grey in the harsh light of an army billet. 'Put some clothes on, and let's get you out of here,' she said, professional to the last, even though her friend was lying dead or dying outside my door.

Sully and Muirann had been woken by all the commotion

and were taken out too. The three of us sat shocked, drinking coffee in another billet. I trembled listening to the Swedish girls as they cried and screamed, and I watched them hug and squeeze each other for dear life. Guilt pulsed through my veins. Could I have done more? Should I have knocked on the girl's window when she closed it on me? Should I have alerted the nurses watching her? It was such a grim night.

It turned out the girl had concealed a spare magazine of ammunition in her billet and simply reloaded her semi-automatic. I've wondered all my life why they didn't take her weapon as well as the rounds. I still have no idea why they didn't.

My presence at the washing line interrupted her when she'd first tried to escape out the window, but she only waited minutes until I had gone to climb out again. I must have been the last person to see her alive. I'm not sure why she decided to shoot herself on my doorstep. Maybe they saw her or perhaps she couldn't bear to live a minute longer. I'll never know.

When I returned to my billet shortly before dawn, the area outside was taped off as a crime scene, much of it blocking my entrance. 'Be careful where you step; that's forensics,' one military policeman said. 'Forensics' seemed a very cold word for the flesh and blood of the girl who'd stood in the next-door window just hours before.

Even now, it sounds extraordinary, but I only heard a 'tap-tap-tap' as if someone had rapped their knuckles softly at my door. I tried to explain this to the Irish military policeman who took my statement as part of the investigation into her death. 'Sure, there's no way you heard that,' he said. 'There's no way she could have got off three rounds.'

'Well, that's what I heard. Tap-tap-tap. And that's what I want to be written in my statement.' I'll never forget the sound as long as I live.

A few years later, I met the same military policeman and we talked about that night. He said the autopsy confirmed the nurse had shot herself in the head three times. This was probably only possible because the Swedes used semi-automatic weapons.

The day after the tragedy, a team of psychologists landed from Sweden and took the nurses into counselling. They remembered that the girl had killed herself outside the Irish girls' billet and invited us to join their counselling sessions.

I admired the caring and respectful way the Swedish army handled the tragedy. The Irish doctor less than an hour away didn't even make a phone call to see if the Irish women were okay, even though everyone knew the nurse had shot herself on our doorstep.

For a long time after, my sleepless nights were haunted by the girl's pale face and twitching feet. I know I should have accepted the Swedes' counselling offer because I never got over the shock of her death. Even recalling the events of that night as I write this has brought on fresh tears. But I was due to go on leave days later, and I was happy to go. I was relieved to escape the bloody scene outside my door.

I expected I'd be able to cope when I returned 12 days later. *People will have moved on, and I will too.* However, I returned to find little had changed. Fresh flowers marked the bloodstains on the parched yellow grass in front of my doorstep. There was no escaping the memory of the nurse's death as I had to step over the fresh flowers and the bloodstains several times a day.

By the third or fourth day, I broke down crying. Between the stress at work and the shock of this tragedy on my doorstep, I wasn't coping.

'I can't deal with funeral flowers and her blood outside my door every day,' I told Sully. 'We need to talk to someone who can sort this out or I need to move.'

Sully must have spoken to the right people because the next day, I returned from work, and the flowers were gone, the grass was dug out, and the step was cleaned. Fresh flowers were laid at the base of the Swedish flag instead.

Days later, I was in the village, when I spotted a cheap keepsake, a small plaque, for sale in one of the shacks. It featuring an image of a smug Garfield carrying a rifle. Proudly emblazoned below the cat were the words: 'I Survived the Mission'.

I must have passed this knick-knack a hundred times without noticing, but its frivolous slogan was disquieting now. *I Survived the Mission.* The faded bloodstain on my doorstep, the memorial rock to the fallen Irish in various missions and the body bags I counted were evidence that many didn't. I couldn't help thinking of all the other people who weren't so lucky.

24

Sourpuss

'I want none of that sourpuss, Molloy. Get over here –
it's hug day today and I'm giving you a big hug whether
you want it or not.' Every day was attempted-hug day or
purposefully-brushing-up-against-me day.

Officer X's behaviour wore me down. It was like being
constantly heckled and bullied by a vile adolescent. The
tragic death of the nurse took a toll and made me less
resilient than I might have been.

I wanted to lodge a complaint but my sergeant wouldn't
hear of it. *It's your problem, not mine*, he more or less told
me.

I decided to confront the officer myself and formally

requested that he stop his behaviour. As I entered his office, he sat back in his chair with a smile. He was delighted for this unexpected opportunity to engage in some early-morning leering. I cut him off before he had a chance.

'Sir, I'd appreciate it if you would stop all this. I don't want to hear comments about my body or my appearance. I don't want you touching me. It's inappropriate and you're making me very uncomfortable in the office. I want this to stop.'

He shook his head in disbelief. 'Ah, Karina,' he said, 'I thought you and I were friends. I've never done anything but pay you compliments. But, I mean, if you feel like that, I'll do my best and won't compliment you again.'

I left the office somehow feeling as if I was being totally unreasonable.

To be fair, the officer stopped his behaviour – for about a week. Then he started again. He'd creep up behind me and, suddenly, I'd feel his hand on my body or his hot breath in my ear. I went out of my way to avoid him but it only made him more determined. 'Please leave me alone!' I said a hundred times a day, but he ignored me.

I wrote to the adjutant seeking a personal interview. I tried to explain that it was a nightmare trying to work with the man, but the adjutant only sighed heavily. 'Well, what do you want me to do about it?' he said.

I said I wanted to make a formal complaint and move office.

The adjutant was having none of it, citing the officer's

outstanding reputation. 'I've no intention of ruining the character of a good officer.'

I blinked in shock but suggested a less formal alternative. 'Well, can't you take him up to the officers' mess for a drink and have a man-to-man talk and tell him to rein in his behaviour? I just want it to stop.'

He exhaled a sigh of irritation. 'Okay, okay, leave it with me,' he said, and I was dismissed.

I left thinking, *Well, that was a fucking waste of time*, and it was. Nothing changed. The adjutant was on his first trip overseas and the last thing he wanted was to confront a veteran officer.

So I did what I always did when trapped in a situation – I shut down. I didn't communicate with Officer X unless he addressed me concerning work. I walked away when he started talking about my backside, breasts, shorts or bikini. This usually meant that I walked out of the warehouse minutes after he entered. It didn't deter him. He'd follow me, berating, 'Ah, don't be a sourpuss, Molloy.'

'Get a sense of humour, Molloy,' I'd hear him holler. 'Don't think you're going to avoid me for the rest of the trip.'

I returned twice more to the adjutant to complain and, when I was ignored, I gave up trying to be the only professional at work. When the officer addressed me, I turned a deaf ear. He was dead to me. My demeanour was icy and I was positively rude to him. The sergeant and the private watched wide-eyed as the tension rose day after day.

The officer didn't know how to deal with this and grew outraged. 'The fucking silent treatment, is it?' he bawled at me.

He started complaining to the lads. 'This is fucking worse than being at home. I'm not putting up with this shit. I get enough of that from the wife.'

Out of the blue, the adjutant called me to his office. This was our fourth meeting, but the first he instigated, so I knew that the officer must have complained about me.

'I take it that you're still very upset,' the adjutant said.

'I've been upset for a long time, sir.'

'I realise now that you're genuinely upset, so we're going to arrange a change of employment.'

'A change of employment when there are only a few weeks to go, sir?'

We had less than a month of the tour left and technically only two weeks because the final fortnight was the handover.

'Yes, I think it would be best for all concerned.'

It might have been best for Officer X, but I knew it wouldn't look good on my overseas report to see a change of employment in the final weeks of my tour. 'No, sir,' I said. 'I'm not accepting a change of employment now.'

'Make up your mind, Molloy. Isn't that what you wanted all along?'

'I wanted it months ago, sir, but you didn't do anything then. I'm about to go home now and I'm not accepting a change of employment now, sir.'

I took a step back, saluted him and walked out the door.

I continued to give the officer the cold shoulder and had the satisfaction of him glaring resentfully at me across the office.

Three weeks later, the handover was in full swing. My replacement had arrived and I was only helping out if necessary. I hardly had to see my tormentor at all. We had a lot of functions during our final week and I returned to my billet at midnight after one such event, relieved that the day was over. The heat was unbearable, so I stripped down to my knickers and lay on the bed.

My eyes had hardly shut when there was an unmerciful bang on my door. 'Molloy!' someone shouted outside. It sounded urgent.

'Who is it?' I said, scrambling into my cotton dressing gown.

I opened the door and Officer X burst into the room.

'Molloy, you've been fucking avoiding me but I'm having you now.'

He grabbed hold of me, pushed me back on the bed and started tearing at my dressing gown. I remember his sweaty paws everywhere and his hot breath, stinking of beer. 'I'm fucking having you now,' he muttered repeatedly.

I never thought I'd be the type of person who'd freeze in a crisis, but I did. For a few seconds at least, I was in shock and then something clicked in my head. *Not a fucking chance are you having me.* I had to summon all my strength to wrestle him and, in the struggle, I rolled off the bed onto the floor. He grabbed for me but missed, and I ran out the door into the camp, panting for breath, still trying to refasten my dressing gown. He didn't chase out after me but no way was I going back inside. *Fuck!* I thought, standing in the dark, wondering what to do. *Fuck!*

If I had been thinking straight, I would have screamed for help. Or I would have turned left to run the short hill to the Swedish guards. I should have let them deal with him. The military police would have been brought in, and no one in the Irish Army would have been able to cover up the incident. But, of course, I would have really gained the reputation of a troublemaker then. I often berated myself after for not going to the Swedish, but I have to remind myself that the reprisals would have been so fierce that I may never have had the career I had if I did.

Instead, I turned right, entered the Irish camp gate and dashed to the billet where the sergeant and private from my office were staying. The men never locked their doors, and I burst straight in. 'Wake up! I need your help! [Officer X] is in my room and I need you to get him the fuck out!'

The sergeant sat up, alert and full of concern – but not first and foremost for me, it seemed.

'You get back over there while we get dressed. Don't let him be seen wandering drunk around the Swedish camp.'

I didn't hurry back. I didn't care if the officer was staggering naked through the Swedish camp blowing a trumpet. Instead, we found him snoring his head off on my bed. I saw them lift him like a dead weight and realised my saving grace was that he was plastered drunk. I saw them drag him backwards, the heels of his boots trailing in the dirt, through the gate into the Irish camp. That was my last sighting of him there.

I don't like to think what would have happened if he hadn't been so drunk. I was defeated by it all that I didn't even try reporting him for attempted rape. What was the point? No one would have listened. I'm sure I wasn't the only woman he sexually harassed and assaulted down the years, but his abhorrent conduct and that of many other men like him went unchecked in the defence forces. As a result, they felt it was their divine right to engage in this behaviour.

As it was, the experience made me even more wary, more anxious, checking and rechecking the lock on my door at night. The army was my workplace. We had enemies out there, but I shouldn't have had to be concerned about my physical safety around my own colleagues.

Our overseas reports were no longer secret by this time. Mine read: 'She is a dedicated and loyal non-commissioned officer. She worked well throughout her tour of duty, is eligible for promotion and is suitable for overseas service.'

Of course, they knew I had the right of reply, and they definitely didn't want to see my reply if they gave me a poor report. A couple of years later, I was strolling through the barracks when a car slowed beside me and the driver sounded the horn. I squinted as I approached, unable to make out who was behind the wheel.

'Molloy, how the hell are you?' he cried out the window.

Officer X sat there, large as life, except by now he'd been promoted. I was stunned. The last time I had seen him he'd burst into my room and sexually assaulted me but, here he was, beaming with delight, as if he'd just been reunited with a long-lost buddy.

'What are you doing here? God, it's been a long time. How have you been?'

I stared in appalled disbelief for a few seconds. 'I'm on a course and very late,' I said sharply. 'Good luck now, sir.'

As I marched away, I heard him yell, 'Hey, Molloy! Do you want a lift?'

I still can hardly believe it.

A few years later, the adjutant got a big promotion, and I was among many staff and former staff invited to celebrate his new command. I was surprised when he approached and said he wanted a quick word with me in private. He steered me outside into the night air.

'Karina, I just wanted to apologise for failing to protect you when we served overseas that time,' he said. 'It was a lack of experience on my part, but I realise I should have listened and done something.'

Well, at least he's man enough to apologise now. 'Thank you, sir. I appreciate it, and I'm glad you won't make the same mistake again if you ever come up against this sort—'

He grabbed me by the back of the neck and planted his lips on mine. He was so fast that he actually got his mouth to mine before I wrenched my neck out of his grip and shoved him away. I was speechless. I stood there staring at him, my mouth opening and closing in complete stupefaction for a few seconds. *Christ*, I thought, *he only brought me out here for a grope.*

He stood there, grinning at me arrogantly.

'What the hell?' I said. 'You're after apologising for inappropriate behaviour and then you do this? Is this a fecking joke?'

He looked at me in vague bewilderment and I gave up in that instant. *What is the fucking point?* We were playthings, property, idle distractions rather than people. I turned on my heel and stormed out of the function, thinking, *Christ, is this ever going to change?*

25

Graffiti

Private Catherina Morris and I stared in horror at our naked likenesses carved into wood in the guardroom of McKee Barracks. No one could deny that the two women depicted in the graffiti were us. The portraits were carved quite expertly, our different hairstyles distinguishing us from each other. And, if anyone was in doubt, the names 'Molloy' and 'Morris' were helpfully carved underneath each figure.

The first image showed Private Morris and me naked and engaged in a lesbian act. However, the artist clearly couldn't decide if we were lesbians because the second image portrayed me nude and pleasuring the pelvic area of an anonymous soldier. The words 'whore' and 'slut' were also carved by penknife into the large windowsill in the guardroom.

If I was more dispassionate about the subjects of the etchings, I might have even admired the artist's skill. However, any hopes I held that female soldiers would receive more respect when we became fully combatant were scrapped as soon as these obscene images appeared.

When I returned from overseas, I'd already decided that working in information technology was not for me. I didn't have the same logical, methodical brain as my gifted platoon colleague Ursula Holly. She became the systems analyst synonymous with computerising the Irish Defence Forces. Meanwhile, I was a fish out of water.

Unfortunately, promotions had almost ground to a halt in the army, and when I applied for any sergeant's position, there were loads of applicants ahead of me. I came second in one interview, but my lack of experience in an infantry unit – experience denied to me – kept coming against me. I had to figure out a new career path.

On the mission, I noted that company quartermasters (CQs), who were responsible for supplies and stores, were rarely tasked with marching soldiers on parade. For an introvert like me, this was a great advantage. CQs also wore the most medals, indicating their frequency overseas. That sealed it. I decided that the CQ path was the one for me and I applied for a General Q course.

Blinded by the overseas medals, I never actually understood that a CQ needs to be able to count. I got an

'F' in my first Leaving Cert maths and improved to an 'E' in my second. Still, I passed the course and applied for the next one.

At the back of my mind, however, was my father's desire that I become an officer. Soon after entering the army, I discovered I couldn't apply for a cadetship because I'd failed Leaving Cert maths. However, after returning from the mission, I met all the criteria to apply for a Potential Officer course for the first time.

I had high hopes submitting my application as there were two places for women. However, I discovered that my rivals included one applicant with a degree and another who was the first female flight attendant on the government jet, and my hopes were dashed. Sure enough, both women got on the course. The latter became the only female commission from our platoon when she successfully passed the Potential Officer course in 1992.

I attempted to get on a Potential Officer course twice later in my career but was never selected. In hindsight, I have no regrets. Having learnt what officers do, I know it was more my father's dream than mine. I would have never experienced the diversity and variety of jobs or had the number of overseas trips I had in my career if I had become an officer.

When I'd completed my Q courses, I had to get practical experience in the stores to stand any chance of promotion. For the next 18 months, I toiled in all the stores, working up my CV and aiming to become the first female company quartermaster sergeant in the defence forces.

Meanwhile, in May 1992 the minister for defence, John Wilson, announced an end to restrictions preventing women from serving in all areas of the defence forces. With little public reaction, the 'non-combatant' limitations on women ended 11 years after I entered as a recruit.

It probably wasn't coincidental that the change came a year after the Gulf War, where many women appeared for the first time on the frontline. The Gulf War showed that modern warfare was no longer dependent on the size of men's muscles but on training, skills, wits and ability to use complex and advanced technical equipment.

Women still accounted for only about 0.7 per cent of defence forces personnel that year – numbering around 110 in total. We could now apply for all appointments and participate in ceremonial activities and duties for the first time.

A letter arrived soon after inviting me to join an infantry unit. I would have been delighted to receive that letter in my early twenties. Nothing could have stopped me from joining an infantry unit back then, doing physical training and being in the great outdoors. I would have been what the Americans call 'a grunt', and I would have loved it. By now, however, things had changed. *Would you ever go feck yourselves*, was my first reaction to the letter. I was almost 30 and, like most men of that age, I wanted a comfortable desk, an interesting job and overseas trips.

The only significant change as a result of our new combat status was we were thrown into regimental duties in the barracks for the first time. The men had always complained about 24-hour duties and resented us for 'avoiding' them. They hated that they could get called for 24-hour duties with two hours' notice and the words: 'The guard commander's gone sick, and you're it.'

'Your weekends will get fucked up like ours for a change,' the guys said. 'Now you'll know what we've been putting up with.'

I didn't care. I was happy about the change in combat status. *Now that we're all doing the same job*, I thought, *attitudes will change.*

As the only female corporal in McKee Barracks, I was invited to the guardroom for a mini-recce shortly after the rule change.

'Have a look around. Is there anything you feel is necessary in this place for women?' the CQ asked.

I glanced into the grubby toilet in the guardroom and flinched, but I knew there wasn't much point in complaining about that. 'We'll need a sanitary bin in the toilet,' I shrugged.

The CQ's flustered reaction was entertaining. 'Oh right, right, right, right,' he said as he buried his head in his clipboard and disappeared.

I hardly slept the night before I started my first 24-hour duties at McKee Barracks on 19 January 1992. I turned up for duty as the guard commander at 08.30hrs without a clue about what I was supposed to do. The last time I'd marched men on the square was during my non-commissioned officer course in 1984 and I'd never performed guard duty as a private.

I muddled through it. I marched the guard on the square and handed over the guard to the orderly officer. Rifles had to be mounted with live ammunition. Then I marched the guard into the guardroom and the off-going guard commander handed me a report of incidents the night before.

After that, my job was to position a soldier 'on the beat', a small Perspex room in front of the guardroom. Soldiers paced the beat while watching the main gate on two-hour rotations. I also had to organise the rest of the guard to patrol the perimeters.

When members of the guard weren't patrolling or on the beat, they played cards or watched TV in the guard house. The duty was long and tedious, and no one was supposed to close their eyes for 24 hours. It meant the sleep-deprived were the first line of defence if the barracks were attacked. (The Irish Army remains one of the few militaries worldwide that still demand 24-hour duties.)

I had some daft idea that women would gain proper respect now that we were doing all the same duties as the men. Then, I found my naked image carved into the big wooden windowsill at the beat window. Several hundred soldiers a month had nothing else to look at but that obscene depiction of me and a female guard for hours at a time. I was angry because it undermined my job as a guard commander. How could I gain any respect from my men when they saw me ridiculed and humiliated in this manner?

I was furious when, despite my complaints, the army

made no effort to remove the offending carvings. Week after week, the pornographic images remained. Catherina Morris and I were forced to request an interview with the adjutant.

We met him and the sergeant major of the barracks, but they more or less shrugged. 'Seriously, Molloy, what the fuck do you expect us to do? Do we give a pot of paint to the guard commander every day in case of a bit of graffiti?'

The adjutant agreed to request that the Board of Works paint over the windowsill etching. Unfortunately, this had the effect of enhancing the relief of the image. We stared at it afterwards in disbelief. I stormed back to the adjutant's office, but his expression told me he thought I was making a big deal out of nothing. *Can't you take a joke, Molloy?*

'Cut out the wood or sand it down!' I said, and he looked at me as if I had two heads. *Sand it down?* Nothing was done about it.

Catherina and I went to the Employment Equality Agency and discovered that the defence forces was one of the few organisations exempt from the Employment Equality Act. They couldn't help us.

The Permanent Defence Forces Representative Association (PDFORRA) was in its infancy, so we approached them. PDFORRA set up a meeting with the adjutant and the CO and told them this was sexual harassment in the workplace and wasn't acceptable.

Finally, a notice was sent out warning the soldiers that anyone caught defacing government property would be charged. The problem was defacement of government property, not sexual harassment. The Board of Works repainted the offending images until they were concealed. But our naked images would probably still be there today if we hadn't kicked up about it.

26

The Italians

Decades later, I still find it hard to come to terms with the tragic ending of my fourth trip to Lebanon. I arrived in Naqoura with the 35th Irish Component in October 1996 and went on to have one of my most enjoyable overseas trips. I was still young and naïve and had no idea that the dreams and the lives we led could be so quickly shattered.

For the first and only time in my entire army career, I was sent overseas on an 'A' appointment. All my overseas trips were Q (quartermaster) appointments in supplies and logistics. They were admin jobs but involved helping to load and unload trucks, so I wasn't always stuck behind a desk.

'A' positions were hardcore administration. I was out of my comfort zone, and I wasn't happy. Days into my new posting in Naqoura, the commandant arrived at my desk. 'We're going to Tyre to collect cash in the morning,' he said.

'Right, sir.'

Great, I thought, a *few hours out of the office*. Tyre was a town about a half an hour's drive north of Naqoura.

'Organise the vehicle and bring it around here for us by 09.00hrs.'

I froze on the spot. 'I can organise the vehicle, sir,' I said. 'But I can't bring it here. I can't drive.'

'You what? You can't drive?' he said. His eyes were on stalks. 'Are you serious?'

Pay clerks had to drive because of the cash collections, but I hadn't been aware of that. And the army had stuck me in an 'A' appointment assuming that because I was 35 years old, I could drive.

It was unheard of to have an officer chauffeuring an non-commissioned officer around in the Irish Army, but I broke the mould again because that's how it was in our office for the next six months.

The only other girl in Naqoura was a gunner (a member of a regiment) called Aideen. Recruited in 1994, she was much younger than me but we got on well. We spent a lot of time in Italair, enjoying the Italian coffee and homemade pizza.

Located across the road from Camp Tara, Italair ran the air-ambulance helicopter service for the UN Interim

Force in Lebanon. The 50 Italians were renowned for lavish parties and looking good while swaggering around the area of operations (AO). They invited all the girls from every contingent into their camp.

We got to know a group of outgoing Italian men, including a pilot known as Pippo, a warrant officer called Massimo and a member of the Italian military police named Daniel. They were brown-eyed, smiling guys in their thirties and most of them were married with children, but they loved female company and practising their perfect English. They had an older friend we called Uncle Raff or Raffaele. They were great to be around.

However, I was always drawn to French men and fell into conversation with a young conscript whom I spotted reading a book on Buddhism in the Blue Beret bar. As soon as I looked into his dark brown eyes, that was it; I was smitten. He was tall, incredibly handsome and eleven years younger than me. He had a degree in psychology, spoke six languages and also happened to be an arrogant chauvinist who warned me not to fall in love with him.

'I know you're looking for a husband, but I can't give you that,' he solemnly told me. 'We can just have fun.'

I laughed and assured him I had no plans to go shopping for a wedding dress.

The French conscript sullenly pouted about my friendship with a group of Italian men, but the parties in Italair continued. On Aideen's birthday, we held a party for her in Italair, with all the women from Irish Battallion HQ attending. I learnt to ski when the Italians organised weekends in the north of Lebanon (which is known as the Switzerland of the East).

The French contingent was on a different rotation to us, so my handsome conscript's tour ended after three months of fun. The night before he left, he broke all the rules to arrive at my billet. Soldiers from his company were outside, urging him to return to camp before he got into serious trouble. It was all very dramatic and French, but I forced him out the door – even though one hand was pushing and the other wanted to pull him back in.

Aideen brought the Italians to her Medal Day Parade on St Patrick's Day, held in Irishbatt in Tibnin. Pippo, Massimo, Daniel and Uncle Raff were introduced to Irish coffees, smoked salmon and soda bread. They watched Irish dancing and had their first taste of Guinness. They had a ball.

For the first time overseas, I would have been happy to extend my trip. But I vowed to stay in touch with them and made plans to visit Uncle Raff and his wife in Sardinia.

Life returned to grey, and I went back to work in the rations stores in McKee Barracks. Cheekily, I threw in my application for overseas duty as I always did, even though I knew I'd have to wait for my turn. I always hoped someone would drop out at the last minute.

Eight weeks after returning home, I was in Sweden visiting my brother when I received news of a helicopter crash in Lebanon.

Best friends Pippo, Massimo and Daniel were killed in the tragedy. I read their full names in the newspaper in disbelief: Pilot Captain Giuseppe Parisi (Pippo), Warrant Officer Massimo Gatti and Sergeant Daniel Forner (Carabinieri). Also killed was Irish soldier Sergeant John Lynch, whom I knew from signals in Naqoura and my first trip in Irishbatt. A fourth Italian officer, a pilot, Antonino Sgrò, also died. None were more than 35 years old.

On 6 August 1997, the Italians were flying in the Irishbatt area, acquainting themselves with the landing pads in the UN posts and testing signalling equipment with John. It was dark when their helicopter crashed in a deep gorge near an Irish observation post. Members of Irish C Company were at the scene in minutes, but all five men were killed instantly.

John Lynch's remains were flown back from Tel Aviv by the Air Corps, and he had full military honours at Baldonnel Aerodrome. Aideen and I attended his funeral at Newbridge in County Kildare.

Controversy surrounded the circumstances of the crash. In the end, investigators blamed pilot error, claiming the Bell-Agusta helicopter hit a power cable after take-off. Pippo's father, a military man, investigated and contested the findings. Eyewitnesses in Irishbatt said they heard an explosion before the helicopter went down, indicating a missile hit.

Whatever the reason, nothing would bring back those men. I was numb and in shock for a long time. Without being able to attend the Italian men's funerals, the tragedy didn't feel real. I still saw them in my eye's mind, joking, playfully punching each other, shouting over each other, but mostly I remembered their good humour, generosity and laughter. I couldn't imagine Italair existing without their cheery presence, yet I was to experience their crushing absence there much sooner than I expected.

27

Fuck the Begrudgers

The phone rang one day in the stores and a senior NCO I knew was on the end of the line.

'Karina, a corporal has just dropped out and I need a good, honest Q [quartermaster] corporal to do rations in Naqoura. Are you interested?'

My eyes widened. Naqoura? Not in my wildest dreams did I think I'd get back to Naqoura so quickly. 'Yes!' I said anxiously. 'Yes, I want the job!'

'Great,' he said, and then, almost as an afterthought, he added, 'You can drive, Karina, right?'

I had to think quickly. 'Yes, I can drive,' I said, lying through my teeth.

He must have heard the hesitation in my answer. 'Do you have a full licence?'

'No, only a provisional,' I said truthfully.

'That's fine. I'll put you down as having a licence.'

As soon as I put down the phone, I booked a block of ten driving lessons. I told my father I had to drive a small rations truck within weeks.

'Sure by week four you'll be reversing, one hand on the wheel and the other over the passenger seat like you were doing it all your life,' he said.

I wasn't so confident.

Before leaving for Lebanon, I had five interviews for company quartermaster (CQ) vacancies in quick succession. I felt quietly confident, even though no woman had ever become a senior non-commissioned officer (NCO) in the defence forces.

I was interviewed by a commandant, a captain and a junior captain for the second vacancy. It was all going well and then the junior captain suddenly sat back in his chair and said, 'You do realise, Corporal Molloy, that the Irish Army is never going to promote a female to a senior NCO rank.'

A stunned silence filled the room. The captain was entitled to think what he liked, but it was hard to believe he'd actually say it to the candidate interviewing for the promotion. The commandant suddenly piped up, 'Corporal Molloy, would you mind leaving the room for a minute?'

When I was called back, the commandant assured me it was a good interview, but he wrapped things up quickly.

I became increasingly angry afterwards. By then, women had been in the army for 17 years and had been fully combatant for five years. Yet some men still thought it was okay to keep women as junior NCOs for the rest of their careers.

I expected that attitude among 'the old sweats' in the mess. *Who the fuck does Molloy think she is going for a senior NCO position?* But the junior captain was in his twenties, younger than me. It made me nearly despair.

I never sought the accolade of being the first female senior NCO, but someone had to push through, so why not me? I refused to be deterred. I vowed to keep sitting through their stupid interviews until they couldn't ignore me any longer.

Three days later, I turned up for another interview and my blood pressure soared to see the same junior captain. I wasn't going to stand for this again. I asked to speak outside with the panel's senior officer, where I explained what had happened in my last interview. 'I want him replaced on the panel,' I said. 'There's no point in me continuing otherwise.'

'We don't have the time,' the commandant said. 'But I'll guarantee that I'll conduct the interview and he won't have a say in your case.'

What could I do? I had to trust him. So I proceeded with the interview, with the junior captain glowering at me throughout.

I didn't have much time to think about the interviews because I was off to Lebanon that week.

On my second day in Camp Tara, I was nervously reversing the truck when a fist hammered on my window. The officer who had driven me around Lebanon stood there, his eyes bulging out of their sockets. 'Molloy, you said you couldn't fucking drive!' he bellowed.

He was steaming, fully convinced I'd lied to him. I had to swear that I'd learnt to drive after I'd returned to Dublin, before he stomped off muttering to himself.

As the rations corporal, I was assigned a driver, Jason. However, he wasn't always available, so I roped him into giving me lessons. Jason was overheard vainly trying to persuade other drivers to take me for lessons.

'Fuck it, I'll take her,' he said in the end. 'I'll be stuck with her for the next six months anyway, so I might as well get used to it. She'll never learn to drive.'

Despite Jason's prediction, I was reversing, one hand on the wheel and the other over the passenger seat, and suddenly I realised my father was right. It was like I'd been driving all my life. It took six weeks rather than four, but I finally stopped panicking when I had to sit in the driving seat.

Uncle Raff was still in Italair when I arrived back in Naqoura, but it was a relief when his rotation ended, and everyone I knew there returned to Italy. Italair was haunted by too much sadness after the tragic deaths.

On 19 November, I received an unexpected phone call from Dublin. A senior colleague told me confidentially that I was about to be the first female in the defence forces ever to be promoted to company quartermaster sergeant. My fifth interview for a vacancy with B Company, 2nd Infantry Battalion had been successful.

I was warned to say nothing until the official letter announcing my promotion reached me in Lebanon. So I got back to my billet and sat on the bed. *I'm the first female senior NCO in the defence forces*, I thought. I'd made a bit of history but couldn't tell anyone. However, the beat of the army gossips' drums reached Lebanon within a day, and my captain congratulated me. Everyone suddenly knew I'd made CQ.

At Irish Battallion (Irishbatt) HQ that week, a forthright battalion commander nicknamed 'The Cowboy' congratulated me with an enormous handshake. He also issued a note of caution that I'll never forget. 'Karina, fuck the begrudgers,' he said. 'There'll be a lot of jealousy and resentment, and they'll forget that you've paid your dues. And because you're a woman, many will think you don't merit the promotion. Fuck them – they'll forget all the years it took to get here.'

What begrudgers? I thought at the time. *Who's going to say I don't deserve this promotion?* I'd paid my dues, as the battalion commander said. I was 17 years a corporal.

Going from a corporal to a CQ involved nine months of rigmarole. First, I had to wait until February to get promoted to sergeant and then serve six months at that rank. My official promotion to CQ wouldn't take place until 5 August, when I was back in Ireland.

I was thrilled at my promotion but half dreaded working among the testosterone-fuelled 'grunts' in B Company, who revelled in their nickname, 'The Vikings'.

By some miracle, I never actually had to work there. Instead, some behind-the-scenes shenanigans took place and I was detached to an admin unit, the 2nd Logistics Support Battalion (2LSB). I was relieved to be back in safe territory and working in the clothing stores at Cathal Brugha Barracks.

Sure enough, the begrudgers' heads started rising above the parapet. The sergeant major of the barracks invited me to attend my first senior NCO conference days before my official promotion. I was a CQ, but I still had a few more days to complete as a sergeant.

However, a company sergeant (CS) in the barracks erupted upon hearing this. 'No fucking way is she coming to this conference,' he announced. 'She's not a senior NCO yet, so she's not coming into this room.' Technically, the CS was correct, so the sergeant major had to back down.

On the morning of my promotion, I was having coffee with GI outside the clothing stores when I saw the sergeant major striding purposefully towards us. 'Here's trouble,' I muttered.

'CQ Molloy, you will report to the NCO's mess for a congratulatory drink at 11.00hrs,' he said.

They served alcohol at that hour back then.

'No thanks, sergeant major, I don't use the NCO's mess.'

'Get your heels together, CQ Molloy. I'm detailing you to be there.'

He saw my face darken.

'Look, Karina, this is of historical significance,' he argued. 'We have the privilege of the first female senior NCO in the entire defence forces in the Eastern Command, and the occasion deserves to be marked.'

I appreciated the sentiment. I knew that not many of the men thought the same way, but I had little choice except to go.

Corporals to sergeant majors packed into the mess that morning, most no doubt as reluctant to be there as I was. The sergeant major made a speech and a toast. 'Congratulations, CQ Molloy,' he said, and all the men raised their beer glasses. However, no stampede of well-wishers rushed to congratulate me afterwards. Out of everyone in the room, only one brave soul from the 2nd Inf Bn shook my hand.

My poor father became ill with oesophageal cancer soon after, and I cycled to St Luke's every lunchtime to see him. I was home with him in Donegal when he died on Thursday, 25 March 1999. I phoned my battalion quartermaster (BQ) in 2LSB to let him know. He knew my father was dying and was expecting my phone call.

'Will you inform the 2nd Infantry Battalion?' I asked. Technically, I was still attached to them even though I had never worked there.

'Don't worry. I'll take care of all of that,' the BQ replied.

The morning I was burying my father, the phone rang at my family home, and my eldest brother Garry answered. 'Karina, someone from the army wants to talk to you.'

I was in the middle of something with my mother. 'Can you take a message?' I replied.

So Garry returned to the phone, and half a minute later I overheard him say, 'Do you realise we're burying our father here this morning?'

'Who was it?' I asked. Garry had sounded angry.

'He says he's from the 2nd Infantry Battalion. He says to tell you he's left your name on the gate because you're absent from your place of employment. I told him we're burying our father, but he said he wasn't officially informed of that fact and hung up.'

He didn't sympathise with my brother – just told him he hadn't been *officially* informed. He meant I hadn't informed him. He would have known about my father's death even if the BQ failed to tell him. Everyone knew everyone else's business in the barracks.

Everyone there also knew if someone's name was left at the gate. It was like having an arrest warrant waiting for a soldier, and it was a major embarrassment for a senior NCO. It was my father's funeral, and I was upset anyway, but this call added to my distress. A female officer and close friend, who attended the funeral, was able to have my name removed from the gate.

The senior NCO had decided to throw his weight around, and technically he could because I hadn't rung him personally. My father had died, but scoring a point was more important than civility and respect for a fellow senior NCO.

It was just one of many microaggressions over the

years; some of them were petty, some more serious. I'm not sure how much of this bad feeling was fuelled by pure misogyny, but I felt many were hostile to any woman's progression through the ranks.

The animosity towards me was also fuelled by ridiculous rumours. I've always said that army men are worse than women when it comes to gossiping. As far as the men were concerned, I boarded the plane as a corporal and landed back in Dublin as a CQ. *Six months from corporal to CQ? How the fuck did she manage that? Who the hell has she been shagging?* That was all the talk because I heard it from several sources. I was beyond caring. The battalion commander in Irishbatt was right. *Fuck the begrudgers.*

28

Learning Curve

I slid down my mother's kitchen wall and broke down in tears. I hadn't sobbed like that since my father's funeral a year earlier, and I suddenly wanted my daddy more than ever. He would have understood and would have known how to make everything okay. I tried to explain to my mother, but she was gaping at me in shock and astonishment.

'I don't understand, Karina,' she kept saying. 'You're a CQ [company quartermaster]. You're fully qualified for this job. So what on earth are you so upset about?'

I was sick to my stomach and had been since I'd picked

up the phone in the clothing store days earlier. It was a colleague. 'What did you do to Richard?'

I was taken aback. 'What do you mean, what did I do to Richard? Nothing.'

I wasn't about to tell him I'd refused Richard's amorous advances a year before. Richard, a senior non-commissioned officer, was married, and I didn't need that complication with both of us working in Cathal Brugha Barracks.

My colleague had snorted. 'Well, you must have done something because he's just royally fucked you over.'

'What are you on about?'

'Did you know you're one of the CQs recommended for overseas?'

'Oh my God, really?'

I was thrilled for an instant because I'd lobbed in my application for overseas without much hope of success. The disadvantage of going up the ranks was that fewer positions are available. Some missions like Kosovo or Somalia only had a single vacancy for a CQ. But I remembered what the caller had said about Richard, so I braced myself. 'So what did Richard do?'

'You were off to Camp Shamrock as the rations CQ, but Richard stopped it. I heard him. He insisted that you be posted to A Company because he said it would be good for you to get operational experience with an infantry company.'

My heart plummeted and I could have thrown up on the spot. He knew I'd be out of my depth in an overseas infantry company where I'd be handling weapons. In all my years in the army, I'd never even seen anti-tank weapons, mortars or heavy-calibre ammunition.

That weekend in Donegal, the stress got to me, and I collapsed in tears. My mother kept reassuring me that I was qualified and had passed every course. But I knew that didn't make a whit of difference. Through no fault of my own, I had no infantry experience. I had only scratched the surface by working for three months in an infantry battalion store. I panicked every time I thought of the A Company posting and seriously considered pulling out. But the stubborn side of me won out. *I've volunteered, so if it kills me, I'm doing it.*

I received notification of the form-up in Clancy Barracks, and I arrived on the appointed morning, three weeks before A Company 87th Infantry Battalion was due to fly out. I couldn't see my company or any sign of where I was supposed to go. Luckily, I'd completed work experience in the stores there, so I went looking for the battallion quartermaster (BQ) of the barracks.

'Karina!' he said, approaching me. 'Well done! A bloody hardcore job you're going into.'

And then he handed me a big bunch of keys. 'Here you go!'

I looked at the keys in bewilderment. It was one of the biggest ditsy blonde moments of my career. Then the penny dropped. There was a reason why there were no signs, and nothing appeared to be ready for A Company's arrival. It came to me in a flash. *Oh, holy fuck, I'm the CQ. I'm the one who's supposed to do all this.*

One hundred and thirty men were boarding transport all over Eastern Command or were already on their way as I stood there gaping. The CQ's job was to open all the doors, allocate the rooms, make sure the offices were cleaned, have paper and pens on every desk, mark out all the notices, and hang up the signs. I had about 40 minutes before they started streaming through the gates. I had to do this before my commanding officer (CO) and second in command (2IC) arrived. *Shit! Shit! Shit!* I would have been setting up two days earlier if I'd realised this.

The BQ must have seen the stricken look on my face because he guided me as I tore around like a mad woman trying to unlock offices and searching for sheets of paper, big markers and thumbtacks.

'This is the biggest office, so this is normally for the CO,' the BQ helpfully suggested. 'The 2IC is here, and you and the CS can share this office next door …'

I got away with my first morning by the skin of my teeth. However, my CO and the 2IC didn't make any secret of the fact that they couldn't understand how I'd been appointed to A Company. 'We're a bit concerned because of your lack of operational experience. Are you sure you don't want to reconsider this?'

They kept expecting me to quit, but I felt I'd be letting down every woman coming behind me if I pulled out. *I can't fail at this. They'll tar every woman with the same brush if I do.* So I took a deep breath and pulled up my big girl pants.

'I can do this, sir,' I said. 'I'm nervous, but what I don't know, I'll learn.'

I didn't have a clue what I was walking into.

Every CQ going overseas was allocated a storeman-driver, but A Company had trouble finding a volunteer for me. The CQ's job was very physical, hauling goods in and out of trucks and stores. None of the men wanted to work with a female CQ, fearing they'd have to work twice as hard. However, on the third day of the form-up, A Company had a late entry.

'He's coming down from the 29th Infantry Battalion this afternoon, and hopefully he'll agree to the storeman-driver job,' said my 2IC.

I met Corporal Eoin Ward later that day and liked him instantly. Stationed in Monaghan, he was going overseas to raise money as he was getting married to Eileen.

'My mother's name is Eileen,' I said. 'That has to be a good omen.'

In fact, Eoin must have been found by my father because he was heaven-sent. He was a professional who loved soldiering.

A CQ and storeman-driver are together 18 hours a day, so I told him to call me Karina. There was no point standing on ceremony. 'No, I can't do that,' he insisted. Instead, he abbreviated my title to 'Q' and called me that.

During form-up, A Company went to Kilbride Army Camp in Wicklow for weapons and tactical exercises. It was an absolute nightmare for a novice CQ. I had to ensure the camp was shipshape and was also in charge of getting food from Cathal Brugha Barracks to Kilbride daily. Eoin and I were driving to Kilbride one evening bringing several 'hot locks', as they were known, big insulated metal containers filled with hot food. The cook was travelling in the back of the truck, which had no seat belt in those days.

We were late, and Eoin hared it down the narrow country lanes. One of the hazards of the route was sheep, and suddenly a ewe and a lamb wandered onto the road. I could see it all happening in slow motion, and I thought of the cook behind us and heard my father's voice in my head when I was learning to drive: 'Never swerve for an animal unless it's bigger than you.'

'Just keep going,' I said. 'Do not brake, Eoin. Do not brake.'

The ewe made it, but the lamb was a goner, and I heard the crunch as the wheels ran over it. 'Christ,' I said. 'Reverse, and let me clean up the evidence.'

I tossed the woolly carcass in the back. 'Guess it's lamb chops for dinner, cook,' I said. The Department of Defence regularly paid compensation to local farmers for sheep killed on or near the camp. No matter how careful the army tried to be, sheep inevitably wandered onto the range, for example.

I swore both men to secrecy when we got to Kilbride. We should have reported the incident, but this would have triggered a military-police investigation, and we could have been stopped from going overseas. When the shit hit the fan overseas, as it often did, Eoin only had to mutter 'lamb chops' to make me laugh.

A Company went out for range practice in Kilbride one morning, and Eoin and I signed out five general purpose machine guns (GPMGs) and five spare barrels. Serial-numbered items were sacred in the army. If I lost a weapon, I could be charged, fined, lose my promotion or even be discharged from the army. The stores were hectic when the soldiers arrived back with the machine guns later that day.

'Eoin, check that they're all there, they're clean and that they each have a spare barrel,' I said.

Five GPMGs were handed back with their five barrels and put into stores.

Early the next morning, I was woken by someone banging on my door telling me the BQ from Aiken Barracks in Dundalk was on the phone, demanding to speak to me. *What now?* I got up and ran over to the office.

'I'm really sorry, Karina,' he said.

Okay, I'm not in trouble so …

'They're on their way down to you now. The eejit. I gave him a right bollicking and I want you to do the same.'

I had no idea what he was talking about, but I played along. 'Oh, right, right, right.'

'I'm sure you were beside yourself when you found you had the wrong ones. I couldn't believe it when I discovered that stupid young lieutenant took your GPMGs.'

My heart skipped a beat. What was he talking about? *They have my GPMGs? Christ almighty!*

'Yeah, I was about to call you,' I stammered. 'I had to wait for you to come into barracks.'

'Well, I'm in early because I knew I had to deal with this shit. And all over that stupid pup. It's probably best if we just swap them over and say nothing more about it. Is that okay with you, Karina?'

'Oh, yeah, yeah. That's probably best.'

'Jesus, I was dreading this call,' he said. 'Everyone said you'd be raging with me over this, Karina, but you're taking it very well.'

'Mistakes happen,' I jabbered. 'No harm done.'

I put down the phone and felt like throwing up. I still didn't know for sure what was going on. I ran to my stores and opened up. Hands shaking, I checked the serial numbers. *Holy fuck, fuck fuck! I've the wrong fucking GPMGs.* Eoin arrived, and when he heard what had happened he started apologising. But it was my fault. No one told me that there had been another unit – the 27th battalion – on the range the previous day and, fatally, I had failed to follow the golden rule of being a CQ – and never checked the sacred serial numbers.

The young lieutenant arrived, grovelling pathetically. The poor guy was about 19 years old and was expecting me to tear strips off him. He didn't realise I was just relieved and grateful that I hadn't been caught.

My first job as an overseas CQ was a steep learning curve before we even left Ireland.

29

Al Yatun 6-40

As soon as we landed in Beirut on 19 April 2000, I became the first female company quartermaster (CQ) to serve overseas. However, I was still racked with trepidation about the tour of duty ahead.

A Company was located at post 6-40 Al Yatun uphill of Irishbatt company headquarters at Camp Shamrock. Someone in good shape could run from Camp Shamrock to our post in 20 minutes. The drive took ten.

The Al Yatun post was smaller and more cramped than Camp Shamrock. Spread over maybe an acre, it was a barren place. My first impression was dust, sandbags, barbed wire and blast walls. A machine gun overlooked the entrance checkpoint and another was located high at the rear of the post. The camp, sited on the top of a hill, had spectacular views of the Irish area of operations (AO), but I rarely had the time to admire them.

Because of Al Yatun's vantage point, the Battalion Mobile Reserve (BMR) of 50 personnel was also located in the same camp. The BMR was the Irish equivalent to the UN's Interim Force in Lebanon's Mobile Reserves. They were a rapid-deployment force in the event of an attack anywhere in the Irish AO. A Company also had responsibility for eight outposts around its AO.

Usually, the CQ and the company sergeant (CS) become bosom pals overseas. However, deprived of his usual drinking buddy, my CS seemed resentful at having to work with a female CQ. He was cold, curt and dismissive, someone I had to work around. During form-up and overseas, he only spoke to me when he had to.

It was standard practice for the outgoing CQ to hand his room to the incoming CQ. As the CQs were in charge of stores, their rooms always had a few extra luxuries like a microwave and a decent kettle. It was one of the few perks of the job. Of course, being a female CQ, I couldn't stay in the outgoing CQ's room as it was in the male lines, but I got permission from the CO to move the contents to my billet.

However, the outgoing CQ was a dedicated member of the old boys' club. He stripped his room of anything of worth and gave it to my CS. I quietly fumed but there was nothing I could do about it.

Peacekeepers in A Company were even more restricted than in Camp Shamrock. We had a couple of ramshackle mingi shops across the road, which provided a steady supply of ice-cold Coke and 'double-double' sandwiches of fried eggs in 'mingi bread'. In the evenings, the canteen only served beer and opened for two hours every night. I'm sure the other non-commissioned officers (NCOs) had sessions in their billets at night but, of course, I was never invited.

As with every camp, the girls erected their own fenced-off area for sunbathing. The lads erected a crudely painted sign reading 'The Aviary' outside it. It quickly became camp jargon: 'Anyone know where the CQ is?'

'She's up in the Aviary with the girls.'

Apart from that, the work was hectic and relentless. Every week I had to set aside an entire day to conduct an ordnance check for all the weapons and ammunition in the camp. My second in command (2IC) and Eoin joined me on the square each time for this ordeal. Weapons had gone missing in Lebanon and, when they did, someone got shafted and the CQ's reputation was tarnished.

My job was to check the artillery, personal weapons and ammunition for all 130 members of A Company and the rest of the men in the outposts. Even though the BMR had its own CQ, the CQ of A Company was also responsible for its heavy weapons and ammunition.

Eoin was my knight in shining armour because I had never seen the heavy weapons they unloaded on the square before me. I literally didn't know one end of a short-range anti-armour weapon (SRAAW) from another.

Eoin laughed. 'Don't let anyone see you carrying it like that,' he said. He turned it around. 'This is how you always hold a SRAAW.'

The BMR had a type of heavy machine gun called a 'point five' (.5), short for the M2 Browning .5s, mounted on their armoured vehicles. Two BMR guys delivered the .5s and boxes of ammo containing five belts of 50 rounds. Eoin had completed a heavy-weapons course and knew how to identify and manoeuvre everything into place. I would have floundered without him as it required a special knack for counting the ammo and getting the belts back in their boxes. He was always at my elbow, patiently teaching me about what I was handling.

The rest of my week was spent requisitioning, collecting and delivering everything from food rations and freezers to toilet paper. We loaded up in Camp Shamrock twice a week and, with Eoin driving our big UN flatbed Renault truck, we delivered and unloaded rations three times a week to A Company and its eight outposts.

Lebanon had a hierarchy of postings. The top of the pecking order was Naqoura, while Camp Shamrock was the prime deployment in Irishbatt. Down the pecking order were postings in A, B or C companies, but they were still ranked more desirable than rotations in remote outposts. Three of A Company's outposts, nicknamed 'The Crib', 'Fraggle Rock' and 'The Black Hole', were infamous flashpoints and rated the worst of the eight. No one wanted rotations there.

I enjoyed my job as I was always on the road and out of the cramped confines of the camp. It was a very physical job, and we usually had a 'shotgun', someone detailed to help with large deliveries. The shotgun position was popular as everyone else wanted to get out of camp too.

One morning, persistent shelling in the AO meant we were on 'Garryowen', meaning we couldn't leave camp. Maintaining camp facilities was another duty under the vast umbrella of my responsibilities, so I decided to do an inspection. Of course, Eoin, a well-seasoned soldier, slipped out behind my back and tipped off the camp.

When we arrived at the first shower block, the cleaning detail was coincidentally rushing out the door, but I nabbed the corporal for a toilet inspection. I spent many years living in a B&B working to my mother's exacting standards, so of course the lick-and-a-promise style of the army cleaning crew would not do.

'Oh my God, do you call this clean?' I roared at the corporal. 'This place is filthy! What's needed here is some elbow grease. Get them back in here, put some bloody elbow grease into it. Clean that again! I'll be back in half an hour and it better be sparkling!'

As I walked out of the block, it suddenly hit me that I had turned into my mother. I was so distracted by this awful realisation that I didn't see the panicked young corporal run after Eoin. He was wide-eyed with urgency. 'I don't have any of that stuff she wants!' he said. 'Do you have any of that elbow grease in the stores?'

Eoin and I laughed for hours afterwards, and our CO admitted he got endless mileage in the officers' mess telling them how a female CQ sent his corporal into a frenzy searching for elbow grease.

One evening, as Eoin dropped me off at my billet, I saw Catriona, a signaller from Donegal, sitting on my doorstep.

I hopped off the truck and, immediately, saw a look of panic cloud her face.

She pulled me into her room. 'Jesus, I thought this was yours! So who owns it?'

She pointed to the holstered 9mm Browning automatic in her locker. Officers and senior NCOs were issued with these pistols. Catriona had found it lying on the cistern in the ladies' toilets and had kept her mouth shut for the whole day, presuming it was mine. However, she spotted my pistol on my hip as soon as I got out of the truck.

But I knew straight away who owned it. A young female officer from the BMR was billeted right behind me and we shared a bathroom. I also knew the panic she must have been feeling. I left an ambiguous message on her door, reading, 'I have it.' I never got a more grateful hug in my life when she returned from patrol. She was sick, praying and hoping she had left it in her room. It would have been a disaster for her career if she had lost her personal weapon.

On 24 May, less than five weeks after we arrived, the Israelis pulled out of South Lebanon. The implications didn't dawn on me initially. I was absorbed in learning my new role and keeping up with the workload.

Suddenly, I was called in for an operational conference in the camp. Amid fears of an upsurge in violence, the United Nations in New York made a decision to secure the blue line with a new post, and the post fell within A Company area of operations.

Wow, I thought, *what a massive responsibility for the company commander and the 2IC.*

But with growing horror, I realised that setting up the new post was delegated to the 2IC and me. And much of the job to build Post 6-50 from scratch had just landed in my lap. I felt like I'd been flattened by a steamroller when I emerged from the meeting. All hell broke loose after that.

Getting from A Company to the new post should have only taken 40 minutes. However, the Israeli outposts were heavily mined. The only way in entailed an eight-hour round trip through Israel. The new post was immediately manned, and the troops were sent ahead, living under tentage and sleeping on fold-up American cot beds. It was raw soldiering, living in basic conditions and dusty surroundings as the construction of the concrete pillar boxes started around them. Eoin drove eight hours to bring basic supplies and rations, anything we could find to improve their living conditions.

Meanwhile, I spent day and night requisitioning everything needed for a proper post. As soon as we got a working generator to Post 6-50, we sourced a large tent and brought a kitchen for a canteen. We needed everything from fans to mosquito nets to pots and pans and chemical toilets. I needed 15 lockers for the troops but was told I had no chance of getting them before Christmas. I wasn't popular when I raided the rooms and removed illicit second and third lockers. I'll hold my hand up and admit I removed my spare locker too.

The Ukrainian minesweepers got to work and cleared a route wider than the trucks so we could drive to the post. That meant I could lead what was called a Q convoy through the minefield to the post. Truck after truck took off from A Company bringing up all the requisitioned supplies for us to set up a proper post. The conversation died in the cab as Eoin and I approached the post and my heart beat a little heavier. There was always an irrational fear that the Ukrainians missed a mine or the wheels of the truck might edge off the cleared track.

Building a new outpost was a massive challenge and incredibly stressful, but I loved every second of the experience. I had to juggle a lot of balls. I was in charge of rations and ordnance for A Company and its eight outposts, while building the ninth outpost.

Setting up a new post on the blue line was a big responsibility for Irishbatt to be tasked with. It was a bigger thing for me to be able to say that I set up a post in Lebanon from scratch. It's still there now, although it has concrete buildings these days.

With six weeks to go, I got a 60-hour pass and arranged to meet Sergeant Kereena Hayes in Naqoura. While Kereena was doing her hair and make-up, I went ahead to the Blue Beret bar. As soon as I arrived, a sergeant major nicknamed 'The Prince of Darkness' greeted me. (The moniker was due to his striking dark features rather than any Satanic leanings.) He was stationed in Camp Tara for the trip.

'Karina, come over here! What'll you have to drink?' he cried from the bar, like we were old mates. 'Drinks are on me tonight!'

'Drinks are on you? Why's that, major?'

'You made me a lot of money. A LOT!'

I was bewildered. 'How did I make you money?'

'Did you not know they opened a book on you in Dublin?'

'What?'

'They opened a book on how long you'd last.' The Prince of Darkness laughed heartily. 'Some of them bet you wouldn't last form-up or board the plane. I was the only one to bet that you'd last the whole trip. So, good woman, you did it, and I won the bet. The drinks are on me!'

So that's how much faith the guys had in me. I can hear them all now. *What the fuck is she doing going to A Company? She hasn't a clue. Stupid cow is never going to last.*

There wasn't any point in being offended. To be fair, the Prince of Darkness had more confidence in me than I had in myself in the beginning.

Weeks later, on 2 December, we were on the buses, impatiently waiting to drive out the gate. Our mission had been extended by two weeks already and I, like everyone else, just wanted to get home.

Suddenly, the 2IC head appeared on the bus. 'CQ Molloy, I need to talk to you. Get off!'

What the fuck?

The 2IC paced outside. 'There's a bloody rifle missing. We need to go and get it sorted.'

I ran back up the steps of the bus. 'Eoin!' I yelled. I'm sure he was cursing me.

I should have told the 2IC, *Look, we've already signed off everything. They're a week and a half into the job now. It's their problem.*

But the 2IC hadn't left the camp yet and didn't want any

potential smear on his reputation. When we returned to the stores, the finger-pointing had already begun. Everyone was shouting and arguing. The new CO and CQ and his storeman-driver were there, among others. My 2IC hurled himself into the row. They were all bickering and I felt flustered. I knew a convoy of trucks and buses filled with the 87th Infantry Battalion had a flight to catch.

'Stop! Stop!' I yelled. 'There's a perfectly logical explanation here. Everyone out except the incoming CQ, Eoin and me!' The officers looked at one another but sheepishly complied and shuffled out the door. However, the fighting erupted again outside.

'Shut the bloody door, Eoin,' I said. 'I can't hear myself think.'

Eoin looked at me as if I was mad. The ordnance store was in a stifling hot metal container. In all my six months at the camp, I never shut the door from the inside. It was only pulled closed from outside when I was locking up for the day.

So Eoin shut the door. 'Is this what you're looking for?' he said, pointing to a rifle which had been concealed behind it.

I tossed the weapon to my replacement. 'Check the serial number,' I said. And sure enough, it was the missing rifle.

'Good luck now. Let's get the hell out of here, Eoin.'

We had to push our way through the knot of men still furiously arguing about who was getting the blame for this. 'We found it,' I said.

To this day, I wonder if that was done to harm me or the incoming CQ. It seems more likely it was done to harm him because we had already signed everything over. Whatever the aim, it was a dirty trick. Careers might have been ruined before anyone thought to look behind that steel door.

At the end of the trip, I received glowing reports from my superiors. The company commander, nicknamed Perfect Peter for his meticulousness, admitted to some initial reservations in his report:

> *CQMS Molloy came to this mission with very little experience as a rifle company CQMS. She worked extremely hard and displayed good vision, initiative and judgement in anticipating and solving problems. She was extremely conscientious and dedicated to her job … Overall, she had an outstanding tour of duty.*

The lieutenant colonel of the entire battalion gave an equally complimentary report and his overall final performance assessment was 'outstanding'.

The posting to A Company and Al Yatun was an incredible beginning to my career as a CQ. I got the confidence and the operational experience that I might never have had in another post. So, ironically, a man scorned inadvertently did me a huge favour.

30

A Bitch in Bosnia

Wide-eyed amazement registered on my face as I wandered around sprawling Camp Butmir in Bosnia. It seemed more like a well-heeled American town than a military camp.

From the outside, the camp looked like any military installation, with its huge perimeter marked by double rings of chain-link fence and barbed wire. However, life within was almost decadent compared to anything I'd experienced overseas in the past.

The place was filled with white-rendered concrete buildings with red-tiled roofs rather than the shabby prefabs of most overseas camps. But the dining hall was the first real revelation of the life I'd enjoy for the next six months. My mouth watered as I scanned endless succulent dishes and delicious-looking desserts.

When I entered the American PX, a retail outlet for the military, I gasped. Like a vast duty-free department store, it was nothing like the versions I'd seen in Lebanon. The Norwegians, Italians and French had their own PXs – all immense warehouses filled with everything from gourmet food to luxury goods.

My head swivelled as I spotted a Burger King and passed buzzing bars, a pizzeria and other eateries with more tempting spreads of food and snacks. The facilities included a massive, fully equipped gym with all sorts of aerobics classes and weight training, which I would need to work off the excesses of the food around me.

Lebanon was like a medieval dust bowl in comparison. My first days in Sarajevo in July 2001 were like discovering a new world. *Wow, the Americans know how to run a camp*, I thought.

Fifty Irish troops went to Bosnia and Herzegovina as part of an international military police (MP) company. The Irish were among thousands of peacekeepers in the Stabilisation Force (SFOR) headquarters just outside Sarajevo, under a NATO-led command. The mission had a National Support Element (NSE), including one vacancy for a company quartermaster (CQ), so I'd flung in my application.

Unfortunately, the army had a system of allocating overseas posts to the 'longest back' from previous trips. The system drove me mad. Occasionally, great trips came along, like to Darwin, Australia (the support element for troops in East Timor). Those who had avoided the more arduous overseas trips like Lebanon were always 'longest back' and were rewarded with the plumb postings, so I wasn't optimistic about Bosnia.

Soon after volunteering, I heard another CQ got the post. Someone suggested he had returned from his second trip to Bosnia *after* I had returned from Lebanon. This meant I was the longest back. I rang the office that dealt with overseas postings and spoke to a captain there.

He checked the files. 'Sorry, CQ Molloy, he got back two weeks before you. Better luck next time.'

'Fair enough,' I said. 'I can't fling my dummy out of the pram so.'

Two weeks later, I got a call from the same captain. 'Are you still interested in Bosnia? A new admin job has come up.'

The Americans had increased the establishment (strength of personnel on a mission), and offered the new job to Ireland. I had to leave that week, but with no husband, children or dog to worry about, I could just lock up my apartment in Dublin and go.

Unfortunately, by the time I landed in Sarajevo, the job no longer existed. The Americans had changed their minds. I went to Irish House, our headquarters in Camp Butmir, one of the few impermanent structures there. Irish House consisted of two metal containers on top of each other with a rec room, offices and a popular Irish bar on the ground floor.

'Well, the accommodation is set up, and we've done all

the admin for you,' my commanding officer said. 'Stick around, and a job will be found for you.'

The flags of many NATO nations – Britain, Canada, France and Turkey – flapped in the breeze at Camp Butmir. Non-NATO nations like Ireland were also in the mix because the mission was UN mandated. However, the Americans ran the camp, and they were obsessed with 'operational briefings', so I reported to Building 200 for a mandatory day of newcomers' briefings. I recognised one of the Irish MPs from Naqoura, even though it was her fourth mission to Bosnia.

'Brace yourself,' she warned. 'You're about to experience death by PowerPoint.'

During a lecture on rules of engagement (ROE), she kicked me under the desk. 'Stay quiet. Don't ask questions, and prepare to have your mind blown.'

The American lecturer outlined a hypothetical scenario where we were in downtown Sarajevo and a rowdy mob approached us. 'They're angry, screaming at you, throwing stones,' he said. 'They're a threat. So, what do you do according to our ROE?'

He looked around the room, but it was a rhetorical question. 'You verify who the leaders are and you shoot them.'

The Americans in the lecture hall nodded and murmured with approval. The collective jaws of European and Canadian contingents hit the floor. *What the hell? Civilians are throwing stones at you and your response is to shoot them?* This shoot-first-and-ask-questions-later approach was alien to our training. Irish troops are trained to avoid inflating a conflict situation and are renowned for their diplomacy and peacekeeping skills.

A new job vacancy arose, and I became one of three military personnel working among Bosnian civilians in the main warehouse. I was in my comfort zone again. I remember being baffled by the Americans' constant requests for sandwich-makers. The dining hall was open almost 24 hours, yet they preferred to eat at their desks. They went into the office at 08.00hrs and didn't leave until 18.00hrs. They had a fantastic work ethic that the rest of us admired but had no desire to emulate.

The Irish didn't carry personal weapons around the camp, but I had to go and sign for a pistol. I'd been warned that the other Irish CQ was on the warpath, accusing me of trying to steal his job. As I approached the weapons store, I saw him outside on the steps, his face like thunder. *Crap*, I thought.

'I know all about you,' he started yelling before I'd even walked up the steps. 'Tell me what you were doing ringing the overseas room about me. You tried to take my fucking job!'

He was smaller than me but blocked my way by planting his feet wide on the steps, and his spittle-flecked rant continued in my face. I had a full view up his flared nostrils as he jabbed his finger at me. It was 35 degrees outside, and his features, contorted with rage, grew redder and redder. *Jesus*, I thought, *I don't need him dying of a massive coronary.*

'Are you not going to say anything?' he finally roared.

'I was waiting for you to finish,' I said calmly. 'I made a phone call to confirm who was the longest back, but that's it. I didn't take your job, so there's no reason to get worked up about it. So, can I sign for my weapon and get back to work?'

At Christmastime in the Irish House, he apologised to me. 'I'm really sorry,' he said. 'You know, you're a lovely woman behind it all. You don't deserve your reputation.'

'Thanks, I think,' I said.

So many men told me over the years that I had a reputation for being a difficult bitch. I still don't know where it came from. I never ordered soldiers about like most senior non-commissioned officers (NCOs). 'Would you mind doing that?' I'd ask. Or 'When you have a minute, could you run up and do this for me?' I was never comfortable barking orders at anyone.

I only reprimanded a soldier once in my entire career. When I was CQ in A Company in Al Yatun I approached a transport driver and explained I needed a few items in a hurry. 'Would you please drive to Camp Shamrock and pick them up?'

The sergeant was dismissive. 'I'm busy,' he said, and sauntered off. It was the height of disrespect and I knew he would never have done it to a senior male NCO.

I stood to attention and bellowed after him. 'Put your heels together, sergeant!'

He turned around immediately and stood to attention. Despite my 'reputation', I never charged anyone with insubordination in my 31-year career. I never abused my rank. I believe the only reason I had the reputation as a 'bitch' was because I fought my corner when I had to.

Most of the time, I liked to do my work peaceably and go home. That's why I revelled in the freedom of Camp Butmir. After the day's work, we hung up our uniforms and wore civvies like normal people. At night, we could head into cosmopolitan Sarajevo, a quick journey in a taxi, whenever we wanted.

The war had ended years earlier, but the city was still battle-scarred. Skeletons of shelled buildings loomed like grim reminders of the past, and the walls of the town were pocked by mortar and tank rounds.

Yet, the city was alive and vibrant and streets were lined with expensive designer stores from the West and bazaars and minarets of the East. I was amazed at the strikingly chic Bosnian women as they click-clacked in their stiletto heels over cobbled streets. Bistro tables filled the pavements and coffee drinkers smoked hookahs and cigarettes. Everyone in Sarajevo smoked and drank strong Turkish coffee.

One Tuesday afternoon in September, I was on a coffee break with a few of the MPs from Cathal Brugha Barracks. We went to a café called Echos, close to the warehouse where I worked. The Americans did everything on a large scale and immediately inside the door was the biggest TV screen I'd ever seen.

We walked in just in time to watch a plane arc

towards a skyscraper and then a fireball explode from the building.

'Wow, this must be a trailer for a new movie!' I said to the MPs.

'Honey, that's no movie,' a guy replied. He was one of a handful of American military watching, grim-faced. 'This is live – and it's happening in New York.'

It was 11 September, and I had just seen the second plane, United Airlines Flight 175, hit the South Tower of the World Trade Center.

We had no time for coffee. As we gaped at the giant screen in disbelief, sirens started howling through the camp. This was our cue to start running for our body armour, helmets and weapons. The same procedure was happening in every single American military base around the world.

I had to tear myself from the screen, run for my billet, get my gear and report to my contingent. The camp was mayhem, full of frantic Americans barking orders. Within minutes, they started shutting down all the premises. The Bosnian civilians, who worked as support personnel such as cleaners and bar and restaurant staff, were rounded up and escorted out. Everyone not in uniform was suddenly a potential terrorist.

The Irish MPs had work to do, but the rest of our contingent gathered in helmets and body armour and waited for instructions. We watched dumbfounded as the 9/11 tragedy unfolded on the TV in the rec room.

Security had been tight around the camp before, but after 9/11 the American military raised the drawbridge. America was under attack and the military was locked in a siege mentality.

A lot of our freedoms at the camp disappeared after 9/11. The American contingent remained in body armour and helmets for weeks. However, every contingent had to hunker down behind heavily fortified gates. It was a number of weeks before they lifted restrictions and let us out to Sarajevo in the evenings. Civilians were regarded as suspect, so we were not allowed to wear civvies. (I wouldn't wear them again until I returned to Ireland in January 2002.) Camp Butmir was only a microcosm of what was happening everywhere. Unfortunately, the whole world changed after 9/11.

31

Eritrea

Shortly after arriving on my first mission to Africa in December 2002, I realised I hadn't researched the destination properly. *It's Africa, so it's hot*, I thought, flinging lots of shorts and T-shirts into my bag. I sighed with pleasure as we touched down in Eritrea just weeks before Christmas on a balmy sunny morning.

By nightfall, however, I was frozen. I didn't know that Eritrea's capital, Asmara, had an altitude of 7,700 feet, which meant we could get sunburnt by day and shiver in near-zero temperatures at night. I had to make an urgent call to get my army-issued fleece sent out on the second chalk.

I landed with Number 3 Irish Guard and Administration Component, as part of the United Nations Mission in Ethiopia and Eritrea (UNMEE). Our job was to monitor the ceasefire between the two East African countries. The 220-strong contingent of Irish Guards provided security and escorts at UNMEE force headquarters in Asmara.

However, my job title was 'travel officer', which sounded glamorous but usually entailed sitting for hours in the travel agents' office while they booked everything by phone and hand-wrote every ticket. I sorted out flights, accommodation and foreign exchange for the 200 soldiers when they wanted to go home or travel to places like South Africa on holiday.

The Irish camp, called Camp de h-Íde, after Ireland's first president Douglas Hyde, was little more than a collection of prefabs on the main road in Asmara. The camp was dismal, and there wasn't much for the soldiers to do in their free time. However, our contingent had 18 women, the largest number of women I'd ever served with overseas. *This is going to be great*, I thought. *I'm going to have the company of lots of women for the first time.* Ironically, I never felt so alone as I did in Eritrea.

All the women had joined after 1994, when they were fully combatant and trained in mixed-sex platoons. They were all at least a decade younger than me, all infantry and laser focused. The female platoon sergeant was the closest in age to me. She was what I wanted to be in the first ten years of my career – full infantry combatant and rising through the ranks.

However, there was no getting away from a difficult truth. Combatants, male and female, seemed to look down on the first all-female platoon because we weren't fully combat trained. I felt regarded by the other women as more a secretary than a solider, a mere typist in uniform. It was this attitude that irritated me then, and still does.

Our platoon had faced more than ten years of obstacles and discrimination before another single woman followed us. We were only 38 women, but our presence and visibility helped undo inequality in the defence forces. Our platoon broke barriers and paved the way for all the other women, but there was little appreciation of that in evidence.

I still thought I could bond with the girls if I tried, so I suggested we have a monthly girls' night out. The women were on different rotations, but I organised a driver and transport for 11 of us and found a nice restaurant that catered to most tastes. I went to a lot of trouble putting an entertaining night together.

The night was a success but, as I returned from the ladies', I heard my name mentioned amid loud laughter. In the shadows, I watched a girl mock my 'lah-di-dah' table manners as the others laughed. What I thought was just basic etiquette, others found hilarious. I never let them know I'd heard them, but I never organised a night out again.

Asmara city proved a surprise. Built by Italian colonists in the 1930s, it had a faded glamour rarely seen in overpopulated African towns. Giant palm trees sheltered its wide boulevards, and art-deco buildings with peeling ice-cream-coloured facades lined the streets. The city was a busy blend of tastes and cultures. Pizza and cappuccino were available in one rundown establishment and goat stew and Arabic mint tea in the next.

By the time our contingent arrived in Eritrea, several international peacekeepers had been expelled in separate incidents for having sex with minors. Unpalatable rumours circulated about the behaviour of some Irish troops in the two previous missions to the country. (Several Irish soldiers were later disciplined for breaking UN regulations governing sexual fraternisation with locals.)

The sleaze had mainly disappeared in the meantime. Brothels had been shut down and prostitutes arrested in a government crackdown. Hotels and clubs that were popular with those who bought sex had also been closed and fraternisation with local women was completely out of bounds. I overheard many half-in-joke, half-in-earnest laments in the dining hall: 'What are we supposed to do with our time off now?'

My escape from Camp de h-Íde became the luxurious five-star Hotel InterContinental Asmara close to the airport. I bought a six-month gym membership there, and the place became my sanctuary. I wandered through the newly built hotel with its glamorous eight-storey glass and marble interiors. I swam in its sparkling blue outdoor pool and treated myself to cappuccinos or a cocktail at the bar. It was a great refuge, especially on Sundays, a very long and lonely day in a place like Eritrea. I might have lost my mind if it wasn't for that vast anonymous retreat.

I very nearly did lose it for another reason. Early one morning, I went in search of the admin sergeant, feeling mortified. The day before we'd had a heated exchange where I'd been hostile and nasty. *What got into me?* I wondered. I screamed and swore at him repeatedly, something I'd never done to a colleague in my life.

As I launched into a grovelling apology, the admin sergeant looked at me as though I had two heads. 'Sorry for what? You never said anything to me,' he said.

He was baffled, and I wondered, for a moment, if I was going mad.

Then he started laughing. 'You've had a Lariam dream.'

'What?'

'It's the Lariam affecting you. You dreamt the row.'

Lariam was the anti-malarial drug we all took overseas. My 'dream' of fighting with the admin sergeant was so vivid, it was unsettling. Unfortunately, it was only the first of many terrifying waking nightmares. Within days, Lariam dreams became the talk of the camp.

'Jesus, I shot you last night,' one soldier said.

'Well, I fucking stabbed the lot of you,' someone else replied.

All the dreams were violent, vicious and angry. Thankfully all the weapons were locked away at night on that trip.

We hadn't been made aware of the many side-effects, especially mood swings, lethargy and inability to concentrate. Some affected were irritable and angry, and the drug was linked to a greater risk of suicide. For many, it caused sleep disturbances, nightmares and hallucinations; for me, the nightmares became so bad, the doctor prescribed a safer but more expensive anti-malarial.

I had also contracted another, more debilitating, health issue. After eating meat on the bone in a local restaurant, I got food poisoning which resulted in my first experience of projectile vomiting, something I never want to repeat. Within a few weeks, however, I spewed like the child from *The Exorcist* again and had diarrhoea for days. The doctor sent me off to the Jordanian military hospital down the road. They did tests and everything came up clear. But it happened again and again. I was fine for a few weeks, and then I'd have to stagger to the medic. On one occasion, the doctor glanced at his watch as I chucked up in front of him. If he had to work after 02.00hrs, he was allowed to rest the next day.

'It's ten to two, so keep vomiting there, and I won't have to go to that stupid conference in the morning.' Army doctors had a warped sense of humour.

Sometimes, the vomiting was so bad, I was admitted to the Medical Aid Post and put on a drip. Towards the end of the tour, the doctor returned to the mission on a new rotation. I was on the ward and heard him being updated.

'You've got one patient.'

'Oh, let me guess, Molloy's back again,' the doctor replied. I could almost see him raise his eyes as he said it. His bored tone indicated that he didn't believe anything was wrong with me.

Meanwhile, my family was struggling in Donegal. My

widowed mother sold the B&B, and she and my sister moved into rental accommodation near Donegal town while their new house was being built. However, their temporary home was damp, cold and miserable.

My sister, always stoic and not inclined to be emotional, was in tears one Sunday when I called. 'Mammy won't get out of bed anymore,' she cried.

My mother had fallen into a depression since my father's death. It was hard being nearly 4,000 miles from home and feeling so helpless.

Illness, the lack of companionship and my family crisis started to affect me too. After three months in Eritrea, I had never felt so sad or ill in my life. We got one free phone card a month to call home. Each card lasted minutes calling Ireland, but I bought a fistful and poured everything out in a tearful call to Aishling, my former housemate and best friend.

'Come home, Karina. You're sick and unhappy,' she said. 'You did everything to please your father, but he's gone now. So why are you torturing yourself? What point are you trying to prove here? Come home and get well.'

'You're right,' I said. 'There's nothing to keep me here.'

I put down the receiver, determined and relieved. *I'm submitting my application to leave.* But by the time I reached my billet, another voice – the sound of my ego and pride – told me, *No way are you going home early. You're not giving in.*

Three weeks before I was due to go home, the doctor called me to see him. 'I've got results from the hospital.'

'Don't tell me – negative again.'

'No, these came up positive.'

He confirmed a parasitic intestinal infection. The diagnosis was difficult because it only became evident every few weeks when the parasites laid eggs and the cycle of illness began again.

But when the doctor announced he was sending me home to recover, I was outraged. 'I've stuck it out this long, so no way am I going home early now!'

Even if it were for medical reasons, it would reflect poorly on my record to be sent home early. I could hear the mutterings already. *Molloy couldn't hack it.* I always felt I had something to prove. I took the pills prescribed to kill the parasites, but I was determined to stay until the end if it killed me.

The night before we were due to go home, I was relieved. I packed my bags and patted myself on the back. I'd made it to the finish line. The camp was in a buoyant mood, and many drinking sessions were in progress as I went to bed. At this stage, I shared my billet with a young corporal called Rachel, who was still on duty. I was exhausted with illness and never heard a thing until something heavy landed on my bed. It was pitch dark, and I was disoriented and terrified. I struggled to escape the weight slobbering on top of me.

'I love you, Karina. I think you're gorgeous ... I love you so much ...'

I was naked from the waist up, but I managed to turn on a light while keeping myself covered. Finally illuminated by the lamp, I recognised one of the camp's young officers. I'd had no actual dealings with him throughout the trip. But here he was, blind drunk and determined to get into bed with me.

Rachel had returned while I slept but hadn't locked the door.

'Are you okay, Karina?' she said, sitting up in the other bed, suddenly awake. 'Will I get help?'

'I'll deal with it,' I said. I wriggled into a T-shirt while keeping the amorous drunk at arm's length.

'I've loved you from afar all the time ...'

'Yeah, yeah, I know.'

Fending off his octopus hands proved too difficult, and it took both Rachel and I to manhandle him out of our billet, slam the door and lock it.

'You're such a lady. I love you sooo much ...' he continued outside, banging on the door.

Christ.

I felt numb. Drained. I went back to bed and eventually slept.

It was delayed shock again because I woke up upset and furious. *How dare officers think they can continue to do this! Twenty-one years after joining the army, women were still subjected to drunks breaking in while we tried to sleep.*

If the young officer had apologised that morning, I might have been able to set the incident aside, but he didn't. So the unwelcome mauling continued to run through my head all day.

Everyone was gossiping about the ossified officer who

got tangled in a briar bush and a barbed wire fence near the women's billets the night before. They laughed about how two guys in the signals corps had to free him. As soon as they heard he had broken into my billet, it would go around the camp that I shoved him in there.

I was busy sorting out all the luggage and typing the manifest for the camp's baggage but, still, I couldn't get what happened out of my head. *What kind of example was I giving the other girls when I appeared to tolerate this behaviour?* When I broke down crying, I was probably more surprised by the tears than the commandant, who looked up from his desk.

'Jesus, Karina, what's wrong? Are you sick or what?'

I've never seen a man get so angry so fast when I told him.

'The bloody pup,' he said, practically grabbing me and bringing me to the commanding officer's (CO's) office.

However, the CO's response was the polar opposite. He raised his eyes to the ceiling in despair. 'For fuck's sake, Karina, I need this like a hole in the head. We're going home tonight. Do you really want to report it?'

The commandant replied before I did. 'He can't get away with this. I won't have any female being harassed like this. Karina managed him, but what if it was one of the younger privates who couldn't deal with him?'

The CO called me back when the officer was sitting in front of him. His arms and face were lacerated and scratched from his encounter with the briars, and he was flushed and mortified-looking. He apologised, genuinely contrite, his head in his hands half the time. 'Oh my God, I'm really sorry, Karina. I vaguely remember seeing you, but oh God, I don't remember the rest. I've really embarrassed myself and I'm so sorry for scaring you like that.'

The CO drummed his fingers on the desk and glanced at the clock. 'Will you accept the apology?' he asked me. He had our two overseas reports and a nondisclosure form on his desk. In an ill-concealed threat, he told me my report was 'outstanding' but hadn't been signed yet. As an added deterrent, I was told that if I wished to proceed further, the case would be investigated by the Swedish military police, so we would miss the flight home.

What could I do? I accepted the apology, and we both signed a disclosure that the matter would no longer be discussed. The CO exhaled and signed both our overseas reports.

Once again, an officer got a slap on the wrist for breaking into a billet and sexually assaulting a female soldier. Professionally, my report read 'outstanding', but personally, it was not a good trip. And this incident in the final hours was just the cherry on top of a shit cake.

32

Witch Hunt

The minute I sat in front of the military psychologist, I burst into tears. So many emotions were simmering just below the surface. It was 2004, and the truth was I just didn't feel like myself anymore. Between bouts of sobbing, I managed to unload a headful of distress on the psychologist's desk. That day, I shed so many tears and felt so broken, I thought I'd reached my lowest ebb. I was wrong. Within days, I faced being discharged from the army and became embroiled in a fight to save my career.

When a senior person in the unit retired, he recommended I take over the clothing stores. So when I returned from Africa, I went to work as the senior of two company quartermasters (CQs) there. Unfortunately, the other CQ was often missing.

'I'm going for a haircut,' he'd announce and disappear for the rest of the day.

The men were allowed time off to go for a haircut because the army provided a barber in the barracks, while women were expected to have their hair done on their own time. He could go for a coffee and meet his mates, many of whom were more senior non-commissioned officers in the barracks, so I couldn't complain.

My main job as a company quartermaster sergeant (CQMS) was reconciling items on the floor with the numbers on the computer system. My storeman corporal and three storeman privates worked behind the counter while I was often in the office, trying to stay on top of mountains of paperwork.

Thousands of items went out over the counter every week, and it was easy to hand out medium shirts and mistakenly mark them 'small' on the docket. Seven pairs of socks might go out instead of six. Humans worked in the stores, so mistakes were made and, like all manual inventory tracking procedures, it was vulnerable to error. Dockets were forgotten, mislaid or not yet entered.

Theft was never a real issue. Most stock had no value outside the defence forces and all personnel received it for free. But every CQMS and battalion quartermaster sergeant (BQMS) in the defence forces faced the same nightmare with discrepancies in the figures. Everything in the army was black and white, and the figures had to tally. So, I'd been taught by every senior CQ how to reconcile the figures and iron out discrepancies. We had ways to tweak the inventory and tally what was on the floor to the computer system.

Keeping on top of the stock was relentless hard work. I was constantly running on a hamster wheel, never able to catch up. I still wasn't feeling my usual self since the parasitic infection in Eritrea and was exhausted. My normal coping skills were frayed because I also had the added stress of my mother being diagnosed with cancer.

So six months after returning from Eritrea, I applied to take leave for a year, like many colleagues had done before me. It was granted the following month, and I heaved a sigh of relief. *Okay, I'm out of here!*

Of course, it wasn't that simple. As the account holder for the store, I had to complete a thorough stocktake before I could do a handover to a member of staff. However, he kept disappearing during the count. He always had something to do, from medical appointments to coffee breaks. The delays continued. He had another job outside the barracks, and I suspected he didn't want the extra responsibility of the stores.

'I don't have to sign,' he'd say. 'The stock isn't right.'

His mate, also his senior in the unit, further delayed the process. 'I've been looking at your printouts,' he said. 'There are discrepancies. We need to start again.'

All through February and March, I tried to do a handover, but I received no co-operation. Every day, I faced their putdowns and hostilities.

When the commanding officer (CO) started enquiring about the hold-up, he was told the stocks weren't right. To me, he was inferring that I was terrible at my job. I didn't realise there was a worse interpretation.

When I couldn't see a way forward, my stress levels went through the roof. The job started taking a real psychological toll. My anxiety levels soared. I was angry and depressed, and when I couldn't face my work environment anymore I ended up seeing the army psychologist. I was close to a breakdown. I couldn't deal with the constant battle against these implacable forces anymore.

Everything poured out in a rush of tears the first day: how I felt crushed by adversarial colleagues and higher ranks; about the unwanted memories of traumas I'd experienced in the army; my mother's illness; everything that was crowding my headspace. I felt heard at last in that psychologist's office, and I left feeling a bit lighter and with a month's sick leave.

He advised me to forget about taking extended leave. 'You can lie on as many beaches as you like, but your problems will follow you. Stay here, and let's deal with them,' he said.

He was right, of course. However, before going on sick leave, I was called in by a senior person in the unit. 'We need to get this sorted. This is looking very dodgy,' he said.

I froze in horror. For the first time, I realised I had more to be concerned about than difficult co-workers.

'There's nothing dodgy going on here,' I said.

'A handover can't be authorised where I see discrepancies.'

I reeled with shock leaving the barracks, not knowing which way to turn for help. He was trying to crucify me for following accounting practices, at the time, that were not only widespread but standard in the defence forces. I worried that I could be charged with fraud and discharged from the army.

I took a bus and went straight home to my mother in Donegal. Meanwhile, the army sent a driver to my official address at my apartment in Dublin. We were meant to stay home on sick leave. I received a call threatening to charge me for not being at my home address.

After two weeks on sick leave, I was called back into the barracks for another meeting. I was wanted back at work so that they could start an investigation. The harassment was constant, and I was distraught with worry.

While all this was happening, the army drums were beating, and fellow CQs started to hear what was happening. Finally, I received a tip-off from a CQ with a lot of information, and what he told me made me feel instantly better.

A week later, the situation had been sent up the ranks, and I was called in from sick leave for a meeting with the adjutant. He was brusque. 'CQ Molloy, we need an end to this. I've been told the stocks were not what they should be. We urgently require your co-operation with an investigation into your procedures in the stores.'

I had nothing to lose. 'Well, if you charge me, this will go to court-martial; if that happens, I'm taking every single CQ and BQ down with me. I will not be singled out for something every CQ and BQ has to do. And my first witnesses will be two MPs.'

I informed the adjutant that the MPs went to collect

their army-issue skirts from their barrack clothing stores, but according to the system, they had received the items. 'Their signatures were forged on the receipts,' I said. 'They're happy to tell you their stories. They have all the printouts as proof and the name of the CQ.'

I had many other examples that involved other CQs and BQs, including those in Cathal Brugha Barracks. 'So go ahead and charge me,' I said in conclusion.

The adjutant had a good poker face. 'I'll take that under advisement, CQ Molloy.'

I never heard another word about any discrepancies in the stores. All their concerns about the stocks disappeared overnight, and they left me alone for the remaining weeks of my sick leave.

The tip-off from the CQ saved me because the men could not refute or bury the evidence of MPs. They decided not to open a can of worms when they realised I wouldn't go quietly.

When I returned to work after four months' sick leave, they sent me to the barrack service stores which stocked everything from furniture to toilet rolls. At first, they didn't give me access to the computer system. I wasn't even assigned a desk. Instead, I had a chair behind the door and nothing to do. For six weeks, I sat there, doing nothing. I felt it was a reprisal, a punishment for being difficult and threatening to expose others when I'd been called to account before the adjutant.

A week after returning to work, my CO also tried to have me medically boarded and discharged on the grounds that I was unfit for any form of work due to poor health. I only discovered this after receiving my personnel file years later through the Freedom of Information Act. I talked to a combat medic, who said the army medical board was more concerned about men who had been on sick leave for 24 months than someone who was back at work after four months. He said they probably binned the CO's request, wondering why he was wasting their time.

The unit sent me back to the clothing stores. The other CQ had already gone. He'd decided to take retirement rather than the responsibility of the place. However, I refused to become the account holder of the store again. I wasn't going to be their fall guy again, so they had to get someone more junior for the job.

After two months in the clothing stores, I was transferred and put into ordnance in 2nd Logistics Support Battalion (2LSB). My new job meant I was in charge of explosive ordnance disposal (EOD) and the weapons stores of the 2LSB battalion. They knew I was out of my comfort zone, as I was suddenly immersed in a whole new language. But I saw it as an opportunity to get more operational and infantry experience. They also did me a favour because I ended up with a fantastic CO. He was my first boss in the army who could honestly be described as 'an officer and a gentleman'. He was a decent, family man who had a heart. He allowed me an extra hour off to stay with my mother on days she was having chemo and radiation.

I took my new job seriously. When I heard on the RTÉ news that the army bomb-disposal team were dealing with an unexploded device, my first thought was, *I hope he measured the fecking coil correctly.* The EOD experts used coil to detonate devices but invariably eyeballed the lengths and wrote guestimate measurements in their reports.

If an EOD officer wrote that they used seven metres of coil and 25 were missing, I'd have to track him through barracks around the country and have him revise his report. I was now paranoid about any discrepancy. When I couldn't rectify the matter, I went to my new CO.

'Just write it off, Karina.'

'What?'

'Just make the requisition, and I'll write it off.'

He signed for it, so I didn't care. Everyone in logistics had their own process, their own magic wand to even out the inevitable inconsistencies that arose, but they'd tried to bury me for doing the same.

The career progress of each member of army personnel was recorded in an annual report. These reports included a box-ticking exercise where at a stroke of a pen, an officer could ruin a soldier's career. Number three on the annual report form asked the commanding officer's opinion about the soldier's 'potential for promotion'.

The first box that could be ticked was 'Yes', meaning he or she had the potential for promotion. The second was that he or she had the potential for promotion 'with additional experience in present rank'. However, my battalion commander ticked the demeaning and capricious third box: 'Has reached her ceiling for promotion.' He emphasised 'her' with hard biro lines. They always had a way to exact their revenge.

33

Problematic

I waited three years after Eritrea before I was selected for overseas again. It was nearly worth the wait to return to Sarajevo. Anywhere we didn't have to run outside in the rain or the dark to use a toilet was a plumb posting.

I was less gleeful to discover I was the only woman in the Irish contingent. And, once again, the army billeted me to the international female block at the far end of Camp Butmir where I was the only one who spoke mother-tongue English. I felt marginalised because of my gender and had little sense of social or emotional connection in the camp. I remember sitting in my billet some nights with absolutely no one to talk to. Isolation might have been a more significant issue on that trip if my job wasn't so hectic.

I hadn't paid much attention to my new job title – head of Morale, Welfare and Activities (MWA) with the European Union Force Bosnia and Herzegovina (EUFOR). I soon realised the job best suited someone with jazz hands and an extrovert's personality. Even though I didn't fit the bill of a Butlin's camp redcoat, I found my own way of being the 'minister for fun'. I had a hectic schedule organising national-day events, parades, tours, and excursions from river rafting to skiing and nights at the philharmonic. Five thousand soldiers attended the events I organised, and I also monitored more than 20 stores run by Bosnian locals in the camp. With careful delegation to my 12 Bosnian civilian staff, I avoided most 'hi-de-hi!' aspects of the job.

To my intense surprise, I got another job vacancy in Bosnia five months after arriving home. It was largely a desk job, working in customs and excise in Camp Butmir. I didn't care. I was going back to Bosnia. I'm not sure why I was so excited, considering the previous overseas trip had not been great.

I was the only woman on the trip again, and as usual I was billeted far away from the other Irish. Thankfully, I knew a company sergeant (CS) and former ranger called Mark in the Irish contingent. He and his two fellow CSs were like guardian angels – people with whom I could have dinner or a cup of coffee. As the months rolled on, Mark and I grew closer and looked forward to spending time with each other.

However, Mark had a partner back home, and I knew her, so I pulled back. I didn't want the unnecessary complications and heartache an affair would bring to my life, so I never crossed that line. The attraction between us was undeniable, though, so if I committed any crime, it was to leave the door open to the possibility of something more. 'When or if you ever decide to leave, we can try having a relationship,' I said. 'But not before.'

But the sense of isolation from being billeted alone continued to be a problem. I also missed meetings and appointments as a result.

'Everyone was there except you,' said the commanding officer pointedly after I'd failed to turn up at some event.

'That's because no one told me.'

'It was up on the noticeboard.'

They posted notices in the men's billet and expected me to be psychic. The army's strict gender segregation drove me mad at times. Mark and the other guys revealed that they lived on the same corridor as all the British army men and women. Separate toilet and shower facilities were located at the end of the block, so I could have been billeted there too.

But when I said it to the commandant, he almost recoiled. 'Oh, we'd have to think about that,' he said, as if I was asking to move Russian secret agents into the block. 'Why don't you talk to the chief of staff when he comes?'

He didn't expect for a minute that I would, but I made it my business to corner the new chief of staff, Lieutenant-General Dermot Earley, when he arrived. He was the highest-ranking officer in the Irish Army. If anyone could do something about this form of discrimination and segregation, it was him.

I managed to speak with him at the Irish House bar. 'It's very isolating for the women to be billeted away from their compatriots,' I explained. 'Camaraderie binds an army together and helps everyone function effectively, so why segregate the women and disconnect us from the unit? We end up missing meetings and schedule changes. British Army women share tents with their male counterparts overseas, yet we can't share the same block?'

The chief of staff cocked his ear to me and nodded at all the correct intervals, but he didn't interject to say he agreed.

'The Irish Army men are happy to share a block with British Army women,' I said, trying to make light of a daft situation. 'Do you think Irish Army women are a greater threat? Is the army afraid we'll attack the men in the middle of the night?'

The chief of staff chuckled amiably. 'Let me look into it,' he said, moving on to someone else. I felt I'd been given the brush-off.

However, he didn't forget about our exchange. His driver told me about the conversation he overheard in the car between the chief of staff and another senior Irish officer that night.

'What's the story with that one, Molloy?' the chief of staff asked.

'Oh, Molloy,' the officer said dismissively. 'She's just a bit problematic.'

34

Chad

My first shock on arriving in Chad was the intensity of the heat. It was like walking into a brick oven as we disembarked the aircraft with temperatures rising to and exceeding 50 degrees Celsius. N'Djamena was probably the hottest capital in the world.

The Irish contingent landed in the landlocked country in Central Africa on 16 July 2009, as part of an EU mission and UN mandate known as MINURCAT. We were there as peacekeepers to protect civilians and refugees, many fleeing persecution from neighbouring Darfur.

My second impression of the country was its poverty. N'Djamena was a collection of crumbling buildings, ragged children, donkeys, dust, dirt roads and military trucks. Chad was one of the poorest countries in the world then, struggling with drought, famine and a succession of conflicts.

Outside the city, the land was red and barren, with tufts of thorny bushes and prickly trees in the desert landscape. Our home for the next six months, Camp Europa, looked as inhospitable as its surroundings. My first glimpse was its high perimeter wall made with concrete and topped with barbed wire. Within the walls were Portakabins, metal containers and a city of tents on a few acres of scorched red earth. Underfoot was hard and stony, and the men had to use sledgehammers to drive tent pegs into the soil.

Camp Europa was the logistical headquarters of the EU force in Chad. However, most of the occupants were from the African Union countries. Around 700 troops from Ghana, Ethiopia, Senegal and other nations were accommodated in the hundreds of tents within the camp walls.

I really wanted to go to Chad because my brother served there with the French Foreign Legion. *Anything you can do, I can do better*, I thought. I was the only woman among 16 Irish personnel from the 101st Infantry Battalion's NSE. However, as N'Djamena was an international camp, I blithely expected a mix of nationalities and genders like I'd encountered in every other international camp I'd lived in.

'How many am I sharing with?' I asked when told where the female billet was.

The company quartermaster (CQ) looked at me as if I'd asked a daft question. 'Sharing? You're the only female. You're on your own here, Molloy,' he said.

I could hardly believe it. 'There are no other women here at all? Are you serious?'

I was the only woman among a thousand men in this scalding place known as the deep heart of Africa.

The shock of this only added to the bombshell I'd received 48 hours earlier during a briefing at army headquarters.

Chad was to be my eleventh tour of duty and my sixth as a senior non-comissioned officer (NCO). It was also my fifth mission overall during my years of service. I was still the only female CQ in the defence forces, but six women had reached the rank of company sergeant in the army, and within 18 months we would have our first sergeant major.

No battallion quartermaster (BQ) applied for the vacancy in Chad, so I was the most senior CQ of all three heading for Camp Europa. I had more overseas service than the other CQs put together, so naturally I would be made acting BQ in Chad. It was excellent news. It would stand to me to get overseas experience when I applied again for BQ vacancies.

'Okay, lads,' the colonel of the QMG's branch said. 'We have among us a CQ with huge experience overseas, and her experience will be very useful on this mission, so welcome, Karina.' Then, he pointed to one of the other CQs and said, 'Acting BQ on this mission will be ...'

I didn't hear any more. The pounding of my heart filled my ears. *What the fuck?* I thought.

The colonel knew exactly why I went straight for him when the meeting finished. 'I am the most senior of the CQs going to Chad, so why am I not acting BQ?'

'I know, Karina,' he said, shuffling his papers and stuffing them into a briefcase. He couldn't even meet my eyes. 'But it's out of my hands. Chad is predominantly Muslim and as a woman, it was felt you wouldn't be able to relate to the local authorities as well as a man could. They decided you wouldn't be able to do the job.'

In light of what I ended up doing in Chad, it was a bullshit excuse.

My personal life was also up in the air as I left Ireland. Mark's relationship had ended six months after we'd returned from Bosnia in 2008, and we'd taken tentative steps to begin a new one together. I was shocked but elated to discover I was pregnant early in our relationship. However, at 12 weeks, when Mark was overseas, I miscarried at home one weekend. I returned to work on Monday as usual, but when an older male colleague cheerily asked how my weekend was, I burst into tears. 'I had a miscarriage,' I cried. I was devastated.

Even in the short while we had spent together, Mark and I discovered we were remarkably similar. My grandfather would have said, 'As God made us, he matched us.' We believed there was a place for everything and everything must have its place. The army had institutionalised us, so neither of us could walk away from an unmade bed. We were always alert, hyper-aroused. In a restaurant, we both vied to sit in a corner watching the door, ready to run, attack or defend. However, we also shared a mutual love for travelling overseas, something that seemed destined to keep us apart.

Ten days after I left my apartment with my rucksack for Chad, Mark left his new flat for Bosnia. The vast geographic separation was the first test of a budding relationship, and I wondered if we could make a long-distance relationship work.

As usual, my billet in Chad was located away from the cluster of buildings accommodating the rest of the Irish. Home for me was a three-minute walk away to a prefab usually used for the handover periods. Worst of all, however, the closest female shower and toilet block was near the main gate – a round-trip of almost 15 minutes.

When I wanted to use the bathroom at night, I had to put on a dressing gown and slippers and run the gauntlet of 700 soldiers living in tents between my billet and the main gate. Weaving my way through tents in the shadows was nightmarish. The African soldiers rarely seemed to sleep, and they sat smoking and sitting around fires, stopping whatever they were doing to stare as I passed. Even when I made it to the female shower block, it was full of men. I stood outside, coughing, waiting for them to leave. It was a frightening ordeal to make my way through an all-male camp every night.

The rest of the Irish contingent had a solid brick building with sinks, showers with curtains, and an enclosed toilet – no urinals – right beside their billet. The block was a three-minute walk away from my billet.

I asked the commanding officer (CO) for permission to use these facilities at night. 'Only at night,' I pleaded.

He refused. 'You have your own shower block,' he said.

I despaired. I would have expected it from the old sweats, but this guy was in his thirties, and I thought a younger man might be more understanding. I even tried not drinking for the second half of the day, which was crazy in the heat. Ultimately, I couldn't bear the terror of the night-time journey anymore. I bought a basin and had to suffer the indignity of using that as my night-time toilet instead.

Maureen O'Brien (now an Irish Army general) came to Camp Europa for one night at the end of her mission. She was the first woman to serve as the 2IC of a 420-strong infantry battalion when deployed to Chad. Conditions were so challenging for the infantry in Chad that they rotated every four months rather than six like those of us serving with the national support element (NSE).

When Maureen discovered men in the female shower block she went ballistic and rang the quartermaster general in Ireland. She marched into my CO, demanding action.

'That's in the control of the camp commandant,' he insisted. 'I don't have the authority.'

I was dispatched to see the camp commandant, a huge Nigerian man.

He wasn't very interested in the shower-block discussion, preferring to discuss my physical attributes. 'Did anyone ever tell you those are good child-bearing hips?'

The Irish troops were stationed in isolated parts of the country, some five days overland by truck. Conditions were rough. Our jobs in N'Djamena were to support the battalion, and Irish troops loved nothing more than getting parcels of sweets and Tayto crisps from their loved ones in Ireland. Part of my job was negotiating the release of these parcels and paying unofficial 'customs' to the police who oversaw the post office. I had to bargain with the head of police every few days. He presented a pile of parcels every time.

'I counted 16 packages here, and they are $3 a package,' he said. 'I also have two big packages here. They cost $10 each.'

I had to negotiate for every parcel because I only had a certain amount of money to hand over. The army had denied me the acting BQ role claiming I wouldn't be able to relate to Muslim authorities as well as a man could. Yet I was the one sent to negotiate with and bribe the local police several times a week. In fact, my posting was the most junior of all three CQs' jobs in Chad. I was angry and frustrated because a trained monkey could have done it.

I found sanctuary in a five-star hotel in N'Djamena, where I could swim, use the gym and stretch out on sun loungers under parasols. I could almost forget the dusty third-world country outside. No one was permitted to wander through the city, so I depended on the Irish drivers to drop and collect me.

Mark and I managed to stay in touch by texting and Skype, and he related an incident in the first week of his mission that really angered me. He was having dinner with seven senior colleagues in the dining hall. None was aware that Mark and I were a couple.

The most senior sergeant major, sitting directly opposite Mark, remarked, 'Did you hear who got Chad?' He named a few of the men.

'Oh yeah,' he added. 'And fecking Molloy got out there as well. I wonder who she slept with to get that!'

They all had a good laugh until Mark put down his cutlery. 'Do you know that's my partner you're talking about?'

Silence fell around the table, and the sergeant major's face dropped. He started back-pedalling madly. 'Oh God, I'd no idea. I didn't mean anything bad by that. Sure, I love Karina. She's a lovely woman. It was just stupid banter. I'd never say anything bad about Karina. She's a lovely girl. I met her loads of times ...'

I didn't see any humour in it. I felt I should have gained respect after reaching a senior NCO rank. But here I was, a senior NCO for 12 years, and still the subject of their locker-room trash-talk.

Mark and I co-ordinated our leave to meet in Ireland in December but were both back on duty for Christmas. By then, I'd met an eccentric British archaeologist and a few Scottish teachers working in a private international school in Chad. I used to meet them for dinner or cocktails at the hotel bar. The little female community we created in the hotel was my salvation.

The second in command (2IC) held a meeting to decide how to celebrate Christmas Day at the camp. I planned to spend it with the women. 'Why don't we do something civilised and go to a hotel with nice food and a pool?' I suggested. I could kill two birds with one stone.

I was shot down. The men wanted a piss-up in the camp. The CO had gone home for Christmas, and the 2IC was in charge. 'Okay, that's decided,' he said. 'And everyone will attend.'

I had no intention of staying in the camp. 'I'm going to the pool – one of the drivers has offered to bring me.'

'No, you won't,' he said. 'He's entitled to a day off too. He's not driving on Christmas Day. We're celebrating Christmas Day in the camp.'

I changed tack and argued that I was a Buddhist and had no interest in Christmas. I was lying through my teeth because I loved the time of year. But I had studied Buddhism and stayed in several ashrams by this stage. I was attracted to the Buddhist way of life and spiritual traditions largely because I liked to practise meditation. I used meditation in stressful times as a coping mechanism.

But the 2IC was determined to add to my stress and ruin my Christmas. 'You have no transport, so you can't go,' he said.

At the last minute, the driver persuaded the MPs on patrol on Christmas Day to transport me. The 2IC no longer had an excuse to keep me in the camp, but he was not happy. 'Buddhist, my arse. I looked in your personnel file, and it says you're a Roman Catholic.'

I couldn't believe that he'd gone and checked! The truth was I explored the possibility of changing my religion on my personal file to Buddhist, but I was told that unless I could provide an official certificate to prove I'd converted, the army didn't want to know. As there is no official process to convert to Buddhism, there is no paperwork.

Even the Dalai Lama himself couldn't have convinced the army to change my file.

At the end of the tour, I received a glowing report stating I was 'hardworking, conscientious and trustworthy' and kept 'a good level of fitness and high standard of appearance'. I wondered if they commented on the men's appearance in their annual reports.

As we were allowed the right to reply, I took the opportunity to vent my anger.

My considerable UN logistics experience was not utilised to its fullest potential during my overseas mission as company NSE CQMS. The fact that I was the most senior CQMS serving with this battalion was not taken into account. I find serving in the most junior CQMS appointment an insult to my 12 years' service as a senior NCO and my 29-year service in the Irish Defence Forces.

I signed the statement on 7 February 2010.

Every time I applied for a BQ vacancy, they highlighted the fact that I was denied the acting BQ post in Chad. *Oh, I see you're the most senior CQ overseas in Chad, but you didn't get the acting vacancy. What happened? Why didn't you get it?*

I had to give the same rubbish excuse I was given, but it was clear that being denied the acting BQ vacancy continued to have an adverse effect on my career.

35

Leaving

I found an ordinary brown envelope on my desk when I came back from lunch one day. It was addressed to Company Quartermaster Sergeant Molloy. I shared my office as the company quartermaster (CQ) of Ordnance in Cathal Brugha Barracks with the company sergeant (CS), and the door was open, so anyone could walk in. I presumed it was a receipt. But instead, the envelope contained a single page with words that nearly broke me.

Well, CQ Molloy, you're giving us a great laugh in the NCOs' mess these days every time you apply for a BQ's vacancy that you're never going to get. Keep applying and keep us laughing.

My hands shook as I held the page. The letter was anonymous, of course. The script looked so awkward that it must have been done by someone using their non-dominant hand to disguise their handwriting. A ball of hurt and humiliation lodged in my throat. I imagined all my supposed colleagues in the mess, sitting around, laughing at me. *Silly cow. Who does she think she is, applying for BQ?*

Were they right? Was I delusional in applying for a promotion? I was 12 years a CQ at this stage, but was becoming a BQ out of my league? Tears stung my eyes, but I knew I must not be visibly upset. Someone nearby might be watching. Instead, I left and walked across the barracks, trembling, with this note clutched in my hand. I went to the mess president, a man with whom I was friendly. I'd never been to his office before.

'Jesus, Karina, what's wrong?' he said. He only had to look at my face.

I handed him the letter. 'I want that photocopied and enlarged and put up in the mess. I want every NCO from juniors to sergeant major to see what's still going on here.'

He tossed the letter onto his desk in disgust. 'Throw it away, Karina. That's my advice. Don't give it the dignity of a response. It doesn't deserve one.'

But my head continued spinning all afternoon. Visceral contempt leapt off that single page of taunts and I knew it came from one or more of my so-called colleagues. Who hated me that much and why?

By then, I was privately seeing a counsellor, an ex-army medical colonel. Working with the army psychologist had made me realise it was unhealthy to bottle up my distress. I had been traumatised in the workplace for years, and I needed to stop internalising it and blaming myself. I happened to have a counselling session with the colonel that night. I managed to keep it together all day, but as soon as I handed him the letter, the ice broke inside me and I sobbed hard. The words created an image that was seared into the back of my eyes: the men gathered in the mess, laughing at me.

My counsellor was shaken by the meltdown he was witnessing. 'Why are you getting so upset by this, Karina?' he said. 'You've been through so much worse.'

But those few cruel lines of ink were the straw that broke the camel's back. It was the culmination of a thousand microaggressions and systematic abuse I'd experienced daily. It was the lack of respect, the disdain and the hostility I continued to face. I wore a suit of armour daily at work, but the armour had been hit so often and so fiercely that it had finally cracked. I didn't want to go to work anymore.

I'd applied for several BQ vacancies while I was in Chad, applying for a total of eight BQ vacancies in my army career. I've recently seen some of the feedback on my applications through Freedom of Information requests, and it's little wonder I didn't succeed.

She does not have the same degree of operational logistics experience as the candidate selected, having only served but once as CQ overseas. I'd served three times at that stage. *She has never served in an operation unit at home.* I had. *Requires further experience*, as they claimed I hadn't operated and run a rations account for a minimum of 90 days, when I'd run the rations account for ten months. These statements were on my file and all wrong. Was this incompetency? Had they bothered to read my file? Were they being selective in reading my file? Who knows.

Any member of the defence forces who had gone under general anaesthetic could not go overseas for a year. So I had put off having a hysterectomy for years even though my entire adult life was blighted with the heavy and painful period pains associated with fibroids.

'Get a hysterectomy and then all your troubles will be over,' urged the consultant. A year after returning from Chad, I saw the competition for overseas was becoming stiffer. And even though I continued to apply for BQ vacancies, no promotion was in sight. I had nothing to lose. It was time to have the operation.

We had no female doctors in the Eastern Command, so I attended one in the Curragh with a reputation for being conscientious and kind. In June 2011, I went to Holles Street Hospital in Dublin for a hysterectomy. It was extensive rather than keyhole surgery, so the doctor warned me I could be out of work for up to three months.

I had the operation in Holles Street on a Monday and woke up in post-op, burning up in a sweat. I'd been plunged into immediate menopause. Mark flew in from overseas on special leave to take me home the following Sunday. With 55 stitches, I could hardly get into the car. He brought me to Donegal, so my mother could help look after me before he returned overseas. He photocopied my sick leave note and posted the original to the orderly room sergeant at the barracks.

I phoned the orderly sergeant first thing on Monday morning. 'I'm out of Holles Street,' I said.

'So, how much sick leave have you got?' he asked.

'Six weeks, and the letter is in the post today.'

'Great, Karina,' he said. 'That's all done and sorted now.'

I rang my CS in Ordnance and told him I was on six weeks' leave. I'd ticked all the boxes and thought I could relax.

But later that morning, I got a phone call from my private storeman driver. 'Karina, I hate calling you like this, but X has put three charges on the gate for you.'

'He what?'

'You're charged with not staying at your home address during sick leave, not reporting to the barracks after coming out of hospital and producing a letter of sick leave from a civilian doctor.'

Technically, they were legitimate charges. But I wondered if any senior NCO getting treatment for prostrate issues was treated the same. I don't believe anyone in the history of the defence forces ever received charges on the gate after undergoing an operation. The charges were the talk of the barracks because it's so rare that a senior NCO's name is put on the gate, never mind one who had just undergone serious surgery.

I couldn't lift a kettle to make a cup of tea. I couldn't drive. I could hardly make it over a doorstep. But I was meant to come out of hospital on Sunday and climb four flights of stairs to my apartment. Then I was meant to make my way to the barracks on Monday, hand in my sick leave, and then try and get an appointment with the army doctor to countersign the sick leave.

I rang the doctor in the Curragh. She was outraged and she dealt with it. She was a colonel, so she was considerably senior to the man who'd laid the charges at the gate.

'It's sorted,' she said. 'I'll see you in six weeks for your review; in the meantime, just relax and get better.'

When the six weeks check-up was due, my kind commanding officer sent transport to Donegal to bring me to the Curragh and back home again. When I returned to work, I warned my bosses I'd need help in the store until I'd fully recovered. 'I can't do the manual labour and heavy lifting I used to do for a few months,' I said.

'You'll have all the help you'll need,' they assured me.

A week later, as I struggled down the stairs laden with six rifles, I realised that this help would never materialise.

So, for a whole combination of reasons, I thought seriously about leaving the army. I still wanted to stay in the defence forces and defeat the system, to progress and improve things. My attitude was: if you leave the room, how can you influence it? However, I seemed to have hit a glass ceiling. Any career progression had stalled and, after 14 years as a CQ, I couldn't see myself getting to BQ. I woke up on my fiftieth birthday and wondered, *Do I really want to stay here until I'm 60? Do I want to die in uniform?*

At that time too, the country was in a financial crisis, and rumours abounded that those with long service were about to lose the facility to retire after 31 years. Our pensions could be deferred. By then, only six of my original platoon of 38 were still serving, and I had already served the maximum levels of service for a pension. Many of the senior NCOs around me started to leave in a panic.

Mostly, however, I was worn down. I felt exhausted, demoralised and marginalised. I worked among some good men, but they were outweighed by the many vexatious ones, those waiting to stab me in the back at any opportunity. I sometimes felt so unwell that I cried before going to work. I was tired of wading in a river of vicious piranhas. I was battle weary and my combative spirit was spent.

I really couldn't think of a good reason to stay so, for the first time in my life, I followed the lemmings and decided to get out too.

The date of my discharge was 17 February 2012. I never shed a single tear as I handed in my uniforms to the stores. I was numb, sleepwalking my way out of my career. *Thirty years and 278 days is long enough in any job*, I thought. As I walked away, I felt nothing but relief.

36

Crisis

I woke in the dark, my heart pounding with fear. A sense of doom and calamity overwhelmed me, so I was almost paralysed beneath it. Something dark and terrible surrounded me. I was afraid to get out of bed, but I was more afraid to stay. All I could think about was getting to my mother. So I fled to her room, a quivering, sobbing shell of a person. I clambered into her bed with her, willing her to hug me and hold me tight. *I'm safe here*, I thought. *I'm safe with my mammy.*

Not long previously, I had fearlessly driven through minefields. Yet that night, I trembled violently and clung like a baby to my mother in her bed, in the grip of a massive panic attack.

The tremendous period of relief I'd experienced when I first left the army was well and truly over. I'd filled the early days with structure, routine and fun – a gourmet cookery course and a holiday in the sun with Mark and my mother. Then, suddenly, I was in my apartment in the city centre with nothing to do all day.

At first, it felt like the usual sense of anticlimax after arriving home from overseas. So often, I'd gone from a busy job in a hectic camp to turning the key and entering the tomblike silence of an empty apartment. Finding myself alone again was always an adjustment and something I never got used to. I liked being on my own, but this was different.

Coming home from overseas entailed a month-long hiatus. Suddenly, I faced an endless number of empty and meaningless days. I had no goals and no challenges for the first time in my life. I had no battles to fight, but the anxiety didn't go away. I had too much time to think and remember things I didn't want to think about. In hindsight, the deep depression that ensued was partly about not coming to terms with what had happened to me in the army. I'd had some counselling, but not enough, and I had shut down too often and too soon. My first instinct was to bury my feelings and move on, but feelings have a way of bubbling to the surface again. And they really started to surface as soon as I removed my armour.

With my uniform gone, I didn't know how to be, who I

was or what was happening to me. For most of my adult life, I'd never even had to think about what to wear. I'd rarely had to think of food because it was served to me. Now I had all these decisions, chief among them what to do with the rest of my life. Of course, I was also in surgical menopause and, even with an HRT patch slapped on my arm, my hormones were all over the place.

My life, feelings and thoughts seemed out of control. I couldn't deal with it, so I ran home to Mammy and, literally and figuratively, curled up in a ball. My mother was appalled. She had never seen me this way. I was always the practical one, the active one, the one who got things done. I remember having a bizarre conversation with Mark and my mother one evening.

'But what am I supposed to do tomorrow?' I was like a lost child.

'You're supposed to relax and enjoy yourself,' my mother replied.

'But how do I do that?'

Mark and my mother despaired.

For four months after I left the army, I was still on pre-discharge leave. I had packed up, handed back my uniform and physically left. However, technically, up until midnight on 16 February, I could have gone back in and said, *I made a mistake; I'm not leaving after all.* I could still change my mind until that date – and that was all going through my head.

When the date passed, I deeply regretted my decision to leave the army. *How could I have been so stupid?* I berated myself. *I still had a lot to do and achieve there.* I was lost in a fog of confusion and hopelessness and didn't know what to do with myself.

My doctor told me the obvious: I was grieving for my job. He prescribed antidepressants, which didn't seem to help much. I hoped I had finished with counselling but, suddenly, I needed professional help more than I ever did. Once again, I started dealing with all the memories and feelings I'd preferred to bury.

I went to the Passaddhi Meditation Centre in Bantry on a silent retreat for ten days. Of course, I followed normal army procedure – hurry up and wait – and arrived hours before everyone else. The centre had a Buddhist nun from the Netherlands as a guest teacher and I watched her in fascination. She was a towering woman, over six feet tall with a shaved head, who seemed to float around the house as if by levitation and was surrounded by an almost tangible aura of peace and serenity.

When I heard she had been a Catholic nun for 35 years, I thought she was even more extraordinary. We bonded during our time there. As with every crisis in my life, the art of meditation was an excellent coping mechanism now. We meditated for 16 hours a day, and being silent for all those days, constantly being in my own head, helped me step outside of my situation and look at it more objectively.

Had I really made a mistake leaving the army? Does this really deserve all the angst I am currently feeling? Meditation helped put some of my issues and worries in perspective. I stopped beating myself up. *You've left an institution after*

30 years, I thought. *Accept that it's going to be a struggle to find a new way of life. You're being as normal as you can in an abnormal situation.*

When the silent retreat was over, the floating nun presented me with a treasured gift, a little statue of Buddha in a glass case. The retreat was a very positive time during a crisis point in my life.

Still, I remember being in tears and calling a friend one day, not knowing what was wrong with me or what I could do with myself.

'Start doing something constructive with your life, Karina,' she said. 'You always loved studying, so go to college.'

I don't know why I didn't think of it earlier. I had already completed a lot of alternative-medicine courses down the years, like reflexology and aromatherapy massage. I had also completed a special course in cancer-care reflexology. I had explored all my interests in Eastern medicine and wanted to try something different. I began researching college courses and came upon horticulture at Pearce College in Dublin. My mother was an avid gardener and had instilled a similar interest in her children, so that's what I decided to study for the next two years.

I arrived on my first day of the diploma course, looking around at the men in the class, ready to do battle. It took a while to relax in the classroom and realise I didn't have to watch my back anymore. *These guys are not out to get me,* I had to remind myself.

I imagined spending my days in the outdoors, planting

and digging, so it came as a shock that horticulture was a hugely academic course. But I soon found the subject absorbing, and having a timetable and schedule again was like a salve to my psyche. My classmates, male and female, were friendly, supportive and inclusive. I found a sense of belonging and engagement that I had rarely experienced in the army. Studying helped me fill the hours in a way that felt meaningful and worthwhile. For the first time in many months after leaving the army, the clouds parted and the sun began to shine again.

37

Closure

My heart skipped a beat as I read the Facebook post over Mark's shoulder.

> Now is the time to break your silence and end your suffering. Message me with your story … Take a deep breath, be brave … tell me your story. Confidentiality is assured.

Retired soldier Anthony O'Brien posted a message on Facebook early in 2020 calling all serving and retired soldiers, male and female, to add incidents of sexual harassment, abuse or rape in the army to a submission he was sending to the Department of Defence.

'Here you are, now. This is your chance,' Mark said. 'Put all this down on paper, and get it off your chest once and for all.'

The old saying is *Come live with me and you'll know me*, and Mark and I soon realised we'd been damaged by our experiences in the army. I had problems with intimacy and a huge distrust of men. I felt uncomfortable and vulnerable in their presence. The incidents of sexual assault and bullying were always sitting there in my head, and they haunted me in cinematic detail at times.

I also harboured many regrets and 'what ifs'. What if I'd turned towards the Swedish camp instead of the Irish camp after Officer X sexually assaulted me? What if I'd refused to back down when the course commander compelled me to drop charges of sexual assault in the pool? I beat myself up for not doing more to challenge the culture of sexual violence in the army. Mark always tried to remind me that if I had done things differently, I wouldn't have survived 31 years and been one of the longest-serving women there. 'At least you stayed in there and tried to bring about change,' he said.

Yet I couldn't help feeling I'd been weak and too easily intimidated in the face of many assaults. I had a nagging feeling that I'd failed the women who came behind me, that I hadn't done enough.

Mark was right, I decided. I reread Anthony's message, and I did what he said – I took a deep breath and decided to tell my story. This was my opportunity to get what happened to me out there – as the Americans put it, it was a way to get 'closure'. However, I realised I would be naming senior officers, so I was reluctant to share the information with a third party in case I left myself open to litigation. In many cases, it was my word against theirs.

'Make contact,' Mark said. 'Find out what it's all about. But don't send anything in writing until you're sure what's going on.'

Anthony sensed my reluctance to submit my information to him. He suggested I send a protected disclosure to the Department of Defence as an individual, and he put me in touch with a woman who had done the same a few years earlier. I contacted Gwen (not her real name), and we spoke at length about our experiences. This happened during the height of Covid, so all communications were over the phone.

Meanwhile, Anthony went on his own journey. The United Nations opened a formal investigation into incidents reported on his submission in 2022. The accounts were also sent to Minister for Defence Simon Coveney, who then sent them on to the gardaí.

I searched the website of the Office of the Ombudsman for the Irish Defence Forces and found a template for making a submission. It took about ten days for me to recount a dozen separate incidents in total. As I wrote the protected disclosure and went through the timeline from 1981 until my departure in 2012, I found only four years without incidents of sexual abuse, attempted rape, harassment or bullying in the entire 30 years and 278 days of my career.

I wrote a cover email declaring that I was submitting the information under the Protected Disclosures Act 2014. It was a way to protect myself and still tell the complete truth. Mark went off to work one day, and I painstakingly began addressing the email to the taoiseach, the minister for defence, the chief of staff and other relevant Oireachtas members.

I sat there shaking and sweating and, finally, heart beating hard, I pressed 'send'. For some reason, I was really scared to send the disclosure. I heard the sound of a ping almost immediately after. The email had bounced back at me. *Oh God, maybe I'm not meant to do this*, I thought.

I took a deep breath. Gwen had already done it, and Anthony was sending in a raft of submissions. Everything that I'd written happened to me over my 31 years of service. I did not enhance it. I did not exaggerate it. I wrote it clearly, concisely and dispassionately. I discovered I'd misspelt 'taoiseach' in the email address, corrected it and pressed 'send' again. This time it went.

I exhaled. It was in the authorities' hands for the first time. *I don't know why you're getting so worked up about it*, I thought. *Nothing will probably come of it.*

Disclosures had been sent to the department before and ignored. Irish Army captain Tom Clonan had produced research decades earlier when he was still serving, revealing systemic abuse of women in the armed forces. The army turned on him as a whistle-blower and his research was ignored. So I had no illusions that my words would have any impact.

However, within days, I received a reply from a senior civil servant in the Department of Defence requesting a meeting. His response was spammed, and there was confusion before I finally linked up with him. However, Mark and I wondered why I had received a response to my protected disclosure when others hadn't. We could only surmise that the inclusion of a very senior officer's name in my disclosure had triggered alarm bells.

The night before the meeting, I felt really nervous. I didn't know what to expect.

'Well, what do you want from this meeting?' Mark started grilling me. 'It's up to you to decide. So what do you want, Karina?'

'Stop going all interrogator on me!' I snapped.

I really didn't know what I wanted. I wanted things to change, but I'd never thought about how because I never expected my disclosure to get this far.

'Well, make up your mind, Karina. There's no point in meeting this man if you don't have an objective.'

It came to me in a rush. 'I want an acknowledgement that this has happened to me,' I said suddenly. 'And I want an apology.'

'Good, you go into that meeting and tell them that. That's what the meeting is about then.'

I had my two 'A's: acknowledgement and apology.

The civil servant chose anonymous offices of the Intreo Centre in Newbridge, County Kildare, for the meeting, apparently to protect my identity. He and a female colleague arrived, and both were personable and kind, even bringing a box of tissues. I did what I swore I wouldn't do in that meeting and broke down in tears as I related some of the incidents. Still, I emerged feeling good that I'd finally been heard.

I didn't have high hopes. I knew it was unlikely the minister for defence, my former employer, would publicly apologise for what happened. We suspected they were only interested because of a few specific names on my disclosure. As Mark said, 'The Department of Defence wasn't meeting you to see how you are, but to see what you are going to do.'

The response, as we expected, was underwhelming. The civil servant reported that the minister for defence, Simon Coveney, had decided that, 'given the gravity of the allegations', the incidents on my protected disclosure would constitute criminal offences if proven. So he passed the buck, along with my protected disclosure, to An Garda Síochána. The department didn't even ask for my consent.

I duly received a phone call from a sympathetic detective superintendent in Harcourt Street station. 'If it were my daughter, I'd have them strung up,' he said. He invited me to make a statement. By that time in 2021, my mother was terminally ill, and I was busy as her carer. Also, it was never my intention to pursue the perpetrators as individuals. I wanted my experiences to be heard, to get my protected disclosure on the desk of someone in the Department of Defence and make them realise that the defence forces were not a safe place for women. I wanted to ensure the place was safer for the next generation of young men and women starting their careers there. I never intended to hang the old or retired out to dry, so I declined the offer to make a statement.

'Look, I'll leave it with you,' the superintendent said. 'If you decide to make a statement, I'm here for you.' His final words were: 'There is no statute of limitations here. If you decide to come back in a few years' time, that's fine too.'

The chief of staff's aide-de-camp contacted me in July about my protected disclosure and offered to organise a meeting with the army's 'gender adviser'. I was heartened by her words, 'your detailed correspondence outlines serious matters that point to significant failings within the organisation during your service'. It was an acknowledgement, at least. However, I replied, 'It's 30 years too late to be offered a meeting with the gender adviser.'

Around that time, Gwen reached out to someone she knew who had been subjected to abuse in the defence forces. That woman called someone else. Our small group of ex-defence forces women started to grow. One woman reached out to someone else, she did the same, and it went on like that.

Suddenly, I went from feeling totally on my own to becoming a core part of what was essentially a small support group of women. I didn't realise that so many of us existed until then. For years, we had suffered in silence, so it was a relief to meet others. *It wasn't just me*, I thought. *I wasn't the problem. My entire gender was a problem in the defence forces.* Everyone had experienced different levels of harassment, but we were all victims of abuse and most of us were traumatised as a result. Some had lost their careers and were constructively dismissed when they'd tried to battle harassment and discrimination. Women had been raped in the defence forces and their rapists were never punished. Everyone had harrowing stories to tell.

We often shared our stories over Zoom meetings. We were careful who we admitted to our fold as we couldn't trust everyone. We discussed strategies about how we could make a difference. We wanted to share our experiences in the defence forces but we had no clue how to do that.

One member came up with the name Women of Honour, and in March 2021, she set up a WhatsApp group in the same name. From that time on, it became our offical title. Much of what happened afterwards is a matter of public record, and every woman involved is, and has been, integral to the story and our group. However, each has her own story to tell, and many wish to remain anonymous, so to respect everyone's privacy and confidentiality I have omitted their names and the following chapters almost exclusively reflect my perspective of events.

None of us had media experience, and the majority of us were working, or raising and caring for our families. One woman contacted RTÉ presenter Katie Hannon and had lengthy discussions with her. She told the journalist that she had several women willing to relate their incidents of violence and discrimination in the defence forces. Katie invited us to send her our information to see if she had a viable programme to present to her producers. I sent her my protected disclosure, but others had to put pen to paper for the first time, so this all took time.

In the meantime, some strange synchronicity occurred as news of a Canadian and British military #MeToo movement emerged. Women in other countries were fighting back and exposing wrongdoings in their military just as we were coming together and trying to do the same thing. We started to hear the first stirrings of their struggles during those months.

Around this time, the Irish Defence Forces launched a social-media campaign to show its 'inclusiveness'. The theme for International Women's Day 2021 was 'Choose to Challenge'. They marked the day with a video featuring several Irish GI Jane-types working in all aspects of the armed forces. I couldn't help myself. I had to respond.

'Yes, we did rise to the challenge with dignity and determination, but some "challenges" were unnecessary,' I wrote in the comments.

The green light was given for a documentary and the long process began. Katie and I spoke on the phone, and I never felt pressured by her. I felt her caution, care and empathy, which was crucial for establishing a sense of trust. By the time Katie came to Mark's house to record me in April 2021, I felt I was in safe hands. Still, I remember staring at that microphone when she put it in front of me and feeling my pulse pound with nerves. It came to me like a hammer blow that this was happening, and that strangers, maybe many strangers, would listen to me for the first time. Worse, some people who knew me would hear these disclosures for the first time too.

Katie had to stop and start the interview several times. I was more emotional than I'd expected and broke down several times. In the end, she recorded me for three and a half hours. I was drained, emotionally spent, but strangely relieved afterwards. I'd told the truth, and someone had listened, and she would broadcast my truth to anyone else who chose to listen.

But would anyone choose to listen? Would anyone bother tuning in to the programme and, if they did, would they care? I was glad to be a part of the documentary, but I didn't have high expectations.

I also didn't have much time to think about it. My sister cared for my mother in Donegal every second weekend, allowing me to spend a long weekend with Mark in Dublin. Mark had left the army by then and had a full-time job that involved a lot of driving and travelling. He also worked as one of the rangers on RTÉ's TV series *Special Forces – Ultimate Hell Week* and recorded a series in May. They had to run the candidates up a high slope during one scene, and he couldn't understand how he felt so exhausted by it. I also remarked that his face looked bloated. He was so fit and ate so well that I couldn't understand it.

I wondered if he'd had Covid-19 and was suffering the after-effects of it, but he was constantly being tested at work, and had never been positive. Then he started wheezing badly and had to stop training.

'God, you don't sound well,' I said. 'I want you to go back to the doctor.'

She diagnosed him with a nasty chest infection, but I was still concerned. So when I got back to Donegal, I rang

Geraldine, a woman from my platoon who works as an assistant to a cardiologist in the Mater Private Hospital, and I described his symptoms to her.

'That doesn't sound like a respiratory infection,' Geraldine said, asking about his colouring and breathing.

'He can't even go upstairs without being breathless,' I said.

'Oh, that's not good,' she said. 'Come back down to Dublin and bring him in. I'll get him an appointment.'

Thank God for veterans and good contacts.

Geraldine got Mark in to see the consultant, Dr Saber Hassan. The consultant sent Mark for an echocardiogram, and we were ushered back in from the waiting room after the doctor saw the results. I'll never forget it.

'Your heart is only functioning at 10 per cent. You are in heart failure. You need to get into a hospital bed now or you could die.'

I nearly had my own heart attack upon hearing the consultant's words. Mark was 57, a fitness fanatic all his life. I couldn't believe it. We discovered he had already suffered a massive heart attack, which doctors called a 'widow maker'. In hindsight, he realised it must have happened a month earlier when he had sat up all night suffering what he thought was bad acid reflux. He should have died, and he would have if he hadn't been so incredibly fit and eaten so well.

He always told me his father had Alzheimer's when he died aged 54, but he didn't tell me that it was a massive heart attack that had actually killed him. If I'd known his family history, I would have immediately suspected a heart condition.

Mark was brought to St James's Hospital, but it was the middle of the Covid lockdown, and I wasn't even allowed in to see him. All I could do was drop off clean clothes and collect the dirty ones. He had booked a weekend away in our favourite hotel – Farnham Estate in Cavan – for my sixtieth birthday, but he was still in the hospital when the time came.

'Don't cancel it,' he urged. 'You need a break from everything, looking after your mother and running around after me. Just go and have a relaxing weekend.'

I thought about the hotel's lovely pool and realised we could keep video calling as usual. So I spent my sixtieth birthday in Farnham Estate by myself. But I rushed back to Dublin the next day because Mark was released, and I spent ten days settling him back home. However, I was torn between him and my mother, who also needed my attention in Donegal. Three days after I returned to look after her, I started getting chest pains and my blood pressure went through the roof. I ended up in hospital for a week with suspected heart issues, which they decided was all stress-related in the end.

The runup to the broadcast of the *Women of Honour* documentary was an eventful few months, but the stress was only about to get worse. I had no idea how everything was about to explode.

38

The Documentary

As soon as the clock struck noon on Saturday, 11 September 2021, Mark and I cracked open a bottle of Prosecco to mark the milestone event of the broadcast of the *Women of Honour* documentary.

Mark was looking well again. He'd had two stents inserted into his arteries, and his medication had finally stabilised. He was making a good recovery, though we knew he still had a long rehab journey ahead of him. Both of us were still in our pyjamas and dressing gowns as I exchanged nervous WhatsApp messages with other Women of Honour members. The documentary had been postponed as Katie was kept busy standing in for Joe Duffy on RTÉ's *Liveline* show that summer. But it was D-Day at last, and I felt a mixture of dread and excitement. We'd had no preview of the programme, so we would hear the entire thing for the first time when it was broadcast.

After pre-publicity had aired, a post had appeared on Twitter days earlier that shocked me. It stated that the Women of Honour were whistle-blowers who needed protection. *Oh my God*, I thought. *We're whistle-blowers. I'm a whistle-blower!* I don't know why, but it never entered my head before that tweet on 'Whistle Blowers Ireland' was forwarded to me. *Nothing good happens to whistle-blowers*, was my second thought. I remembered when Tom Clonan's research had revealed the dark side of the defence forces – they'd attempted to destroy his career and reputation with a smear campaign.

The TD Peadar Tóibín was proactive too when he heard about the documentary. He contacted us to say it was horrific that this had happened to us and said we were 'brave and courageous'. I ran the words through my head. I never once thought I was either brave or courageous. If anything, I was making up for past mistakes and refusing to remain silent anymore. I was finally speaking out and telling what had happened to me.

So I sat down with Mark to listen to the programme with a sense of nervous anticipation. I knew Katie had a devoted listenership, but this wasn't one of her scheduled shows. It was a one-off documentary and Katie's first. It was also a Saturday lunchtime broadcast, so I was doubtful that many would hear it. I just hoped someone would listen and that something positive might emerge from our painful revelations. A final flurry of messages was exchanged as the seconds ticked towards 1p.m.

'Good luck!'

'We're on now!'

'Talk later!'

Mark and I sat at the kitchen table as the continuity announcer intoned, 'Now on RTÉ Radio 1, a special documentary feature from Katie Hannon exploring the emergence of the Irish branch of the military #MeToo movement.' She warned that listeners might find the content that followed 'disturbing'.

The documentary opened with the sounds of seagulls, and waves crashing on the shore. I looked at Mark, my forehead creasing in confusion. *What's this about?* Then I nearly fell off my chair as I heard my voice from a WhatsApp message I'd shared with the Women of Honour months earlier: 'Oh my God, ladies. Oh my God. Please play back the World News on RTÉ 1 8.17 to 8.20.' Katie's voiceover explained that I was on my way for a Sunday swim when a radio report about Canada's #MeToo military scandal stopped me in my tracks.

I'd been shocked to hear what was happening in Canada that morning. But it was nothing compared to the shock of hearing myself on the radio for the first time. My heart beat heavily throughout the hour as, for the first time, female soldiers, sailors and aircrew talked about everything from discrimination to brutal sexual violence in the Irish Defence Forces. Katie had done an incredible job, weaving all our stories into the hour, all of us relating a series of distressing incidents from early days up to the present day.

I felt highly emotional by the end, necking a glass of bubbly and trying to calm myself with a few deep breaths. It was done. Our experiences were swept out from under the defence forces' carpet at last. Messages of congratulation were flying on WhatsApp, and everyone seemed moved by what they'd heard.

Many of the women were jubilant, and Mark was elated and reassuring. 'It's a powerful documentary – so well-edited, and you were wonderful on it,' he insisted. He also made me laugh, telling me how seductive my radio voice was. I needed that laugh. I didn't even realise how wound up I'd been until the programme was over. I felt a certain relief but was still apprehensive. How was the documentary going to be received?

Many positive messages bearing #WomenofHonour started appearing on Twitter, and congratulatory and supportive WhatsApp messages and texts poured in. Then, suddenly, in the mid-afternoon, Katie rang me. 'Is it okay if we send out an RTÉ camera to you? They want you to do an interview because you're the only Woman of Honour in Dublin.'

'Jesus, no, Katie,' I gasped. 'I'm still in my dressing gown and we're two bottles of Prosecco down!'

She laughed. 'Okay, will you come in for the *Six One News* so? You'll have time to get ready and we'll send a car out.'

I nearly had a heart attack at the thought. I had never done anything like that before and had no desire to appear on television. 'No, sorry, Katie. I'm not going on national TV. Absolutely not!'

By 4.30 p.m. that afternoon, five women serving in the defence forces had contacted me through the Women of Honour Facebook account. The gist of the messages was: *Oh my God, well done. I didn't know this group was out there. How do I get involved? I need to tell you what happened to me.* What shocked me was that most of these women were young and only a few years in the army. It was clear that little had changed 40 years after my platoon first entered the defence forces.

It was bad enough listening to myself on the radio that afternoon, but I was staggered to see my photograph flash up at the start of the *Six One News* on RTÉ TV that evening. The *Women of Honour* documentary was the lead item on that news and RTÉ news at nine. No words can describe how surreal it was to see the photo taken of me wearing my camouflage uniform in a snowy Bosnian landscape on the national news. Retired captain Tom Clonan appeared on the broadcasts to discuss the significance of the documentary.

The next day, I had seven more messages from serving women. Clearly, the programme had triggered some of these women, arousing feelings of emotional distress that they had buried for years. Some needed help, but we weren't a counselling service. We knew someone sympathetic who worked in personnel support services in the army, so we referred them there. The Rape Crisis Centre also came on board that week and offered to help, which was a huge relief.

Within my own family, I caused a lot of shock. I had never told my mother about my experiences. My father knew about the pool incident, but my mother knew nothing. Why would I have burdened her? She'd been dead against me joining the army in the first place. I remember she hugged me afterwards, but she was hurt and bewildered. 'Why didn't you tell me what was going on?' she said.

My brother who had been in the army was saddened but not surprised by what he heard.

My older brother was probably the hardest hit. He listened to the documentary at his home in Sweden via the internet and was shattered by what he heard. 'Oh my God, Karina, why didn't you tell me this was all going on?'

He was my protective big brother and was deeply wounded that I'd never confided in him during all the years. But he was in Sweden, so I never saw the point in burdening him either because there was nothing he could have done except worry. But I felt re-traumatised because of the pain I caused him.

Everything blew up after that, and the ripples from the documentary spread far and wide. News items and discussions and newspaper reports continued. None of us dreamt that we might end up in the eye of a media storm and the focus of a #MeToo movement in the Irish Defence Forces. But that's what happened.

President Michael D. Higgins, the supreme commander

of the defence forces, commended the 'bravery' of all the women who'd told their stories. There was that word again. The documentary was all over *Morning Ireland*. Every time I switched on the radio or opened a newspaper, there was more about it. Many TDs paid tribute to the Women of Honour in the Dáil.

Katie wanted me on her show the following Saturday. I dreaded the prospect but didn't want to let her down. If no one could see me, it wouldn't be so bad.

'It's radio, right?' I said.

'Yes, Karina,' she said. She knew what I was like about dressing up. 'But there is a camera in the studio, so you'll have to run a comb through your hair.'

Like many women, I didn't worry about what I would say. Instead, I panicked, thinking, *What am I going to wear so that I won't look so fat on camera?*

The group tried to put a press release together, but that was a disaster. We didn't know what we were doing. We weren't always available for media and it all became very stressful.

As Katie started to despair of us, she introduced us to a crisis media manager and told us he would help us pro bono for ten days. (He's still helping us.) He taught us how to write a press release and deal with hounding reporters. 'Just tell him to go away,' he said. 'You have jobs. You have children. You can't be at the beck and call of everyone.'

Prime Time wanted me to appear, but there was no way I could face it on my own. 'I'm not that important and I don't have that much to say,' I said when Katie contacted me. 'I'll only go on if I can bring another Woman of Honour with me.'

One of the other women agreed to do the programme. Our interview was pre-recorded, which alleviated some of the stress. I talked to the producer beforehand. 'Will there be someone to do make-up because I don't know how to do make-up?'

She laughed and said they didn't normally do make-up because it would be recorded in the Merrion Hotel rather than in an RTÉ studio, but they would arrange that someone did it for me. Then, I ran around Arnotts, fitting on loads of dresses, dragging poor Mark with me.

'I'm going to be seated for the interview, and the camera is going to pick up all the rolls of fat, so you have to take photos of me sitting down,' I instructed.

I bought three dresses and then sent photos to three friends and my mother. They all said, 'No, absolutely not. You can't wear those on TV.' So I brought all three dresses back and wore an old pair of black trousers and a forgiving blouse and blazer I already had.

Mark suggested I wear my ribbons, which I thought was a good idea. I never wanted to disgrace the army, but some men, by abusing their ranks, were bringing disgrace to the organisation and the system in the defence forces was enabling them to do that. Despite everything, I still love the army and am proud of my service, so I pinned those ribbons on my blazer.

Like the good soldiers we were, the two of us arrived way too early. That was a big mistake as we just got more and more nervous waiting in the hotel. I would have been sick if I had been able to eat something.

However, presenter Miriam O'Callaghan did her best to put us at ease and make us feel as comfortable as we could in the circumstances. 'Listen, don't worry about stammering or getting stuck or saying something wrong; we can cut it out, and we can start again,' she said.

I hated recalling those incidents from my protected disclosure because it was traumatising every time I had to do it. But even when Miriam asked for our biographical details on camera, I had to repeat it three times. I still found it so difficult to talk about myself that I stuttered and stammered my way through it. In the end, however, I was pleased with how they edited my interview. They made my performance on camera look a lot better than it actually was.

Still the media requests poured in. Within two weeks of the radio programme, I remember scrolling through my phone contacts, and it was surreal – it was full of reporters' personal numbers.

Twelve days after the documentary was aired, we were invited to meet the first female secretary general at the Department of Defence, Jacqui McCrum. She had only been appointed in July 2020. 'I have six years left in my term, and I'm 100 per cent committed to finally rooting out this abusive culture once and for all. I want this to be my legacy,' she said. 'I want to get this sorted within my term of office.'

She also told us that the Department of Defence had

the highest percentage of protected disclosures of any government department. This fact was at odds with the post-documentary statement from the chief of staff's office that 'all incidents of harassment, sexual harassment, bullying and discrimination' were 'treated with the utmost seriousness'.

We met with Minister Simon Coveney in Government Buildings five days later. We went in asking for my two As – an apology and acknowledgement. I soon added two more As to our demands – action and accountability – and those four As became the pillars of Women of Honour.

Simon Coveney apologised in a personal capacity for what had happened to us and said he acknowledged what happened. He claimed he was under the impression that the historic abuses had ended. He had been led to believe that they had been eliminated amid the rafts of revised policies about equality and dignity published by the defence forces over the previous 20 years. However, he also admitted that he had spoken with 14 serving female members of the defence forces before meeting with us that day, and that the serving members had confirmed what we were saying was still happening.

To be honest, I thought he was very genuine and earnest in his willingness to make changes. He pledged an independent external review to investigate all the incidents reported to him by Women of Honour. So I was hopeful after that meeting.

'He's listening to us,' I told Mark. 'He's allowing us to have an input into the terms of reference of this review.'

A Dáil debate on the defence forces took place two days later, and Simon Coveney was bombarded with questions concerning the documentary revelations. Within a week, the minister announced that a private organisation, Raiseaconcern, had been appointed as confidential contact person for victims of the defence forces. I thought this was a great initiative, very fast, very effective. But I had to stand by the Women of Honour, many of whom had questions about confidentiality within the private company.

That month, a whirlwind of consultations and meetings with serving women took place in barracks across Ireland. As far as the army was concerned, they had all their dignity charters, policies and procedures and complaint systems in place. Everything was perfect until the Women of Honour documentary, and suddenly the higher ranks were unnerved. I could only imagine the conversations. *Shit, we better talk to these whinging women and see what their bloody problem is.*

Personally, I was disappointed that the highest-ranking female in the Irish Defence Forces, Major General Maureen O'Brien, never publicly raised her head above the parapet and said a word in support or otherwise of the Women of Honour.

During all this, a serving soldier contacted me. 'I have two officers who want to get in touch with you. Can I give them your number?'

The men were retired colonels I had worked with, both decent people. They duly rang and said they admired the Women of Honour for speaking out. *You did a brilliant job, and it's about time someone stood up and did this*, was the general tone of the conversations. The burning issue in both of their minds emerged at the end of their calls. 'Did any of those incidents happen on my watch?'

Anti-bullying campaigns with titles like It Stops Now started popping up on the defence forces' social media. 'Bullying, sexual harassment or discrimination will not be tolerated,' members of the organisation intoned. 'It stops now.'

It stops now? Well, at least you're admitted that it has been happening, I thought, watching the advert.

It took nearly another month after meeting with the minister for defence before the new chief of staff responded to our request to meet with us. Lieutenant General Seán Clancy had been appointed to the role in July 2022 and took over on 29 September following the retirement of Vice Admiral Mark Mellett.

Army HQ set up a meeting with the chief of staff that was an odd, cloak-and-dagger affair in an anonymous hotel in Portlaoise. Lieutenant General Clancy arrived with two female 'henchmen' as backup. In fact, the female commandant and senior non-commissioned officer were supportive, and thanked Women of Honour for giving them a voice.

All three also arrived wearing civvies, which astonished me considering it was a meeting about military matters. 'Why are you not in uniform?' I asked. They said something about wanting to keep the meeting informal and friendly. Nevertheless, I thought the whole arrangement was odd.

However, the meeting was frank and friendly, and I discussed our objectives, the four As – acknowledgement, apology, action and accountability. I spoke about the emphatic response of the Canadians to the #MeToo military movement. I'm sure he flinched when I added, 'The Canadians believe in real action and accountability and have fired two of their chiefs of staff.'

Before the end, I let them know that Katie Hannon had invited me on her show the next day to talk about what we'd discussed. I was astonished that the chief of staff suddenly appeared ruffled. 'Well, I hope you'll say positive things,' he said, and I was hurriedly presented with a sheet of paper containing a list of new policies and procedures to stop bullying, harassment and inappropriate behaviour. Afterwards, I reread it and realised the army always refers to 'inappropriate behaviour'. No one in the army seems to be able to utter the words 'sexual assault' or 'rape'.

I spoke about our meeting with the chief of staff on Katie's radio show, but afterwards she mentioned something about 'our next interview'.

'Do you mean I'm going to be on the radio again?' I said, almost appalled at the suggestion.

'Karina,' Katie replied, 'you have to realise you're going to be on again and again.'

To be honest, I wanted to step back at this stage. *We've done our job. We've opened the floodgates now and handed everything over to the minister*, I thought. *It's now his job.*

My mother's illness was getting worse and she was less patient when her dinner was late in the evening. Our work was done and I wanted to return to normal life.

39

Platoon

Throughout the frenzy that followed the broadcast, there was largely a silence from my own platoon. Three out of our 38 had unfortunately died but, of the rest, only a small number sent texts of support after the documentary.

At first, I felt upset by that. Many of my platoon seemed to have had what I thought of as 'blessed careers'. They appeared to progress through the army, and nothing ever happened. In hindsight, I question that but, at the time, I expected those women to support the others who were not so lucky.

In the end, I shrugged it off. I realised people were busy, and many of the platoon had returned to civilian life years earlier and moved on. Nevertheless, we always made time for a reunion every year, several of which I'd organised in the past. And 2021 was a big one – our fortieth-anniversary reunion. I suggested we hold it in the Curragh where it all started for us as recruits and everyone agreed.

The reunion took place at the end of October, six or seven weeks after the documentary's first broadcast. Twenty-seven members of the number four recruit platoon arranged to meet in the Keadeen Hotel in Newbridge, County Kildare, where our passing-out celebrations had taken place.

I was really looking forward to meeting up with everyone again. On Friday night, we arranged to meet for a few casual drinks before the formal night on Saturday. When I arrived, I was shaken by the rancour I experienced from a few of the platoon towards the Women of Honour and the documentary's revelations. It was the first time I felt the brunt of being a whistle-blower.

What do you think you're doing, Molloy? Do you really think those you're going to make a difference? Nothing's going to change.

I was taken aback then, but I think I understand the reactions a bit better now. Perhaps some were hurting because I had exposed their vulnerability along with my own. I should have understood that some women feel uncomfortable speaking about what had happened to them. One woman said she had never told her husband about her experiences and now he was asking questions as a result of the documentary. I was sorry to hear that she couldn't bring herself to reveal whatever trauma she'd experienced. Internal psychological barriers to exposing assaults and wrongdoing are often more insurmountable than institutional ones. I had felt misplaced shame and embarrassment when I was assaulted, and I understood how hard it was to speak out.

Others correctly perceived that if they had reported abuse in the army, it would have worsened the outcome for themselves. They put on a smile and carried on and minimised the incidents in their minds. I know I tried to do that at times – blanked incidents out, told myself that they didn't matter. Maybe some women never acknowledged what had happened to them and didn't appreciate it when I and other women stirred uncomfortable memories.

And denial can have its uses. A major study cited in the *European Journal of Social Psychology* in 2021 revealed that women who deny gender discrimination have an improved sense of well-being. Refusing to acknowledge its existence or blinkering ourselves to it is an actual effective coping mechanism.

Of course, there may well have been women who did have 'blessed careers', who were lucky enough to work with male colleagues who respected them and treated them as equals. I wish there were more of them. From my experience and that of many women I've come to know through Women of Honour, the culture of sexual harassment and discrimination was so pervasive, very few escaped.

After a somewhat cool reception from some on the

Friday night of our reunion, the Women of Honour debacle was put behind us. The following night was the formal dinner. We heard RTÉ were coming down that afternoon to record a piece about the reunion for the *Six One News*. That morning, I went for a swim in the hotel leisure centre and, when I returned, I discovered that one of the women had been frantically calling me. I'd missed about six calls.

'Karina, I have selected the women who will be interviewed this afternoon,' she said. 'The reporter asked to speak to you but I told her you're not speaking. This weekend is about 40 years of friendship and not about being sexually harassed, bullied or raped. Can you please stay away from the reporter?'

I was in shock for a moment. I was effectively being gagged from speaking about the abuse of women in the armed forces by some in my all-female platoon. *Go ahead*, I thought. *Let's pretend the dark side of the past 40 years in the army doesn't exist.*

I just shrugged. So be it. At least I wouldn't have to have to worry about doing a media interview that afternoon.

That evening, the cameras from RTÉ arrived, and I stayed well away. I watched the report on the news that evening. At the end of the clip, however, the reporter remarked: 'These women are celebrating their fortieth anniversary under a cloud of accusations of sexual harassment and rape.' The gritty truth was still uttered even though a few would have preferred if it wasn't.

40

A Dangerous Place

I woke with a start to the sound of breaking glass in the middle of the night in Donegal. My heart thumped with fright, but I jumped out of bed and ran barefoot down the stairs. From the shadows, I saw a man, head and shoulders through the smashed kitchen window. 'Get fucking out!' I screamed, dashing into the kitchen, eyes darting about for a potential weapon. That's when I saw the two others outside, staring at me, waiting their turn.

The intruder wrenched himself further through the window, and terror pulsed in my veins. The others were bobbing behind him, impatiently urging him on. I knew I had only seconds before all three would be on top of me. I snatched the filleting knife from the kitchen drawer, grabbed a tuft of the intruder's dark hair, yanked his head back and ripped the blade with force through his exposed throat. The blood from his jugular vein sprayed in a wide arc across me and the kitchen.

'Who's next?' I cried, brandishing the bloodied knife at the two men outside.

I woke gasping, panting, sweating, my heart banging hard. I had to run my hands down my nightclothes to convince myself I wasn't coated in thick blood. The nightmare was so vivid and the faces so distinct that I could have identified all three men in an identity parade.

This horror had been part of my morning routine just recently, and the savage nightmares keep coming. No matter how long I've left, the army is never far away because I still live with the legacy of Lariam.

Similarly, it hasn't been as easy as I'd thought to leave Women of Honour behind. After the documentary, I believed our job was done and that everything our campaign sought to achieve was in good hands with the minister. We had blown the whistle, exposed many wrongdoings, and the minister believed us. He was determined to ensure that what we had experienced would never be repeated.

Towards the end of 2021, personal family issues arose around the end of the year as my mother got weaker and sicker and she died aged 88 from complications of oral cancer on 25 November. It was a traumatic few weeks and by the time I'd started to engage again with Women of Honour, the minister was circulating draft terms of reference for a review – without the consultation he'd promised us.

He was considering a 'back-to-basics' judge-led review of policies and procedures that would provide recommendations within months. I tried to wade through the terms of reference, but they were written in legal speak, as I couldn't understand what they were proposing.

I contacted Katie in RTÉ and said we needed help. She came to our rescue again, finding a company of solicitors who were happy to come on board. We learnt that the minister's proposed review could not investigate or compel witnesses who didn't want to participate. So it was nothing like the full independent, investigative, statutory inquiry we'd discussed.

The shelves of the Department of Defence were already laden with white papers that had been ignored for decades. Unfortunately, Simon Coveney seemed to be commissioning another pointless review to add to them.

We arranged a meeting with the minister on 16 December to try and persuade him to change tack. The day before the meeting, I had a bad reaction to my Covid vaccination in Letterkenny. I had to stop the car twice on the drive to Dublin to throw up. The last thing I wanted was a meeting in Government Buildings the following morning. I was breaking out in cold sweats and shaking like a leaf. We met with the lord mayor, Alison Gilliland, in the Mansion House first. My head was spinning but luckily she was tight on time, so the meeting was brief.

When we met the minister afterwards, he claimed to

be still on the fence about the review. He said he'd take our comments on board and insisted nothing had been decided.

At one stage, he sat back for a breather. 'By the way, who came up with the four As?' he asked, referring to the Women of Honour demands for an apology, acknowledgment, action and accountability. 'It's a good concept. I'm very impressed.' All the women turned and pointed to me sitting at the end of the table.

Even though the discussion was all very cordial, I suspected he was more committed to the review than he purported to be.

'As an employer, I have a duty of care to the current 600 women still serving in the Irish Defence Forces,' he said. 'And they have to get this protection in place straightaway. A review would be much faster than a statutory inquiry.'

However, still not over my vaccine reaction, the waves of nausea started to hit again and halfway through the discussion, I thought I was about to throw up. 'Sorry, I'm going to have to stop the meeting,' I said.

I didn't want to return to the overheated room. Deep down, I knew we were wasting our time. *The man has decided what he's doing,* I thought. The civil servants, the chief of staff, everyone had bent his ear, and he'd done a complete U-turn. In the end, we cut the meeting short because I was feeling so ill.

Despite my disappointment with the minister, I wasn't convinced we should wage war against him. I always preferred being in the room to being outside it. However,

I adopted the Women of Honour line on the radio, stammering through all the legalese often contained within official statements. I've never been great at using political language. I only improved when I explained what had happened in my own words.

'We felt we were being railroaded onto an express train that we didn't want to get on. All the other stakeholders have got on that train, but we're still standing on the platform because they've changed the destination.'

We went back to meet the minister again at the end of January 2022 and discovered he had no intention of changing his mind. The review was a fait accompli, and we walked out on him. From then on, we would not engage with his Independent Review Group (IRG). *Oh my God, I really can't believe we're walking out on the Minister for Defence*, I thought as we left.

My personal opinion was, *If you're not in the room, you can't influence the room*, but I was part of the Women of Honour, so I had to take one for the team.

However, I also realised I'd been naïve about the minister. I thought he was genuinely concerned at first and had been blindsided by our revelations on the *Women of Honour* documentary. In hindsight, this should have been difficult to believe as he'd received many protected disclosures before mine. In the end, I had to accept he's a politician, and all politicians revert to type. He was reminded that his first duty was to look after himself, his department and the defence forces, and that's what he did. I believe he was afraid of leaving the department open to compensation claims, even though that was never on the agenda of Women of Honour. In all our time together, I never heard the issue being raised by a single woman.

We had a meeting with Taoiseach Micheál Martin a few days later, though only two of us from Women of Honour were available to attend, along with the head of our legal team. I wasn't even nervous because there was little at stake. The IRG had already begun work days earlier, and the taoiseach was never going to overturn the minister's decision. It was merely a courtesy meeting as a result of political pressure. He gave us the floor but I could see his eyes glaze over and could almost read his mind: *Are these women ever going to stop talking?*

'Why can't you run a statutory inquiry at the same time as the review?' I asked.

However, he swerved smoothly around that. 'If the IRG recommend a statutory inquiry at the end of their review, then I can assure you I will sign off on a statutory inquiry.'

I knew that was unlikely to happen.

As soon as we emerged from the meeting, a microphone was stuck in my face. I could feel a cold trickle of sweat running down my back. I would never get used to speaking publicly. I never wanted to stand in front of troops, and I certainly never wanted to be on national radio or TV.

Afterwards, I had to face another live interview with Claire Byrne on her radio show. She said she could hear that I was 'deflated' – deflated was a good word. And tired. And fed up. I felt like saying, *Right, that's it. Now get me out of here. I never want to be in front of a camera or a microphone again. I've had enough.*

After so much hope, stress, sweat and tears, it was crushing to feel we had made no progress. The Department of Defence had decided there would be no investigative process, no statutory basis and no true independence in setting the terms of reference. The minister's department appointed the review panel. The review wouldn't even attempt to get to the root of the problem. It was just another whitewash.

Yet, when I received a letter from the IRG in September 2022, asking me to participate and give my submission to the review board, I felt I had to do it. The other Women of Honour did not participate in the review or engage in the process. But I thought of my protected disclosure sitting in a file, gathering dust in a garda station. The Department of Defence had swept it out of their door, so there was no record of me submitting a complaint. I wanted my submission to be on the record somewhere, so I decided to submit it as an individual. To align myself as closely as possible to the Women of Honours' position, I did it through email rather than a personal submission in the room with the IRG.

I spoke to one woman who had joined the army more than a decade after me. We knew each other in service, although we never actually worked together. She had joined as part of a mixed platoon, was fully combatant and had fought her way up the ranks. Yet she wrote a far lengthier submission than mine, for the IRG. I always assumed things improved for those following us, but she was emphatic. 'No, Karina. It's actually getting worse.'

However, the minister didn't even have to listen to

Women of Honour to understand what was happening. The department's own report on the defence forces, which came out in 2022, was highly critical of what it discovered in the organisation. The *Report of the Commission on the Defence Forces* described the defence forces as a 'very uncomfortable place for females, and lower status males or minorities to work'. It bluntly stated that the organisation has a culture 'that scapegoats women with children' and damages their 'future promotion opportunities'.

The commission noted that a threshold of 35 per cent of female participation was needed to 'overcome the negative effects of a lack of gender balance'. They wanted to see this rate on all command and career courses by 2025. Unfortunately, this seems like a pipe dream. Women are 42 years in the defence forces and still only account for around 7 per cent of the personnel or just over 600 out of 9,500 employed there.

This was underlined at the press conference to launch the report in July 2022, when the chief of staff admitted that only 15 women had been recruited to the defence forces that year.

Responding to queries about how to attract women into the army following the Women of Honour exposé, he spoke about tackling abuse 'from misogyny right down to inappropriate language and behaviour'.

Once again, I marvelled at how leadership in the defence forces seem afflicted by an inability to form the words 'rape' and 'sexual assault'. The chief of staff soon had enough of the media asking awkward questions. A female defence-forces official stepped in and told the press to stop asking about the Women of Honour and culture issues in the organisation. I was stunned reading this. It doesn't augur well for change in the culture when they try to gag the media in the middle of a press conference.

Despite the veneer of political correctness and the 'gender advisers', the defence forces still doesn't do humility well. They continue to bristle in the face of criticism, preferring to remain blinkered and in 'Crisis? What crisis?' mode.

In the face of the rising numbers of shocking disclosures from women and some men, serving and retired, they remain in denial. At the Permanent Defence Forces Representative Association's annual conference in October 2022, the chief of staff finally acknowledged that discrimination, including sexual harassment against female members was not just historic, it was ongoing. Yet the defence forces is still trying to keep these incidents under wraps. I have been reliably informed that, over a period of 18 months during 2021 and 2022, several women have settled cases with the Irish Defence Forces and have been awarded sums of up to six figures for discrimination and harassment. All the women had to sign non-disclosure agreements.

It requires real bravery to change an organisational culture that thrives on secrecy, obfuscation and cover-ups, but there is little evidence of this happening. The defence forces has never referred anyone convicted of sexual assault or rape in a court-martial to the sex offenders register during the 20 years the register has been in operation. Instead, it prefers to sweep issues under the carpet or circle its wagons around the perpetrators who abuse their rank.

Despite everything we tried to do, the minister's decision to pursue a review of policies and procedures is only contributing to this mindset of secrecy and concealment. No one will be responsible or held accountable. The review will not address what happens to members of the defence forces after they make a complaint – the isolation, the coercion, the reprisals, lack of promotions, how they are frequently 'left behind'. Another forest will be felled to produce another hefty paper full of recommendations that will be shelved in the Department of Defence – yet the status quo will be maintained.

I had hoped that our disclosures might be a game-changer but, despite all the lip service about change, the Department of Defence and the Irish Defence Forces have raised the drawbridge again. As long as the department refuses to countenance a statutory, proper investigatory review, the toxic culture that presides within those battlement walls remains protected. The women, meanwhile, are not.

Military sexual trauma (MST), which refers to psychological trauma resulting from sexual violations while serving on active duty, is recognised as a major public-health concern in the United States and Canada. Their militaries now understand that MST is an underlying cause for many debilitating health conditions and that survivors often take many years to heal from its impact. Many, for example, suffer from severe post-traumatic stress disorder and depression and are constructively dismissed because they can no longer tolerate their dangerous work environment. Veterans in America receive medical-disability pensions and compensation for psychological distress and other conditions related to MST.

The profound implications of a hostile and dangerous working environment on people's health and wellbeing are now widely recognised and accepted on the other side of the Atlantic. However, by their inaction or limited actions, the Department of Defence and Irish Defence Forces continue to be complicit in traumas being inflicted on many of their employees.

While my worst nightmares are confined to dreaming these days, unfortunately many women face the nightmare of working in a hostile workplace every day and continue to be scarred by these experiences.

The severe levels of abuse I experienced haven't stopped, and the perpetrators haven't gone away, but neither will I nor many members of Women of Honour.

A reporter once asked me what justice would look like for me, and I replied from the heart. Justice for me simply means that the next 18-year-old female and male who walk through those gates will be protected, and that no one will ever again have to deal with the physical, sexual and psychological abuses we experienced.

And if any 18-year-old asks me if they should join the defence forces, my answer, sadly, remains the same. Hold off until there's real protection in place. It hurts me to say this but, in the meantime, this organisation remains – as it proved throughout my 31-year-long career – a dangerous place for women.

Appendix

Irish Army Ranks

OFFICER
- lieutenant-general
- major-general
- brigadier-general
- colonel
- lieutenant-colonel
- commandant
- captain
- 2nd lieutenant
- 1st lieutenant
- senior cadet
- cadet

OTHER RANKS
- sergeant major
- battalion quartermaster sergeant
- company sergeant
- company quartermaster sergeant
- sergeant
- corporal
- private 3 star
- private 2 star
- recruit

Acknowledgements

I wish to send heartfelt thanks to Katie Hannon. Thank you, Katie, for giving us, the Women of Honour, our voices – and subsequently giving every other serving member and veteran a voice too.

A special note of appreciation is due to Anthony O'Brien. Thanks, Anthony, for getting the ball rolling and giving myself and many others the courage to step forward.

Thanks too to my publisher and editor Ciara Considine for taking a chance on me and convincing me that my story was worth telling.

Thanks to Kathryn Rogers – my wonderful co-writer. Thank you for helping to craft so many official documents, notes, overseas reports, assessments and personal diaries into my story.

To my brothers Garry and Alan: thank you for your encouragement. To my darling little sister Geraldine: even though you're sometimes overshadowed by older, louder siblings, you've always been a true light for me whenever it matters.

To Kevin Barnes: thank you for inspiring me and helping me get my first job in UCD, and on the first step to my career.

To my overseas colleagues, Jason Whelan and Eoin Ward: you guys protected me when I needed it most. You have no idea how much support you gave me. Thank you.

Special thanks are due to Caroline (Strawballs) Hayes, Catherina Tupponi and Geraldine Cassidy: thank you for all your honest advice, help and support during this process.

To Anne O'Sullivan (Sully), Geraldine Lupini (née Acheson), Margaret Doyle, Patricia O'Shaughnessy, Ann Molloy, Sharon McNamara, Aideen Mulhall, Kereena Cahill, Ursula McCloskey (née Holly), Maeve Quigley, Bernie Curran, Mary O'Riordan, Muirann O'Connell, Georgina Kane, Rachel Snee, Catriona Gallagher, Eddie Costigan (Cossie), Paul Collins (GI), Geoffrey Dickson (Jock), Paula McCosker, Janet Peakin Callery and Anthony O'Regan (Taz), Sonya Kennedy: thank you all for your help and contributions.

To DH: thanks for the debrief!

Thanks to my fellow Women of Honour for their steadfast courage and ongoing advocacy for change.

To my fellow Wild Atlantic Dippers: thanks for listening and all your amazing support during difficult times.

Last but never least, to my darling, wonderful, long-suffering partner Mark: thank you for your endless patience, support, editing, spellchecks, dinners, countless cups of coffee and for being by my side through all of this.